AN ANVIL ORIGINAL
Under the general editorship of Louis L. Snyder

SIMÓN BOLÍVAR
AND SPANISH AMERICAN
INDEPENDENCE: 1783–1830

JOHN J. JOHNSON
Professor of History, Stanford University

with the collaboration of
Doris M. Ladd
Stanford University

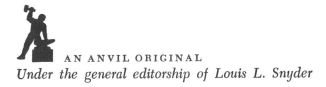

KRIEGER PUBLISHING COMPANY
MALABAR, FLORIDA
1992

To Maurine

Original Edition 1968
Reprint Edition 1992

Printed and Published by
KRIEGER PUBLISHING COMPANY
KRIEGER DRIVE
MALABAR, FLORIDA 32950

Library of Congress Cataloging-In-Publication Data
Johnson, John J., 1912-
      Simón Bolívar and Spanish American independence, 1783-1830 /
   John J. Johnson with the collaboration of Doris M. Ladd.
         p.   cm.
      Originally published: Princeton, N.J. : Van Nostrand, 1968.
      Includes bibliographical references and index.
      ISBN 0-89464-687-7
      1. Bolívar, Simón, 1783-1830. 2. South America--History--Wars
   of Independence, 1806-1830. I. Ladd, Doris M.   II. Title.
   F2235.3.J72 1992
   980'.02--dc20   91-36882
                                                        CIP

10   9   8   7   6   5   4   3   2

Preface

Simón Bolívar, liberator of five nations from Spanish tutelage, is one of the towering public figures that our hemisphere has produced. Bolívar was at once a visionary, soldier, statesman, political prophet and internationalist. His vision made it possible for him more than anyone else to see the potential of America, and he more than anyone else was responsible for keeping alive the idea of independence in the face of overwhelming odds. As a soldier he gave warfare in America a new dimension by establishing that makeshift forces, if imaginatively led and with grass roots support, could triumph over better drilled, better equipped external armies. His contemporaries compared him to Washington. As a statesman he embraced the political and social philosophies propounded by revolutionaries in Anglo-America and in France, but he always gave those philosophies his own interpretations. He probably sensed better than anyone of his age the kinds of political systems best suited to the new republics burdened as they were by their colonial inheritance. As a political leader he preferred conceptualization to administration. He accepted presidencies on many occasions but invariably he left to his vice-presidents the responsibility of implementing official policies. As a prophet Bolívar saw with uncanny insight the future of Spanish America. He predicted the segmentation of Spanish America. He forecast that Chile would prove to be the most orderly of the new republics. He identified the forces that would lead to instability, and he prophesied with a remarkable accuracy the role that the military would play as a force for political stability or political anarchy. As an internationalist Bolívar was responsible for the calling of the Panama Conference of 1826. It fell short of his expectations but it was nonetheless the forerunner of the Organization of American States. Some internationalists credit Bolívar with planting the seeds of the League of Nations and the United Nations.

Today Bolívar's political creations, Bolivia, Colombia, Ecuador, Peru and Venezuela, are being carried along by the nationalist revolution of our time. In their search for identity, they have once again turned to the Liberator and have made him a symbol around which to rally. Other nations of the Hemisphere pay him homage. The followers of Fidel Castro often seek to associate his name with their cause.

My collaborator, Doris M. Ladd, worked with me throughout this project. I am most deeply indebted to her for her invaluable research assistance, sharp criticism and constant encouragement. It gives me considerable pleasure to acknowledge my thanks to Mrs. Marjorie Sowers and Miss Rebecca Baird for their thoughtful suggestions, for typing the manuscript, but most of all for their patience and understanding as the three of us worked simultaneously to administer Stanford's graduate program in Latin American Studies and to prepare "Bolívar" for submission to Van Nostrand and Company. My thanks also go to Mr. George Evangelauf, a graduate student in Latin American Studies at Stanford, who read the galley proofs on the volume and who assumed primary responsibility for indexing it.

Professor Gerhard Masur, whose *Simón Bolívar* is the standard work in English on the Liberator, read the manuscript. He made several suggestions that I incorporated into the manuscript.

On several occasions I solicited help from Mrs. Esther Barret de Nazarís of Fundación Vicente Lecuna, the internationally known center of Bolivarian studies. She went out of her way to be helpful. I am indeed indebted to her.

J.J.J.

Table of Contents

PART II—READINGS

Part I

SIMON BOLIVAR AND SPANISH AMERICAN INDEPENDENCE: 1783-1830

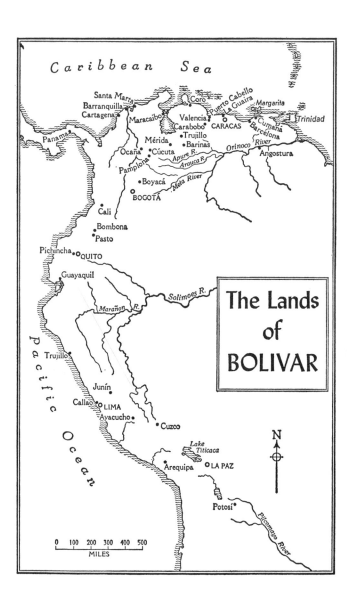

The Lands of BOLIVAR

CHAPTER 1

Introduction

Simón Bolívar was born in 1783 into an era of reform and revolution.[1] In that year the American Revolution was successfully terminated. Six years later the French Revolution initiated a generation of upheaval in Europe which reverberated throughout the western world. It was an age of military glory, of political innovation, of nationalistic stirrings, and of international alliances. In many respects Simón Bolívar personified the great trends of that age, for in his lifetime he played the varied parts of Jacobin conspirator, military hero, state-builder, nationalist, and hemisphere leader. This book proposes to show Bolívar in his many roles within the context of his time, for only by placing him within the framework of the Enlightenment reform which preceded the Independence movement and Creole reaction which followed, is it possible to evaluate his achievement.

More than any other individual, Simón Bolívar knew the meaning and the price of the international wars and civil conflicts that ravaged Spanish America between 1808 and 1825. The international struggles, with autonomy as their final aim, occurred in three major theaters: Mexico, northern South America and southern South America. Some, for example in Chile and Argentina, were plotted from cities; others, as in Uruguay and Mexico, were directed from the countryside. Each followed a different but similarly uncharted course. Final outcomes were unpredictable for more than a decade. The loss of lives and property varied widely from one area to another, with success costing least in La Plata and Central America and most in northern South America. Collectively, the struggles collapsed Spain's American Empire, leaving Madrid in control only of her oldest American colonies, Española (now the Dominican Republic), Puerto Rico, and Cuba. From the territories lost by Spain, there

---

[1] Gerhard Masur's seven-hundred page *Simón Bolívar,* Albuquerque, 1948, is the best one-volume biography of the Liberator. I have relied heavily upon it in the preparation of this chapter.

arose new political entities led by Creoles, who considered themselves Americans, rather than by Peninsulars, who knew that they were Spaniards. When the new rulers failed to dominate the war-torn societies, the emerging nations lapsed into a generation of chaos and anarchy.

Localism and Regionalism. From the first there was never at the local level unanimity of opinion on the merits of revolution and evolution. Everywhere there was parochialism born of Spain's imperial system. A kind of individualism, which Américo Castro calls "personal separatism," [2] set one man against another, previewing the personalism that later dominated the politics of the emergent republics. These underlying currents produced civil disputes of various kinds. Some pitted partisans of independence against loyalists who often were as "American" as their opponents. This was the case in Chile, Mexico, Paraguay, and Uruguay. Some local conflicts, like those of Venezuela, turned race against race, as the masses, moved more by instinct than reason, battled against Creole and Spaniard alike, siding first with the mother country and then with their former masters. Still others, particularly in Colombia, arrayed district against district. In Argentina the strife was rural-urban; in Peru, Bolivia, and Ecuador, mountain against coast. The variety of internal conflicts testifies to the fact that struggles for home rule were also struggles over who would rule at home. No matter what was at the root of any specific struggle, its effect was to divert the resources which could be directed against Spain and to nourish rivalries which later plagued the new nations.

These conflicts dominated Bolívar's entire adult life. They commanded the use of his numerous talents. They absorbed his prodigious physical energy. Yet he in turn dominated them. Never once did he compromise his ideal that his native Venezuela should be independent. Initially he helped to generate radical Independence struggles against Spain; later he, at times almost single-handedly, guided a large part of South America along the road to freedom. Civil wars sometimes forced him to postpone victories or, as at Ayacucho, to absent himself from triumphs. At other times they destroyed the fruits of his vic-

[2] *The Structure of Spanish History,* translated by Edmund L. King (Princeton, 1954), pp. 619-620.

tories. His triumphs in the name of liberty and his refusal to be diverted from his ultimate objective by domestic differences made him the epitome of a generation who fought for freedom. He was *the* Liberator.

Bolívar's Revival. Simón Bolívar died near Santa Marta, Colombia, on December 17, 1830. A few days earlier he had expressed the wish to be buried in Caracas, Venezuela, where he was born July 24, 1783, the year Great Britain recognized the independence of the United States of America. But so hated and feared was he by the political and military leaders of his strife-torn native land that twelve years passed before his family dared remove his body to Caracas, where it remains enshrined. For much of the rest of the century the name Bolívar was practically forgotten or alternatively made the symbol of controversy.

When the nations which owed to him their freedom from Spain were indifferent to him, it was because in the course of their efforts to be Europeans, something they were not and never could be, they had lost their cultural orientation. And Bolívar's essence and character, his life and works are intelligible only within the framework of the Spanish American culture which had formed him. When Bolívar became a symbol of controversy, it was because centrifugal tendencies—national rivalries, the ambitions and treacheries of lesser men, and, sometimes, gross ignorance—were relentlessly undermining the foundations of his life's work.

In this century Bolívar's political creations—Bolivia, Colombia, Ecuador, Peru, and Venezuela, have been caught up and carried along by the Nationalist revolution of our time. In their frantic and often frustrating search for identity, they have again turned to the Liberator and have again made him a symbol, this time a symbol around which to rally. Love, adoration, reverence for the resurrected Bolívar, moreover, does not end at the borders of those republics most directly indebted to him. All nations in Latin America pay him homage, as well they might, because Bolívar, except for brief periods when he suffered from profound depression over what he considered his "failures," thought in hemispheric terms. And beyond the boundaries of Latin America his stature, never greater than at present, continues to grow in magnitude.

There were many others without whose efforts Spanish America would have remained longer under the tutelage of the mother country. José de San Martín, Bernardino Rivadavia, Bernardo O'Higgins, Francisco de Paula Santander, José Antonio Páez, and Antonio José de Sucre readily come to mind. But not one of these independence leaders fought Spain as tenaciously or for so many years as did Simón Bolívar. Not one of them won as much territory away from Spanish arms or freed so many people from colonial status as did Bolívar.

The Leader. Bolívar was more than a simple soldier, more than a nationalist or an internationalist. He was a man and a leader of many talents. It is the man and the leader that initially compel attention.

Bolívar, the man, was born into the Venezuelian Creole aristocracy. Orphaned at the age of nine, he inherited one of the greatest fortunes of all of colonial Spanish America: a half-dozen houses in Caracas and the port of La Guaira, huge agricultural estates, vast herds of cattle in the valleys of Aragua and Tuys, and the rich copper mines of Aroa. All the material comforts and social privileges that the Creole aristocracy had won for itself were his. But he eschewed the traditional past and embraced the cause against Spain, pouring his vast personal fortune and his still greater abilities into the long and bitter and ultimately successful effort to free the North and South American mainlands from Spanish colonialism.

Bolívar was a changemaker, not an opportunist. By keeping faith with his ideals and exhibiting rare qualities of leadership, he ultimately moved his people to want freedom. Once the desire was aroused, he could exploit those of his qualities which made others see him as their savior. If in the discussion below no effort is made to emphasize one quality at the expense of others, it is because Bolívar's greatness lay in his ability to draw simultaneously upon all of his personal resources.

Generosity was one of the characteristics that Bolívar exhibited throughout his public career. That he contributed his great personal fortune to the cause of liberty may be evidence of the generous strain in him or it may have been a reflection of his indifference to money, which as a youth he spent lavishly and which as an adult he handed out to nearly every petitioner. That with his health broken, he fought as convincingly for political unity as he had fought earlier for liberty may be a more important testimony to his generosity towards his compatriots. His generosity is also manifested in his praise of his comrades. After being officially proclaimed *El Libertador,* the title he cherished above all others, he created the Order of the Liberators, to give his lieutenants a feeling of equality with him. Later he was unstinting in his praise of General Antonio José de Sucre, whom he called "the sword of Ayacucho . . . the avenger of the Incas . . . the liberator of Peru." [3] Sucre was, among Bolívar's many officers, the one whose stature most nearly approximated his own.

At times Bolívar's generosity towards those who fought by his side may have contained an admixture of flattery "for the general good." Assuredly, Bolívar could have known about flattery from his own receptiveness to it. For the most part, however, his praise was an honest expression of his feelings. This is true if for no other reason than that throughout his career he believed in men and in personal, creative action rather than in laws and institutions. With such an approach to progress, he had to have a generous view of those around him. Also, the continued dedication and loyalty of his subordinates to him and their ability under his inspiration to rise repeatedly to new heights suggests much more than a response to mere flattery.

Bolívar's readiness to share glory with his subordinates did not keep him from reacting sharply when his orders were not honored or his decisions disputed. He understood better than anyone that the *llaneros,* the cowboys of the Venezuelan flood plains, respected only the authority of a single individual at a time. This meant that the person in command either exercised authority absolutely or surrendered it completely. Bolívar's generosity could not, then, extend so far as to forgive those who were bold enough to be insubordinate. As the case of his lieutenant Manuel Piar proves, Bolívar was not above having a man judged and shot in the field for challenging his orders. Nor was

---

[3] Simón Bolívar, *Selected Writings of Bolívar,* comp. Vicente Lecuna, ed. Harold A. Bierck, Jr., translated by Lewis Bertrand, 2 vols. (New York, 1951), II, 497. Hereinafter this extremely valuable and often-used source will be cited as Bolívar, *Selected Writings.*

Bolívar as generous toward the leaders of the Plata areas as he might have been. Their contributions to the cause of South American independence were probably more significant than the Liberator was ever willing to acknowledge publicly.

Bolívar had a slight body gifted with incomparable energy and a seemingly infinite capacity to absorb punishment. Long before independence was won, his restless activity had become legend. He could march, sit in a saddle, or engage in battle throughout the daylight hours and then, after a change of clothes socialize throughout much of the night. This was true even when responsibility weighed most heavily upon him. At public functions he especially enjoyed dancing, and the livelier the step and the larger the audience, the greater his enthusiasm. It was as if he needed constant activity to release a perpetual tension. His endurance appealed tremendously to his tough, hard-riding cavalrymen, who expected their leaders to outstrip them in everything. Because he excelled in feats that captured the imagination of the working man, he was able to transform primitive, brutal, undisciplined hordes into armies that triumphed in the name of freedom.

His faith in his ideal and in himself gave Bolívar the courage to face adversity as few men in history have faced it. Defeated on many occasions, he never once admitted defeat during the fifteen years that he battled to overcome Spain. What is remarkable and also a measure of the man is that from each reversal at the hands of Spain and its allies he emerged stronger than before.

Latin American intellectuals historically have preferred to dwell upon Bolívar the visionary or the inspirational leader or the heroic man. (*See Reading No. 1.*) Admittedly, his grand design for the emancipation of Spanish America was the work of a visionary. No hard-headed practical realist could have entertained such a dream. Foreseeing anarchy, he pleaded for a kind of confederation that would amalgamate Creole power into a continental articulation of Spanish American interests. From his pen in 1812 came the "Cartagena Manifesto," northern South America's first great document of hemispheric unity.

Bolívar's ability to work and fight with all types of men was truly remarkable. His personal charm disarmed his critics. His readiness to attempt the heroic, inspired men to subordinate their conduct to the welfare of the cause. A consummate orator, actor, and writer, Bolívar was able to divert inspiration and heroism to wherever it was most urgently required: on the battlefield or in the halls of Congress, to a constitution, a treaty, or a battle plan.

However great his qualities and however outstanding his achievements, Bolívar was above all a man of action. His personality in fact compelled him to act, and as a man of action he was not faultless. He could be inconsistent. On occasion he made poor judgments which first affected the course of the Independence movement and later the evolution of the republics he brought into being. These will be pointed out with no intent to detract from the character of the man as a whole or to deny him any of the credit he so richly deserves.

Although Bolívar did not remarry after the death in 1803 of his bride of a few months, he was seldom without one or more women. Some individuals, more often foreigners than his own compatriots, have felt that Bolívar's "amours" and his flaunting of custom somehow made him a lesser leader than he otherwise would have been. I do not. Nor do I see how, in the past, elucidations of his private "affairs" have contributed significantly to an understanding of his public career, except perhaps to call attention to the fact that he was very much a man of those Byronic times.

But if Bolívar should not be faulted for the way he handled his private life, he can perhaps be criticized for his failure to win control over himself while so successfully controlling others. He seldom, for example, could keep his vanity within recognizable limits. On the occasion of his meeting with General José de San Martín at Guayaquil in 1822, he offered this toast: "To the two greatest men in America, General San Martín and myself." Flattery would nourish him when all else failed. He needed clear and continued evidence of approval. After he had liberated five republics, he gloried in the processions, titles, and statues struck in his honor. This meant that around him sincerity did not always reap its just reward. He also sought glory and power with determination. He was constitutionally incapable of visualizing himself in the role of a simple moderator. His ambition, however legitimate, however human, however natural, literally knew no bounds. (*See Reading No. 2.*)

On occasion wrong, sometimes dangerously wrong, Bolívar was one of those men who appear at long intervals to accomplish what is impossible for the ordinary man. Seeing the future and the past with equal clarity, he arose amid the passions of a romantic era. He was talented and he was determined, but he was also shackled to the environment in which he lived. Most of those with whom he worked were guided by beliefs and values formulated while Spanish America was under the domination of Bourbon Spain.

The purpose of the chapter which follows is to examine the reactions of Spanish Americans to the swiftly changing events of the late eighteenth and early nineteenth centuries; to present those aspects of the Spanish American past and the Northern European and Anglo-American present that made some men, among them Bolívar, willing to favor revolution and others to prefer the kind of conciliation they believed would guarantee peaceful development and progress.

CHAPTER 2

Reformed Spain, Responsive America

Almost one hundred years before the uprisings of 1810, the French Bourbons secured their claims to the crown of Spain. The Treaty of Utrecht gave Philip V dominion over a metropolis and its subject American colonies, all in the throes of a century-long decline. It also stripped Spain of Gibraltar, Minorca, the Netherlands, Naples, Sardinia, and Sicily. Concession of a slave *asiento* gave England access to Spanish American commerce. The new rulers' primary imperative was to defend Spain's imperial status against Great Britain, then riding to new heights as a European and colonial power. Their goal was to create wealth which could be transformed into military resources.[1] The Bourbons instituted a series of reforms based upon humanistic teachings and enlightened despotism. In America, the reforms brought prosperity; in Spain they produced a vigorous revival of rationalism.

Bourbon Economic Policies. By 1800 Bourbon economic reforms, without having changed the basic colonial economic structure dating from the sixteenth century, had produced the highest level of prosperity that the colonials had ever enjoyed. Mining, notably in Mexico, was strongly stimulated through the application of up-to-date scientific and technical knowledge first brought by scientists from Europe and later disseminated through a College of Mines, which began classes in 1793. Despite a considerable increase in mineral production, the principal source of Mexico's riches was agriculture, as Alexander von Humboldt noted from first-hand experience during his visit to the New World from 1799 to 1804.[2] In most areas of the Empire export agriculture prospered as never before. The sale of hides, jerky, and tallow pumped life into the pampas of La Plata. The export of wheat helped to make Valparaiso, Chile, a leading Pacific port. The "Marquises of Cacao and Tobacco" glutted the legal Venezuelan market with their products and sold what they could of the remainder to smugglers operating primarily from the nearby Dutch islands.

Mineral and agricultural expansion combined with relaxed trade regulations to effect an era of unusual commercial pros-

[1] The Bourbons' international wars included: The War of the Spanish Succession, Spain and France vs. England, the Netherlands, Austria, and the Holy Roman Empire, 1702-1714; Spain vs. England, Austria, the Netherlands and France, 1718-1720; Spain vs. England, 1727-1729; the War of Jenkins' Ear, Spain vs. England, 1739; The War of the Austrian Succession, Spain, France, Prussia vs. England and Austria, 1740-1748; Spain and France in "Family Compact" vs. England and Portugal in the Seven Years' War, 1762-1763; Spain, France, and the United States vs. England, 1779-1783; Spain and England vs. Revolutionary France, 1793-1795; Spain and France vs. England, 1796; Spain and Napoleonic France vs. England and Portugal, 1801-1802; Spain and Napoleonic France vs. England and Portugal, 1804-1808; Spain and England vs. Napoleonic France, 1808-1814.

[2] Alexander von Humboldt, *Political Essay on the Kingdom of New Spain,* translated by John Black, 2nd ed., 4 vols. (London, 1814), II, 356.

perity. The monopoly of Cádiz collapsed before an increasingly liberal policy that by 1790 opened all ports in Spain, the Balearics, and the Canaries, and twenty-four littoral cities in America to Empire commerce. Certain customs duties and protective tariffs were reduced. Under the impulse of change La Plata, Chile, and Venezuela moved from stagnant backwashes into the mainstream of colonial trade. C. H. Haring calculated that between 1778 and 1788 the total value of commerce increased 700 per cent.[3] Successful merchants invaded the power structure and, before the end of the eighteenth century, were increasing the political influence of the commercial sectors at the expense of mine owners and agriculturalists.

Bourbon Political Reforms. Like their economic policies, the Bourbons' political reforms had as a major objective increased efficiency in the creation and collection of wealth. Political reforms had an added objective: to secularize authority and to consolidate power so as to reinforce direct Crown administration. Political changes bolstered royal authority by substituting Crown agents for churchmen and making key officials at all levels of government directly responsible to the Crown. The net result was that the imperial political structure was differentiated and specialized, while political functions were at one and the same time consolidated and confused.

The Bourbons extracted from enlightenment thought justification for the centralization of power and conveniently ignored that part of intellectual reasoning that denied blind obedience and emphasized a social compact. The result was a colonial system predicated on "everything for the people, but nothing by the people" (*todo para el pueblo; nada con el pueblo*), a kind of enlightened bourgeois despotism which contrasted to the humanistic royal absolutism of their Hapsburg predecessors.

The Bourbons undertook the first major overhaul of administration since the mid-sixteenth century. Their purposes were three: to modernize administration in view of the complexities of the colonies, to prepare the Empire for international wars which they correctly predicted would increasingly be fought in America, and to catalyze inert areas. Special defense problems (for example, the construction of elaborate coastal fortresses), economic retardation, and sheer isolation dictated that northern

[3] *The Spanish Empire in America* (New York, 1947), p. 342.

South America be made into a viceroyalty. This was done in 1717. Called Nueva Granada, the viceroyalty was abolished in 1724 but restored in 1740. At one time or another it included modern Colombia, Ecuador, and Venezuela, the three states that Bolívar later insisted must be maintained as a unit, and also Panama, where the Liberator would have located the capital of his "Greater America." In 1776, La Plata, languishing economically and threatened militarily by the Brazilian-based Portuguese, infested by smugglers from Great Britain, Portugal, Holland, and the United States, was made into a viceroyalty with Buenos Aires as its capital. Captaincies-general and military districts were created in both North and South America in order to tighten control over and foster development of areas distant from viceregal centers.

The most radical political innovation of the Bourbons was the introduction of the French intendant system. Cautiously tried in Spain itself, it was then imposed on America in stages. Only after it had proved successful in Cuba (1764) and in Argentine and Venezuelan rural areas (in the 1770's), did it become general. After 1786 Mexico was divided into twelve intendancy districts; Peru and La Plata into eight each; and Chile, Central America, and northern South America into fewer divisions.

The intendant system was part of the larger and continuing effort of the Crown, through its chosen agents, to exercise direct and, hopefully, more responsible secular control over ever smaller components of its vast New World holdings. To this end it was successful. Intendants injected a personal factor into administration that was previously lacking except in a few major centers. In response to the urgings of the more able intendants many districts underwent a political, economic, military renascence, while urban renewal beautified cities.

Perhaps most important, the intendants curtailed the authority of the *corregidores,* those local officials who, because of their generally corrupt practices and tyrannical treatment of the natives, had come to epitomize the worst in colonial rule. It was against a *corregidor* that José Gabriel Condorcanqui (Marqués de Oropesa), who assumed the title "El Inca, Tupac Amaru," led his essentially Indian following in a revolt near Cuzco, Peru, in November 1780. Tupac Amaru attracted some 80,000 to his standards, and before his uprising was cruelly suppressed, it had racked the heart of Spanish South America's wealth-producing region from Central Bolivia to southern Colombia.

Bourbon Secularism. Under the Hapsburgs, the Catholic Church had exercised considerable political influence through its close ties with the Crown. A politically influential Church was, however, incompatible with Bourbon centralist and secularist views, and the new dynasty early set about to reduce the ecclesiastical base of its temporal power. Before very long the "peculiar interpenetration of Church and State," which had marked Hapsburg rule, collapsed. And more or less to the degree that the Church lost political authority, it lost its power to coerce, both in Spain and in the colonies.

Philip V initiated the secular movement. On assuming power he surrounded himself with advisers from France where the current of secularism was running strong. When the time came to replace them, the Bourbons did not select representatives of the old Catholic Hispanism but turned to a new generation of Spaniards, who looked outside the Church for fresh ideas and who gave top priority to material progress.

By the late 1750's anticlerical elements were clearly in the ascendancy at Court. The Count of Aranda, one of the able ministers of Charles III, was the first in a series of outstanding individuals who, as agents of the Crown or advisers to the King, were strongly influenced against the involvement of the Catholic Church and particularly the Jesuit order in secular affairs.

The Jesuits felt the full impact of the new secular mood in Court when, in 1767, they were expelled from all of Spain's American colonies.[4] Various explanations have been advanced as to why the highly controversial measure—for so it continues to be considered—was carried out. Some individuals, including officials close to the king, believed that the Jesuits, who were regarded as the most successful agriculturalists, traders, and bankers in the colonies, possessed considerable wealth. Charles III undoubtedly had in mind the possibility that if the Jesuits did in fact have great treasure, it would revert to him. Also the Court was concerned that the Jesuits' disciplined organization and their opposition to "the divine rights of kings" might lead them to attempt to create an empire within the Empire. But

[4] The Jesuits had been expelled from Portugal and the Portuguese Empire in 1759; the Order was suppressed by the Pope in 1773.

apparently the decision to expel the order was above all a part of the continuing Bourbon effort to reduce the colonials' reliance upon the Church and to strengthen their ties with Madrid.

Church influence over secular matters received another, although milder, blow when the intendant system was established in the colonies. Intendants brought to their posts broad powers over economic and social matters. Those were areas of human relations where Churchmen, especially in the outlying settlements, historically had acted as moderators in a way that gave prestige to the institution they represented. In La Plata, intendants took direct action, exercising the right of *patronato* to select high Church officials.[5] There were other blows against the Church in favor of temporal authority. In 1774 the collection of tithes in America and the Philippines was taken from Churchmen and assigned to royal appointees. About the same time the Crown made limited encroachments against the sanctity of ecclesiastical *fueros* (privileges) by extending Crown jurisdiction over all common crimes and cases involving Church-related foundations.

Bourbon Social Objectives. In the social sphere the Bourbon reforms were more theoretical than were their decisions on economic, political, and Church matters. Since the Creoles already had legal equality with Peninsulars, social reforms were primarily directed to improving the living conditions and/or the social standing of the Indians and colored castes (*pardos*) and protecting bonded Negro slaves from the worst abuses of their masters.

The social reforms represented a Spanish humanistic response to the increasing number of uprisings involving people of color. Both liberalism and realism suggested that positive measures were demanded to prevent the further alienation of the submerged elements. With a thinly veiled hope that somehow short of politicizing the people of color they might be converted into potential Crown allies against disgruntled Creoles, the Bourbons set about making amends. The *encomienda, mita,* and *repartimiento* systems, under which the Indians almost from the founding of the first colony had been forced to labor, were

[5] John Lynch, *Spanish Colonial Administration, 1782-1810, the Intendant System in the Viceroyalty of the Río de la Plata* (London, 1958), p. 280.

definitively abolished during the reign of the enlightened Charles III (1759-1788). In Peru, wages of Indian miners were raised by law. As an aftermath of the Tupac Amaru uprisings (*see p. 19*), Indians were increasingly assigned to prestigious posts in essentially Indian communities, and a Peninsular intendant replaced the hated *corregidor*. In 1804 Charles IV rescinded a 1752 decree which excluded mestizos, zambos, mulattoes, and quadroons from the universities of Peru. Other new regulations permitted half-castes to enroll in seminaries and gave them equal rights with Creoles to purchase the title of "don." After 1797 men of color could be admitted to medical practice.[6] A decree of 1784 abolished the practice of branding slaves. This advance was followed in 1789 by a new "black" code. Meanwhile, the Bourbons struck at aristocratic privilege by imposing an inheritance tax aimed at subverting the practice of primogeniture and entail.

Well aware that Creole society had despised trade and manual labor, the Bourbons attempted to confer new status on those areas of activity in the hopes that they would create the kind of middle class that would insure an achieving society. In 1783 Charles III dignified skilled labor in a decree which was in a sense the most revolutionary change in emphasis of the century. Blacksmiths, tailors, shoemakers, carpenters all who distinguished themselves in commerce and industry, were to be considered not debased but "honest and honorable" and worthy of being nobles.

Bourbon enthusiasm for the progress produced by enlightened absolutism was mitigated by a fear of what the populistic theories that the Enlightenment also taught might provoke in the colonies. Thus successive kings freely exported the most up-to-date ideas for environmental development and governmental reform but resisted the introduction into their Spanish American Empire of doctrines they felt might undermine their aggregating authority.

Charles III, in 1767, ordered an end to the teaching in the universities of the doctrines of regicide and tyrannicide and in 1771 suppressed all Jesuitical teachings. In 1794 Charles IV

---

[6] François Raymond Joseph de Pons, *A Voyage to the Eastern Part of Terra Firma, or the Spanish Main, in South America, During the Years 1801, 1802, 1803, and 1804,* translated by An American Gentleman, 3 vols. (New York), 1806, I, 173-182.

suppressed all courses dealing with natural law, popular sovereignty, and popular law.[7] Viceroy Teodoro de Croix of Peru (1784-1790) forbade public spectacles showing the beheading or dethroning of nobles. Direct relations between Mexicans and inhabitants of the United States were prohibited, and news of political developments in the former British colonies was systematically suppressed. Spanish officials disseminated propaganda depicting the citizens of the new republic as pirates and outlaws without respect for religion or morality. Under Charles IV blows to Enlightenment thinking in Spain were felt in America in the form of increased censorship of revolutionary literature.

The Conflict between Goals and Achievements. Bourbon reforms and Bourbon restrictions did not always turn out as the Spanish Court hoped they would. All breaks with tradition had their price, and the enforcement of restrictive legislation often proved nothing less than a fiasco.

Economic reform cut several ways. Spain did not respond to economic innovation in the same positive way that the colonies did. This gave disgruntled elements in Spanish America opportunities to capitalize on the fact that it was the Peninsula, not America, that constituted the major obstacle to economic progress. Colonials railed against commercial companies to which the Bourbons had granted monopoly privileges in certain areas in return for loans and defense assistance. As early as 1748, for example, contentious Creoles in Venezuela rose against the most famous of the monopoly operations, the Basque-controlled Caracas Company. That company remained on the defensive thereafter, and private corporations with monopoly privileges in Honduras, Cuba, and Santo Domingo were brought under attack by residents of those colonies. Crown tobacco monopolies in Mexico, Chile, and Cuba and a royal alcohol monopoly in Ecuador yielded huge revenues but enraged Spain's New World subjects. Protests against monopolies and taxes sometimes led to violence, as in the case of some 20,000 *comuneros* who marched on Bogotá in 1781, demanding a change of administration and fiscal policy, and nearly toppled the local royal government.

[7] See Camilo Torres, "Memorial de agravios o representación del cabildo de Bogotá a la Suprema Junta Central de España [1809]" in *Bolívar, Camilo Torres y Francisco Antonio Zea* (Biblioteca Aldeana de Colombia) [Bogotá, 1936].

The prosperity which was directly traceable to economic reforms often exacted a high price. Domestic craftsmen suffered from cheap imports. The rise of Buenos Aires meant that Peruvian trade declined. Prosperity and contraband established new consumption patterns which increased a demand for goods that only foreigners could supply. But perhaps most important, Bourbon reform from above taught colonials that economic well-being could be directly influenced by political decisions. After 1810 advocates of separation from Spain insisted that independent states could legislate in their own economic self-interest.

Political reforms worked against Spain in a number of respects. The creation of new administrative districts whose authority, as it turned out, overlapped, produced such profound antagonism between Crown officials that by 1800 a true "crisis of administration" existed.[8]

The intendant system, the most imaginative measure in the political sphere and the one which, given time, might have proved the most successful, in the end did more than any other decision to create discord. Empowered to act in areas formerly delegated to others, intendants sapped authority from top to bottom of the old colonial hierarchy. No less important, the intendant system, with its declared objective of development of fringe areas, challenged the entire political structure. In practice that structure had confined Spanish authority largely to the more important administrative centers, while allowing Creole landlords free reign on the forgotten frontiers. Political reforms indeed centralized the Empire. But the intendant gave smaller areas an administrative, judicial, and financial focus which in the end tended to legitimize the local.

The intendant system struck at the Creoles from at least four other directions. First, like earlier administrative reforms, the system meant greater numbers of bureaucrats. Their influence, salaries, and superior attitudes all tended to add heat to long-standing conflicts between Crown officials and revenue-producing Creoles, who resented the loss of "independence" they had enjoyed under Hapsburg rule. Second, the intendants tightened law enforcement and the collection of taxes. Third, they weakened still further the already debilitated *cabildos*, those municicpal institutions borrowed from medieval Castile, which had main-

[8] See Lynch, *op.cit.,* Conclusion, pp. 279-289.

tained an echo of traditional local reform and self-government. By the late eighteenth century the *cabildos* ordinarily had neither program nor policy and their functions were primarily ceremonial. Still, seats on them were much sought after because they were the only administrative posts readily open to Creoles who, as a group, were always desperately concerned to enhance their prestige. Fourth and most important, when the time came to appoint the intendants, Spain named Peninsulars rather than Creoles. In showing its continued preference for those born in Europe over those born in America, the Court missed its last major opportunity to give ambitious Creoles the prospect of a greater voice in the direction of affairs of prime concern to themselves. Thus, like the other reforms which improved colonial administration, the intendant system removed Spanish subjects still farther from the source of power which determined their destiny.

Nor were the Bourbon victories over the Catholic Church complete ones. The increasingly secular definition given to authority by Charles III deepened the discord between "Creole spirit" and Spanish domination. This was because the rich and conservative Creole classes, historically the chief support of the Crown, tended to remain devoutly Catholic. In this sense the expulsion of the Jesuits, who had numerous ties with the Creole elites, marked the breaking of still another "spiritual link." In several respects the Order represented the "best" to be found in the colonies, and many Creoles appreciated this. Jesuits were the best educators. They were recognized leaders of society, the richest proprietors, the most enterprising farmers and industrialists. They wrote the most valuable accounts of the area's natural history and state of development. They were the most active missionaries. On the northern frontier of Mexico, they protected royal domains against French and British intrusions and on the frontiers of Peru and Paraguay from Portuguese invasions. They were, in the words of the Argentine scholar, José Luis Romero, "the strongest prop of authoritarianism in the colony" and more than any other element, they traditionally had provided a spiritual doctrinaire justification of Spanish Crown hegemony.[9]

[9] José Luis Romero, *A History of Argentine Political Thought*, translated by Thomas F. McGann (Stanford, 1963), pp. 51-52.

However, if the Jesuits suffered under Bourbon reforms, many other Churchmen found in the new environment a freedom to study and teach the new physical, natural, and political sciences. They prized that freedom and drank so deeply of humanism that when the Catholic hierarchy remained loyal to the Crown after 1808, some of the lower clergy in America rejected their superiors in favor of association with reform-minded lay groups.

Bourbon social reforms, which in effect meant trying to improve the lot of the underprivileged while simultaneously constraining the privileged, earned Spain little gratitude from any quarter. Not one of the lower social groups had good cause to be indebted to the mother country.[10] Crown officials in America had neither the power nor the will to enforce the laws which would have ameliorated the conditions of the African slaves. Their welfare, consequently, continued to depend largely upon the temperament of their masters. The basic condition of the Indians did not improve despite the legislation in their favor. Few from the mixed castes were able to take advantage of the opportunity to purchase titles of status or to enter the professions through education. Those few who did were ordinarily confronted by a Creole-erected color bar which the Spanish officials were unable to lower.

Creoles, for their part, restrained from above and threatened from below, were embittered by royal measures which encouraged the castes to invade the universities and professions and gain the degrees and decorations that Creoles had monopolized as a way of distinguishing themselves from "commoners." This serves to remind us that if before independence the Creoles fought the *de facto* segregation which kept them from attaining status equal to that of the Peninsulars, both before and after independence they fought no less ardently to maintain the checks that kept the mixed masses from attaining Creole status symbols.

If the Bourbons were disturbed by the failure of their social reform measures, they did not show it. Spain could profit from promoting the general welfare within the existing colonial social order. It could gain nothing from a radical reshuffling of the

[10] It should not be assumed that because the masses did not feel indebted to Spain they felt indebted to their Creole masters. This was not the case. As is developed in chapter 4, during the independence struggles the masses often fought on the side of Spain to rebel against the personal tyranny of their overlords.

local social classes. But Spain could benefit from keeping alive low pressure antagonisms between classes, and the Creoles, by socially ostracizing people of color, contributed to that end.

The Flow of New Ideas from Europe. Spain's efforts to keep revolutionary literature out of the colonies ended in monumental failure. Viceroys, Captains-general, and lesser bureaucrats were too few, when not unwilling, to man the levees hastily thrown together to stop the flow of ideas from Europe. In fact, Spain's attempts to exclude the revolutionary classics from America seemed only to intensify the determination of the Creoles to read them. The Church's attack upon Raynal enhanced curiosity about him in America. Once Rousseau was put on the Index in 1756 he became a "best seller" in the colonies. Earlier Spanish theorists such as the Dominican, Francisco de Vitoria (1480?-1546), and the Jesuits, Luis Molina (1535-1600), Juan de Mariana (1536-1623), and Francisco Suárez (1548-1617), from whose writings Rousseau may have drawn some of his ideas, were less well known than might have been expected. Creole intellectuals were by no means limited to the teachings of Raynal and Rousseau. Disgruntled Creoles found ready-made inventories of grievances in the works of Voltaire, Montesquieu, Diderot, Helvetius, Adam Smith, Locke, Bentham, Paine, and Jefferson. Intellectual salons (*tertulias*) were common and were held more or less openly. Despite restrictions on what could be produced in theaters, considerable revolutionary thought issued from the stage. Economic societies, patterned on those in Spain, promoted some interest in commerce, agriculture, history, and morality.

Inflammatory ideas were introduced into the colonies by the stream of Spanish, French, and German scientists who came to America on expeditions sanctioned by and often supported by the Spanish Crown. Among those who through direct contact most influenced Creole thinking were Jorge Juan, Antonio de Ulloa, José Celestina Mutis, Fausto d'Elhuyar, and Felix de Azara from Spain; Charles de la Condamine and François Raymond Joseph de Pons from France; and Thaddeus Hanke, Baron von Nordenflicht, and Alexander von Humboldt from Germany.

Political pamphlets from abroad were still another source of French views. In Colombia, Antonio Nariño, as early as 1793, had acquired a copy of the Declaration of the Rights of Man and was having it translated into Spanish for printing and distribution throughout South America. By the turn of the century sailors from the United States were preaching the virtues of independence in Chile, and their officers were distributing texts of the Constitution of the United States and the Declaration of Independence. Propaganda from the United States reminded the Creoles of what they already knew: Spain, in having supported the thirteen Anglo-American colonies against Great Britain had in fact sanctioned revolt against legitimate authority.

Reform and Revolt. The crucial question remains equivocally to be answered. Were the outbreaks of 1808-1810 and the subsequent declarations of independence from Spain caused by Bourbon Reforms and the introduction of radical political and economic theories into the colonies? Or were they fortuitously stimulated by the Napoleonic invasion of Spain?

Strictly on the basis of grievances arising from the reforms and Creole exposure to the thinking of eighteenth-century theorists, it appears unlikely that the uprisings would have occurred as early as they did. But without the continuous exposure to reform and theory, the Creoles probably would not have come to emphasize those characteristics which distinguished them from Spaniards, a highly important factor in the Independence struggle. Nor would they have ventured, in the manner of their contemporaries in Anglo-America, France, and Haiti, to give concrete application to the theoretical lessons they had learned.

Economic issues could not have provided a firm and lasting basis for union against the mother country. Although lists of complaints against Spain invariably included economic grievances and although Napoleon, once he invaded the peninsula, tried to play upon the Creoles' economic desires, the fact remains that Spain's New World subjects were far from agreed on their reactions to the measures taken by the Court to make America richer.

Militant opposition to change emanating from Madrid was often begun not by the "white" elites but by the popular elements—Indians in Peru and Bolivia, Negroes and mulattoes in Venezuela. The effect of those populist revolts which had strong racial overtones was not to divide Creole and Spaniard but to unite them in defense of their privileged position. And when it came the Creoles' turn to conspire in 1810 they were careful not to bridge their movements to the earlier mass-supported ones.[11]

Furthermore, as noted above, the elites themselves were deeply divided on the advantages and disadvantages of reform. The commercial regulations that benefited some ruined others. Those who prospered under relaxed trade restrictions were little inclined to plead the cause of those who suffered. It is worth recalling that Peru, which declined most from Bourbon economic reformation, was the last major continental area to be freed from Spain.

Creolism. Creoles were not ready to rebel against Bourbon administrative practices. They were embittered, to be sure, over the Court's decision to employ Spaniards instead of Creoles as intendants. But it is significant that while the intendant system was designed specifically to tighten royal control in hitherto "autonomous" areas, Creole *hacendados* accepted intendant impingement with remarkable docility. And when Creole discontent broke into the open, the spokesmen were ordinarily residents of the cities, not rural planters. In general the latter group followed rather than led. Only after the expulsion of Spain and the collapse of the commercial class through exile or from competition from British merchants did the rural land-holding elite usurp power from the urban elements who had initiated and kept alive the struggles for independence.

In much the same way that Creole elites bowed before the attacks upon their privileged status, the Catholic hierarchy accepted inroads on what churchmen had come to consider religious domains. The Church at no time offered sustained opposition to multiple assaults upon its prerogatives and to the Crown's determination to secularize political authority. When the disturbances of 1810 came, the higher clergy and a large share of the lower clergy, from conviction or apathy, remained in favor of continuing to take instructions from Spain. On the basis of currently available evidence, priests in Mexico like Miguel Hidalgo and José María Morelos were the exceptions rather than the rule.

A point is often made of the Jesuits' efforts to arouse colonials against Spain in retaliation for the expulsion of the Order from America. Some Jesuits did lend their prestige and vast knowledge

[11] Mexico was an exception. There, Hidalgo's predominantly Indian following terrified urban Spaniards and Creoles, who forgot their differences and joined together in loyal conservatism to oppose the patriotic pretensions of the provinces.

of the colonies to Spain's enemies. (*See Reading No. 3.*) Still the Jesuit effort against the Crown can hardly be hammered into a significant link in the chain of events leading to the developments of 1810. There is the added consideration that while the Jesuits had a following among the colonials, since many of them were sons of colonial families, they also had their influential enemies both civilians and ecclesiastics, as they would continue to have well into the modern period. One of the points on which nearly all American and Spanish representatives to the liberal constitutional Cortes of Cádiz in 1812 agreed was that the Jesuit order should not be re-established.

Neither reform nor social inequalities were prominent in the decisions of 1810, except for the already mentioned conflicts of interest between Creoles and Peninsulars. The Indians and *pardos,*[12] apathetic, lacking in ideas, and without common interests were incapable of organized action. Furthermore, at the start of the Independence movement the Indians' allegiance was more apt to be with the king than with the Creole elites whom they knew personally. For the Creoles to have involved the masses in political discussions would have run counter to the entire colonial tradition. Bolívar and others could, later on, enlist the support of the masses in a desperate effort to debilitate Spain; but if anything can be said with certainty, it is that the welfare of the masses was the farthest thing from the minds of men taking their first cautious steps on the road to political emancipation.

The influence of the intellectual climate is the hardest of all to measure. There is no doubt that it was important, but how important it is impossible accurately to determine. The new teachings from Europe had torn away some of the curtains of superstition and ignorance and had revealed several of the imperfections of colonial society. They had undermined the Church, especially in its temporal role. They had raised doubts about the status quo. They had challenged Spain's cultural monopoly and its prestige as the fountainhead of reform ideology in the colonies. They had given the elites a new rhetoric and an exciting new set of slogans. They had made the small intellectual elite aware that the world of

[12] The terms *pardos* and "castes" generally referred to free men of part-Negro blood, although occasionally mestizos were included. See James F. King, "A Royalist View of the Colored Castes in the Venezuelan War of Independence," *Hispanic American Historical Review*, XXXIII (Nov., 1953), 526-537.

thought and the world of politics were in revolt. What the new learning had not done was to offer solutions or acceptable alternatives to basic problems. In short, from the outpouring of theories the Creole elites had learned some of the things they were against but not as yet what they were for.

Although antagonism arising from political, economic, and social conditions and an introduction to the natural and political sciences did not of themselves produce revolutionaries, they did contribute to making the Creoles more aware of their own abilities as a class and of their own uniqueness. This consciousness of difference was a prior condition to breaking Spain's spell over them. I shall call this feeling of identity "Creolism" rather than the then new and mystifying nationalism which became meaningful only after independence. The distinction is important because Creolism provided a basis for hemispheric solidarity but little basis indeed for national consolidation. Between 1810 and 1814 nationalism would not have permitted, as Creolism did, loyalty to the Spanish Crown while denying loyalty to the Spanish nation.

Certain authors, for example the Mexican, Fernando Benítez, date Creolism from the rifts which developed between the descendants of the original conquerors and the officials sent from Spain to administer the colonies.[13] There is no doubt that the American experience acted upon individuals in a way to make them feel different from Spaniards (a term which suggests a unity that in fact did not exist) who remained on the peninsula. Even so, Creolism was an essentially passive phenomenon without political portent until the eighteenth century.

Creolism and Bourbon reforms began to show results at about the same time. The Frenchman, François Raymond Joseph de Pons, visited Venezuela from 1801 to 1804 and returned home to write that Creoles scarcely remembered that Spain was their mother country. "They are confident that they inhabit the happiest land upon the globe. . . . Intoxicated with this opinion, they feel a sense of pride at being born on the soil of a New World." [14] Humboldt observed that after 1789 Creoles preferred to be called "Americans." (*See Reading No. 4.*) Bourbon policies gave Creoles

---

[13] *The Century after Cortés,* translated by Joan MacLean (Chicago, 1965).

[14] de Pons, *op. cit.,* I, 112.

access to the work of foreign scientists who had discovered a rich and diverse natural environment in Spanish America. Once conscious of America, Creoles also became conscious that they were permanently asociated with it in contrast to the "transient" Spaniards. They contrasted the richness of America to the poverty and decadence of Spain. If for Humboldt, America was great and rich, for Colombian propagandist Camilo Torres that meant that it was mature and worthy of being free.

Loyalty and Disloyalty. Assuming that the colonies had become the principal and Spain the accessory, the question followed, "Why should 'Americans' remain subject to Spain?" Those few who opposed the continued relationship found ready answers to the question. By 1808 there were few survivals from the set of mutual interests that had for so long linked Creole to Spaniard. For centuries the Crown had commanded Creole allegiance through its control over land and Indian labor. However, as the colonial era drew to a close, Creole claims to possession of their estates in perpetuity was a fact in practice if not in theory. Although the Bourbon kings had decreed legislation designed to mitigate the condition of the Indian, he remained subject to the caprices of his masters. In their turn, the masters had come to fear the loss of Indian labor more through uprisings than through the courts.

Two and a half centuries earlier, the original settlers, Catholic zealots that they were, could with good reason trust equally zealous Spanish kings to protect them from aggressive Protestantism. By the beginning of the nineteenth-century Protestantism no longer seemed so threatening because the bitterness of the Reformation and the Counter-Reformation had abated as both Catholic and Protestant learned something of toleration. Also, the Spanish Catholic Church seemed less important because the secularist policies of the Bourbons had undermined its political-economic-social role.

Before the outbreaks of 1808-1810, it was apparent that Spain was declining as a world power. Decadence invited disloyalty from its overseas subjects. Sixteenth-century settlers knew that they could depend upon a mother country that was a formidable military power with the world's greatest land army and dominion of the seas. By contrast, eighteenth-century Creoles knew that Spain could not defend itself, much less the Americas, as Great

Britain already had proved. In a single generation England had stripped Spain of the Falklands and Trinidad and had driven Spain's frontiersmen from Nootka Sound, its outpost of Empire on Vancouver Island.

The Spain of the early Hapsburgs had produced goods and provided markets. The Spain of the late Bourbons could do neither with any degree of consistency. When at war with England, Spain was so effectively cut off from its American subjects that it turned to neutrals to supply them. Thus in 1797 colonial ports were opened to neutral shipping. This was followed in 1799 by efforts to limit imports from neutrals to foodstuffs. In 1801 the colonies were opened to licensed ships, only to be entirely closed in 1802. In 1804 they were again open to trade. Such capricious enforcement testified to Spain's decline. Reduced to the status of a "powerless power," [15] Spain was losing undeclared wars.

Even when Spain was at peace with its neighbors, smugglers took advantage of colonial connivance and official cupidity to flood the empire with contraband. Smuggling was so prevalent in La Plata that it became a cherished "natural right." The debility of Spain on the one hand and the daring of the *contrabandistas* on the other combined to produce a kind of amoral flexibilty that was conducive to expediency.

Spain, with its back to the wall, became a subject of vilification. Creole journals such as *El Mercurio peruano* and *La Gaceta de Mexico* not only called attention to local issues; they began to evoke the Indian past and revive the Black Legend. Mexico's foremost liberal, José María Luis Mora, recalled that phrases like "the barbarism of conquest" and "three hundred years of slavery" were repeated over and over. By 1811 the Caracas Declaration of Independence avenged a century of metropolitan arrogance with a phrase of contempt:

> It is contrary to the order of nature that territories so much more extensive and a population so incomparably more numerous should be subject to and dependent upon a peninsular corner of the European continent.

As they negated their Spanish origins, as they flattered themselves that "culture" had progressed more rapidly in the colonies than on the peninsula, Creoles moved closer to the perilous con-

[15] Daniel Cosío Villegas, *American Extremes,* translated by Américo Paredes (Austin, Texas, 1964), p. 37.

clusion that would deny them identity: progress was French
or English; to progress was to imitate.

Meanwhile the Creoles manufactured, as all revolutionaries
sooner or later must, a kind of moral justification for their
actions. They contrasted Spain's degeneracy with their own youthful receptivity to change and used the results to justify the escala-
tion of unrest to revolt. What commenced as uprisings against
Napoleon's usurpation evolved into rebellions against Spanish
domination and eventually into civil wars. As some fought to
break away from the mother country and others to cling to it,
the disintergration of the enormous American Empire set in.

Creolism was indeed a sense of uniqueness. It did exist.
Intellectuals did read and discuss the world's rebels. And yet
neither alone sparked rebellion. It took powerful stimulants
from the outside to transform Creole grievances and political
theories into justifications for direct action. The strongest stimulants from abroad were the independence of the United States
of America; the French Revolution; the Haitian Independence
movement; and the divisive influences growing out of Napoleon's
occupation of the peninsula. The influences of these four developments invite at least two observations. The Spanish American
Independence movements were fulfilled by isolated episodes of
civil war. Yet, they were in themselves processes which were dy-
namically linked with movements and currents that were flourish-
ing in other parts of the western world. And the most Jacobinist
of the Creoles shared the vocabulary and the aspirations and
pursued courses that other peoples were pursuing.

Creoles had almost immediately grasped the philosophical implications of the revolutionary upheavals in Anglo-America and
France, and from them had spun their own doctrines of political
liberalism. Now those who believed in action as well as words
were learning the very concrete lessons of applied political science
that the revolutions taught them. To the man of action, each
provided abundant proof that legitimacy could be successfully
challenged, that oppressive regimes could be toppled by the citi-
zenry in arms, that the power of monarchs could be returned to
the people; in brief, that colonials could break their bonds.

Haiti, on the other hand, dampened the rebels' enthusiasm.
There an aroused population composed overwhelmingly of illiterate slaves and ex-slaves shouting slogans invented by Parisian

mobs and trusting force rather than theory, nearly exterminated the "white settlers." In the process, they wrested independence from Napoleon in 1804.

But the United States offered proof that an ex-colony could survive as an independent nation. This fact was of special significance because in the final analysis, independence would be the truly popular cause since it was the easiest for the masses to grasp. Also, the misgivings raised in the minds of some Creole aristocrats by the excesses of the French and Haitian revolutions were, to paraphrase Salvador de Madariaga, laid to rest by the spectacle of men like Washington and Jefferson living like patriarchs in comfortable wealth among slaves.[16] *In toto*, the example of the United States offered the activists promise of political success and economic security of the kind that no amount of abstract reasoning could. As would prove important later, the United States experience also gave to revolutionary thought a narrower, more national, more personal character than did the French revolutionaries, whose ideas of liberty, fraternity, and equality had a distinctly universal quality about them. Throughout the long struggle for independence, Bolívar and other revolutionary leaders leaned first toward the one and then the other, undecided as to whether they were essentially Nationalists or Internationalists.

It is all too easy to equate the forces of discontent or even the forces of change with the forces of revolution. In those years from 1808 to 1810, as Napoleon overran Spain, the majority of Spanish Americans remained as vociferously loyal to King Ferdinand VII as did peninsulars. Their inertia, a comfortable feeling of stability and prosperity, testified to the ultimate success of the Bourbon reforms. They deposed viceroys, captains-general, and governors not in the name of liberty but in the name of the captive King Ferdinand, *El Deseado*. Humboldt, writing in 1799-1804, had predicted why. They saw in revolution only loss: loss of privilege, loss of slaves, loss of status, loss of wealth. Above all they hated equality and dreaded domination by their social inferiors. (*See Reading No. 5.*)

The Bourbons' final failure was not their inability to hold America. It was their inability to hold peninsular Spain itself.

[16] Salvador de Madariaga, *The Fall of the Spanish Empire* (New York, 1948), pp. 304-305, 323.

Bent on bringing Spain into his orbit, Napoleon forced Charles IV to abdicate in favor of Ferdinand VII, then lured both to France and imprisonment. On June 6, 1808, Joseph Bonaparte was crowned King of Spain. The Spanish people refused to acknowledge him. Instead, they declared their fervent loyalty to Ferdinand and to the integrity of the monarchy. Spain's subjects in America took the same stand, their Spanish Catholicism originally triumphing over their franco-philosophy. Their pledge to Ferdinand represented the last Hispanic American hemispheric consensus. Never again would all the colonies or all of the nations speak with a single voice or join in a united acclaim.

CHAPTER 3

The Making of Creole Radicalism

Between 1808 and 1810, loyal insurrection convulsed Spain and Spanish America. At issue was the matter of accepting or rejecting the several councils in Spain that claimed to speak for Bourbon authority against Napoleonic power. In South America every major colonial administrative district divided over the issue, with the larger centers tending to favor the creation of their own autonomous *juntas* to act until the king was restored, and provincial towns often showing a disposition in favor of peninsular *juntas*. Nowhere did the issue create greater division than in Venezuela, where Bolívar and a small group of like-thinking individuals injected into the regency question a demand for complete and immediate independence.

Bolívar's Early Development. The future Liberator first publicly declared himself unalterably opposed to further domination by Spain in 1809. His statements during that year made clear that he had completed the transformation from aristocrat to revolutionary. However, the route which led him to his decision is unclear for at least two reasons. First, Bolívar never took time out from his busy life to analyze in full the experiences which determined him to become an embattled crusader for freedom.

Second, at the moment he became a revolutionary, he was still far from having developed either a systematic philosophy of life or a coherent political theory.

The inconsistencies and the intellectual disorderliness apparent in 1809 dated from his early youth. As a child, Simón was, we are told, unruly and given more to physical development than to study. His lack of learning was apparent in 1799 when at the age of sixteen he traveled to Spain for the first time and members of the Madrid branch of his family noted that his intellectual poverty contrasted sharply with his material well-being. But whatever his lack of learning, it did not keep him from having a spirited year in the capital of Spain. He took advantage of family connections to establish contact with the degenerate Spanish court dominated by Queen María Luisa, wife of the incompetent Charles IV. Under the urging of the Marquis de Ustariz, his protector, the young Bolívar developed an appreciation for reading. Finally, he fell madly in love with María Teresa, daughter of Caracas-born nobleman Rodríguez de Toro.

Within a year Bolívar was out of favor at court and, under the admonition of his family to grow up a bit before claiming María Teresa, he set off for Paris. There he enjoyed for a few months the festive life that hid the cares of a France shaken by Napoleon. Early in 1802, Bolívar, age eighteen, returned to Spain, wed María Teresa, and took her directly to Venezuela, where she died on January 22, 1803.

The experiences of his first European sojourn might have headed the youthful Bolívar on his way to becoming a revolutionary. He could have been shocked or embarrassed, as some Creoles already were, by the corrupt Spanish court, by Spain's material and intellectual backwardness, by the widely-held view in northern Europe that Spain was no longer a first-rate world power. His serious introduction to the reading of books might have inspired him to search out a philosophy of his own. What Napoleon was doing to France could have sparked Bolívar's political ambitions. Any one of the above could have happened, but they probably did not. He was still very young and while it is reasonable to assume that he stored up impressions which he later drew upon to support his case for freedom, when he headed for Venezuela with his new bride, revolution was probably the farthest thing from his mind.

The death of María Teresa may have influenced Bolívar's development as a revolutionary. It is conceivable that had she lived, he might have taken a more passive role in the Independence movement. However, it should be noted immediately that not one of the several women whom he was later to have as confidants and mistresses ever influenced him for long. This being the case, his wife's death in and of itself was probably not as important a determinant as was the fact that it occurred when it did. It released him of all family responsibility at a time when in Spanish America agitation was on the upsurge, and mail from Europe indicated that the brilliant Napoleon was almost daily setting new standards of achievement for those who would seek glory by the sword. (*See Reading No. 6.*)

Within a few months of his bride's death, Bolívar was again en route to Europe. It was 1803. When he reached Madrid, he discovered that in his absence young Creoles idling away their time in the capital had begun thinking revolutionary thoughts against a decadent Spain. Bolívar, however, was still content to listen and observe.

He left Madrid for Paris, where he saw Napoleon crowned emperor. The young Venezuelan aristocrat was perhaps more impressed by the Corsican's personal success than by his threat to freedom. The coronation may have aroused in Bolívar such a driving desire for glory that it could be satisfied only by doing something as spectacular as liberating America. He was quite capable of thinking in such grandiose terms.

In Paris, he felt the currents of new freedom and lively cultural activities. He also read extensively in Montesquieu, Voltaire, Rousseau, Locke, Condillac, Buffon, D'Alembert, Helvetius, Hobbes, and Spinoza. He studied the Anglo-American and French revolutions. He talked on at least two occasions with Alexander von Humboldt, probably the leading scientist of the day. Humboldt had recently returned from an extended trip to Mexico and northern South America, including Venezuela, convinced that the area and its people were different and worthy of a separate existence. That is what he told Bolívar.

Bolívar's expanding horizons led him briefly into Freemasonry through a Paris lodge. The order was in the forefront of revolutionary thinking and would play an active role in the Spanish American Independence movements, particularly in La Plata and

Chile, where General José San Martín of Argentina and Dictator-President Bernardo O'Higgins of Chile were members. Seemingly Masonry's elaborate ritual was more than Bolívar could abide, and he apparently soon disassociated himself from that order. His rejection of Masonic ritual is sometimes noted as evidence of his developing democratic idealism.

In the spring of 1805 Bolívar decided to leave Paris and make his way to Italy. He joined his favorite childhood tutor, Simón Rodríguez, an eccentric disciple of Rousseau, who accompanied him to Rome. Years later Rodríguez was prodded by Bolívar to recall that it was on Mount Aventine, in the Eternal City, that he had vowed to liberate his country. Whether or not Bolívar actually made the vow is uncertain. What is certain is that somewhere between Madrid and Rome, sometime during 1804 and 1805 he became less the observer and more the activist. We do not know, probably will never know, what was uppermost in his mind: a burning desire to free Hispanic America or the personal glory that would accrue to the individual who achieved it.

Early Venezuelan Radicalism. When Bolívar returned home in 1807, Venezuela like most of the remainder of Spanish America was ripe for conspiracy. While the future Liberator was still in Europe the town council (*cabildo*) of Buenos Aires had deposed a viceroy named by Spain and installed one of its own choosing. By early 1808 the level of discontent was rising rapidly. In July residents of Caracas rejected emissaries of Joseph Bonaparte. Two months later Montevideo elected a *junta* to reign in the name of captive King Ferdinand VII. In Mexico a *junta* in partnership with the Creole *cabildo* and Frenchified Viceroy José de Iturrigaray took a cautious step towards autonomy by voting not to recognize the Junta of Seville.[1] However, on the night of September 15, 1808, some three hundred conspirators backed by the Archbishop, the Grand Inquisitor, the Audiencia, landowners, and Vera Cruz and Mexico City

---

[1] Mexico waited until a Central Junta, formed in the name of all peninsular juntas, declared war on the French, September 1808 at Aranjuez. It fled to Seville, then to Cádiz, and on January 29, 1810, turned over its authority to a regent Council of five on the Isla de León. It was this last group, the Regency, that called America to the Cortes which wrote the liberal Constitution of 1812.

merchants deposed Viceroy Iturrigaray in the name of Ferdinand VII.

In January 1809 loyalist troops in Buenos Aires frustrated an attempt to form an autonomous *junta*. In June, July, and August, disgruntled elements in Chuquisaca and La Paz (now Bolivia) and Quito (now Ecuador) created *juntas* to protect themselves against the pretensions of Carlota, Ferdinand's sister, whose intrigues were further complicated by her position in Brazil as wife of Dom João, exiled King of Portugal. Royalist forces crushed both Carlota's supporters and her autonomist opponents.

These initial outbreaks were followed in 1810 by another series of revolts that are today generally recognized in Latin America as marking the true beginning of independence. First in Caracas on April 19; then in Buenos Aires on May 25; Bogotá on July 20; Dolores, Mexico on September 16; and Santiago, Chile on September 18, insurrections in the name of autonomous *juntas* took place. They foreshadowed the beginning of the end of Spain's American Empire and the initiation of Creole rule.

Bolívar welcomed with mixed feelings the course of events in Caracas where the Captain-General was forced to resign and a *junta* was formed. That body in turn declared itself independent of the French Usurper but under the scepter of Ferdinand. Bolívar would have preferred a declaration of absolute independence under a republican form of government. And he was undoubtedly disappointed that he had not been one of the leaders of the movement despite his misgivings about its direction. He was already displaying those qualities which throughout his life made it nearly impossible for him to compromise or graciously to submit to someone else's leadership.

Few of those most directly involved shared Bolívar's view that the Caracas *junta* had not gone far enough. More moderate men easily gained control of policy-making during the months following the creation of the *junta* while radicals of the Bolívar variety were largely excluded from principal posts in the government. The districts of Coro and Maracaibo in the west and Guiana in the east, distrusting even the moderates, turned down an invitation to join with Caracas and remained loyal to Spain. In making that decision the three Venezuelan provinces were in effect joining with numerous other outlying districts in all parts of Spanish America in a precedent-setting action that made disunity based upon regionalism a primary deterrent to the wars for independence and to the development of viable governments afterward. In Europe the Regent Council declared the *caraqueños* and their provincial adherents in rebellion and took measures to reassert Spain's authority.

Bolívar in England. Confronted with opposition from elements of their own social-economic group, from small towns which insisted on their own autonomy, and from those provinces that remained loyal to the Regency, the Caracas *Junta* sought the protection of Great Britain. Bolívar, still disapproving of the *junta*'s moderation, was entrusted to lead a mission to London to solicit the assistance of Great Britain. The mission failed in its objective. Bolívar, inexperienced in diplomacy, went beyond his instructions to request the support of Great Britain for complete independence. Foreign Minister Richard Wellesley could not sanction, much less approve, a policy that might threaten England's Spanish alliance against Napoleon. In fact, Wellesley urged the Venezuelans to recognize the Regency, a proposal that Bolívar rejected peremptorily. This was not the last time that the Spanish American colonies would fail in their efforts to win support for their cause. They would in fact fight and win their battles for freedom with little assistance from Europe or from the United States, although, as will be made clear, the contribution of Great Britain was important in a number of ways.

While in London, Bolívar met for the first time Francisco de Miranda, widely revered as the "Precursor of Independence." Although his instructions explicitly stated that he should not make deals with Miranda, Bolívar convinced the Precursor that he owed it to Venezuela and the rest of America to return and lead a liberating movement. The next two years of Bolívar's life were inextricably tied to Miranda's. The relationship did not increase the stature of either man.

Miranda was a dedicated professional revolutionary. Born into the lower gentry in Venezuela in 1750, at age twenty-one he went to the Peninsula to become a soldier in the Spanish forces. For a decade he fought in the Old World, in Africa, and in the revolution of the thirteen Anglo-American colonies once Spain joined them against Great Britain.

Despite his services on behalf of the Spanish Empire, Miranda determined that Spanish America should be free. He turned to

Europe for aid. Between 1789 and 1792 he sought to interest the British government in his projects. Unsuccessful, he went to France where he served in the French forces and intrigued against Spain for several years before being imprisoned by the Jacobins. He was exiled from France in 1797 and thereafter divided most of his time between Great Britain and the New World, including the United States.

Independence was a passion with Miranda. Wherever he could find listeners among the young Creoles traveling and studying in Europe, he appealed to their "Americanism" and exhorted them to revolt against decaying Spain. He supplemented his personal contacts with a steady stream of correspondence to his acquaintances in America in the same vein.

Failing to win support in France or England for his schemes, Miranda sailed to the United States in 1805. With subsidies from various sources he obtained the sloop *Leander,* and headed south with about 200 adventurers. He added reinforcements in Haiti and proceeded to Coro where he landed in April 1806 and proclaimed the independence of his fatherland. Revealing the conservatism they affirmed four years later in accepting the Regency, the residents of Coro greeted the Precursor with apathy. Miranda re-embarked and in August, under the guns of a British squadron, made another attempt near Puerto Cabello, where his Coro experience was repeated. In despair he sailed for England only to find British interest in Spanish America had been distracted by the urgent need to contain Napoleon's advances on the continent. Miranda's fortunes were at a low point, and he had become little more than a pawn of British diplomacy by the time Bolívar contacted him.

The Return of Miranda. Miranda reached Caracas on December 10, 1810, a few days after Bolívar's return. His appearance sharpened the dissension among the Creoles. Those who favored complete independence from Spain quickly made him their spokesman. But the moderates distrusted Miranda. They felt that he had been out of touch with Venezuela so long that he had no real appreciation of Creole thinking. Their opposition to him increased when by his behavior he gave the impression that he was the polished sophisticate, and they provincial rustics. His efforts to woo a personal following convinced some that he was nothing more than a soldier of fortune and others that he was a tool of the British, who had designs on Venezuela. And while certain Creoles wanted freedom from Spain, they did not want it at the price of becoming subjects of Great Britain or any other power.

Elected to Congress, Miranda became the champion for absolute independence. On July 3, 1811, he proclaimed, "We ought to declare our independence: so that we may enjoy the advantages of it; in order that European nations may make alliances with us, which will aid us by engaging directly the forces of our enemies." [2] Two days later Congress voted in favor of the Miranda proposal, thereby declaring that the provinces they represented were and ought to be by act and right, free, sovereign, and independent states. The document recalled the evils of the colonial regime by passing over them in "silence" and declared that the usurpation of Napoleon had destroyed the legitimate link that had bound them to the Spanish Crown. It censured the Regency for having responded to Venezuelan actions of 1810 with acts of war rather than of understanding. The imprescriptible rights of a people, it affirmed, included the right to destroy every pact, convention, or association that did not fulfill the purpose for which governments were established. The radicals within the upper class had triumphed over the moderates of that same class. With slight modifications, and with varying degrees of emotionalism, those justifications for independence were repeated from Mexico to La Plata.

Independence declared, the Venezuelan Congress began writing a constitution. The charter they completed six months later, on December 21, 1811, manifested Creole concern for the preservation of economic privileges and demonstrated their sensitivity and receptiveness to political idealism. In defense of private property the document retained African slavery, but except for Negro slaves, all persons regardless of color were declared equal. Indian tributes and corporate privileges (*fueros*) were abolished. As strongly as it defended individual liberties, it denied religious freedom by making Roman Catholicism the religion of the United Provinces.

With independence proclaimed and a constitution promul-

[2] William Spence Robertson, *Rise of the Spanish-American Republics as Told in the Lives of Their Liberators* (New York, 1918), pp. 62-63.

gated, the problems of Venezuelan patriots had only begun. The masses did not understand what had taken place or why. To them it mattered little whether their masters were Creole or Spanish. The swift-moving events had deepened the divisions within the oligarchy. Then, as if the problems of the patriots were not sufficiently great, an earthquake laid waste Caracas and several other towns, on March 26, 1812. The quake did irreparable damage to the cause of independence. What optimism remained turned to deep pessimism as the Regent Council, which had taken advantage of Coro's dispute with Caracas to land troops, now launched an offensive. Threatened with military defeat, the Venezuelan Patriots quickly foreswore those idealistic provisions of their constitution which had sanctioned a high degree of local autonomy and dependence upon a multiple executive. They gave Miranda powers that made him a virtual military and political dictator.

The Precursor had displayed little modesty in discussing his military and administrative abilities, but when given absolute power, he proved incompetent and indecisive. Unable to forget the modern armies of Europe with which he had fought, he instinctively distrusted the rag-tag Patriot forces and their poorly trained Creole officers. More basically, he was unwilling to lead a true social revolution for fear that it would give rise to slave insurrections which might destroy the liberal framework that he envisioned. Bolívar, on the contrary, would prove many times that he was willing to take that risk.

Miranda's attitudes, combined with military pressure from Spanish forces and desertions which swelled their ranks, caused Patriot support to dwindle rapidly. On July 25, 1812, by the Treaty of San Mateo, Miranda surrendered Venezuela to the Spaniards. Counter-revolution had triumphed. Miranda prepared to flee the country with a considerable share of the Patriots' meager funds. Before he could make his escape he was seized in the port of La Guaira and turned over to the Spaniards by a group of patriots who included Bolívar.

The Miranda Incident. The surrender of Miranda climaxed several months of increasing enmity between him and Bolívar. The future Liberator had been responsible for Miranda's return to Venezuela and had freely acquiesced when the radicals named Miranda their spokesman. Both men had been instrumental in bringing about the declaration of complete independence from Spain and subsequently they had argued in vain for a strong centralized government. But as early as the Declaration of Independence in July 1811, if not before, they had begun to grow apart. The sixty-year-old Precursor believed that the Spaniards in Venezuela should be protected; the twenty-seven-year-old Bolívar wanted them expelled. Personal antipathy strained the difference of opinion to the breaking point. Miranda sensed that Bolívar was vying for power and tried to keep it from him. When neighboring Valencia rose in revolt against Caracas, Miranda chose to quell the rebellion himself and to keep Bolívar from sharing any of the glory. However, the younger man had important connections, and Miranda was compelled to permit him to join the campaign. Bolívar showed skill and bravery in leading his troops. Miranda commended him but also promptly ordered him off to Puerto Cabello and away from the centers of action. Bolívar accepted the assignment as a duty but believed that Miranda acted out of personal vindictiveness. Bolívar's frustration was heightened when he lost the port to the royalists, at least in part because of his failure to take routine military precautions in the handling of prisoners. It is not known how this loss affected the worsening relations between the two men, but it seems clear that the capture of Puerto Cabello by the monarchists directly influenced Miranda's decision to give up the struggle against Spain.

The Liberator's motives in surrendering Miranda to the Spaniards are uncertain. He may have believed that the aging Precursor had committed treason by signing the Treaty of San Mateo, or he may have considered Miranda's attempt to flee with the "national treasury" treasonable. He later observed caustically, "I had Miranda arrested to punish an infamous person for betraying his country." [3] A less generous view would be that Bolívar had reached the point where he could no longer abide taking orders. At any rate Miranda's imprisonment eliminated a major contender for power.

Without either condemning or justifying Bolívar's action, it

[3] Daniel F. O'Leary, *Bolívar y la emancipación de Sur-América: Memorias del General O'Leary,* translated from the English by his son Simón B. O'Leary, 2 vols. (Madrid, 1915), I, 147. See also pp. 138-141.

may be said that the cause of independence did not suffer from
Miranda's incarceration. For nearly two decades before 1810,
his had been an undeniably notable contribution to the movement. More than any other single individual, he had propagated
the idea that America should be free. However, by 1811 he had
lost touch with America and with the revolutionary spirit of the
times. More imaginative men than he, men who knew America
and the changing Creole mentality better than he, were needed
to counter Spain's determination to keep its empire intact. As
for Bolívar, he never publicly regretted his role in the act that
sent Miranda to chains and three and a half years later to
death in a dungeon in Cádiz. (*See Reading No. 7.*)

Miranda's imprisonment was a personal tragedy. For the
people of Venezuela the greater tragedy was that his arrest
heralded the appearance of pretorianism in their midst. When
Bolívar and some of his fellow officers put the head of the
Venezuelan state and their Commander-in-Chief under arrest
without orders from Congress, they in effect asserted the "right"
of the armed forces to change the administration of the nation
and to place military concerns above constitutional arrangements.
On a number of occasions following the Miranda episode, Bolívar not only made clear his belief that the armed forces deserved
a special status in society; but also that in military-civilian con-
troversies he would personally show a strong disposition to consider himself first of all a soldier. Such views became standard
for most high-ranking officers who dealt with civilians on a
continuing basis. Like Bolívar, the great José San Martín, who
was primarily responsible for liberating much of southern South
America, not infrequently disregarded instructions from his
civilian superiors. Before all the republics had won their freedom,
the presumed power of the militaries to unseat civilian regimes
and involve themselves in basically civilian matters was well on
its way to becoming institutionalized. Thereafter for a century
military-civilian disputes were the most politically unsettling
factor in the life of the new nations. Armed forces, not constitutions, often provided the final code of rules for national politics.

While Miranda was being taken to prison, Bolívar, through
the intercession of a Spanish friend of the family, was given
safe conduct to leave Venezuela. He chose to go to New Granada (now Colombia), parts of which were still in the hands of

Patriots. Stopping for a short time at the Dutch island of Curaçao, he reached the Magdalena River port of Cartagena in October 1812. Behind him was his failure as the head of the diplomatic mission to London, his share of the responsibility for the loss of strategic Puerto Cabello, his role in the surrender of Miranda. With him were his regrets over the fall of the First Venezuelan Republic. Before him was a lifetime of soldiering and statesmanship predicated on one fundamental postulate: that Spanish America and Spanish Americans were unique and must therefore be made masters of their own destiny. That meant the expulsion of Spain.

Ironically, the Spain that Bolívar opposed was, from 1811 to 1814, liberal and extraordinarily responsive to Hispanic American demands. (*See Reading No. 8.*) In the Constitution of 1812 and by its legislative acts the Spanish *Cortes* of Cádiz began to rectify a number of the grievances which Spanish Americans had enumerated in their declarations of autonomy and independence. Colonial status was swept aside, and Spain and America were proclaimed a single nation. American Spaniards, Creoles, and Indians were granted equal opportunity to political, ecclesiastical, or military rank and office. If in 1809 Camilo Torres had advocated the removal of bureaucratic parasites, in 1811 Spain promised that all civilian and military officials would be removed, subjected to review, and, if necessary, replaced by Regent appointees. If Spanish America had requested free agriculture and industry, a suppression of monopolies, and the right to trade directly with other American ports, by 1813 Spain had adopted legislation endorsing those privileges. If Creoles like Miranda feared "black power," the *Cortes* responded by denying Negroes citizenship and representation. Venezuela's federalism was matched by Spanish decentralization procedures. Both areas adopted a doubly removed indirect electoral system. The unicameral Spanish legislature reiterated the Bourbon effort to protect Indians from forced labor, either public or private. It abolished press censorship. It abolished the Inquisition.

This, then, was the Spain that had declared Venezuela to be in rebellion. This was the Spain that Bolívar had determined to expel from America.

CHAPTER 4

Bolívar as Soldier and State-Maker

Bolívar reached Cartagena convinced that Spanish America would not be free until Spain had been defeated militarily and he determined to devote his life to that end. He had a cause but not an army. When the insurgents in New Granada embraced his cause and lent him aid, they launched him and all of Spanish America on a great military crusade that did not terminate until December 9, 1824 at Ayacucho, Peru.

The intervening years extracted a terrible price from the former colonies. More than a decade of constant war left enduring scars upon an exhausted and demoralized society. The classes who lit the torch of war were decimated by the opposing forces and destroyed economically in support of their own armies. The masses left for war without permanent values and returned without homes or families. A generation grew up inured to battle. For them fighting was a habit, brutality a commonplace. On every side violence bred more violence. Vengeance begat vengeance.

Warriors carved out of Spain's empire new nations, only to shackle them with militarism. Force assumed the role of law. The objective—independence—produced a superficial spirit of political unity that made final victory possible. But the forces of disunity were never far below the surface and in the end they "Balkanized" the continent.

Bolívar knew well the cost of Spain's bitter resistance because he almost singlehandedly directed the course of developments in a large part of Spanish South America. Long before final victory was won he had identified himself so completely with the cause of liberty that his name and the word "freedom" became identical. His genius gave meaning and unity to the America which was trying to express itself. His talent welded together Creole, mestizo, Indian, mulatto, and Negro and constantly rediscovered for them a hope for ultimate success in the ruins of repeated defeats. Between Cartagena and Ayacucho, Bolívar was at times a statesman and political theorizer. For the most part he raised armies, waged campaigns, and used his great influence, won as a freedom fighter, to cajole civilians into providing men and funds for his ever-expanding war effort. It is with Bolívar the soldier and military leader that this chapter is concerned.

The First Campaign. Between La Guaira and Cartagena, Bolívar embarked upon a new stage in his career. He had left the Caribbean port a Venezuelan patriot, whose radicalism had deceived him into expecting quick victories and blinded him to the importance of acknowledging social-economic realities. He reached the Magdalena River port an internationalist and a moderate, prepared for a protracted struggle and ready to compromise with those who wanted an independence generated from within the established framework of social and economic institutions. Henceforth, for him the achievement of independence would take precedence over the resolution of inherited inequities. From those convictions there followed logically first that New Granadans owed it to themselves to help liberate Venezuela and second that the first fruits of independence would be essentially political in nature.

On December 15, 1812, approximately two months after landing at Cartagena, Bolívar issued his famous "Manifesto to the Citizens of New Granada." A rich blend of intellectual idealism and political common sense, the Manifesto was an eloquent call for unity within and between the entities that comprised the Spanish Empire. It was also a plea for offensive war, with the immediate aim of liberating Venezuela. The doctrines contained in the Manifesto—unity and attack, and no reconciliation or compromise with Spain—were persuasive. But Colombia was torn by the very dissension that Bolívar had urged be resolved in the interest of his broader objectives. As in Venezuela before and after the fall of the first Republic, Centralists were contending with Federalists, province was fighting province. The contest between Cartagena and Bogotá was especially heated. Under such circumstances only a few leaders heard Bolívar's admonitions above the din of political debate, and the civil wars it spawned. Bolívar made opportunities from the limited support which men like Camilo Torres, outstanding Federalist leader of New Granada, could extend to him.

Given the rank of Commandant and assigned to Barranca, a small river port garrisoned by some seventy men, Bolívar on his

own initiative and against the orders of his superiors raised his
personnel to 250 men and began a campaign that in eight months
carried him all the way to Caracas. It took him less than two
months to clear the Magdalena River from Cartagena to Ocaña,
which fell to him on February 28, 1813. At that point New
Granada commissioned him to use its sons in Venezuela. In ordering its troops into Venezuela, the future Colombia in effect assumed a commitment that was not fulfilled until its soldiers had
figured prominently in the independence of Venezuela, Ecuador,
Peru, and Bolivia.[1]

On May 14, near Cúcuta, Bolívar crossed the Venezuelan
border and on May 26 entered Mérida. Victories brought volun-
teers—as later defeats would bring desertions—and Bolívar left
Mérida and headed for Trujillo with approximately 700 troops.
Trujillo surrendered on June 10.

At Trujillo, Bolívar issued his famous order *"Guerra a
Muerte"* (War to the Death). It called upon all to join the patriot cause and threatened those who did not with extermination
as enemies. (*See Reading No. 9.*) In proclaiming it Bolívar
clearly had in mind retaliation against the Spanish military for
atrocities perpetrated before and particularly after Miranda's
surrender. Bolívar later observed, "I resolved to wage war to the
death in order to take from the tyrants the incomparable advantage that their destructive system gave them." [2] He believed that
the order would force natives and foreigners alike to declare their
intentions. The order did not have that effect. Rather it was used
by Patriot and Royalist alike to reduce the war to barbaric levels
as each side at times seemed determined to outdo the other in
showing disregard for human life.

There is no condoning Bolívar's decision on this occasion.
To say that he had no choice but to fight terror with terror, that
he lived and fought in an era of brutality, that he figuratively
turned his head so as not to see the savagery with which his
own troops sometimes fought, or that he was quick to renounce

[1] Vicente Lecuna, *Crónica razonada de las guerras de Bolívar,* 3
vols. (New York, 1950). This set contains quite good accounts of
all the military campaigns in military theaters under Bolívar's command.
[2] Simón Bolívar, *Cartas del Libertador corregidas conforme a los
originales,* ed. Vicente Lecuna, 12 vols. (Caracas, 1929-1959), I,
64.

the order once the tide of victory turned in his favor, does not negate the fact that the order was an inhuman, premeditated act on his part. The records are filled with evidence of atrocities committed in the name of order. We know that it was premeditated because Bolívar was considering the possibility of such a declaration at least as early as the Cartagena Manifesto in which he decried his compatriots for their "blind . . . tolerance" of those, particularly the "European Spaniards" who committed crimes against society and the State.

Continuing his triumphal march with victories over superior forces at Barinas and La Victoria, Bolívar returned to Caracas on August 6, 1813, just a year after his ignominious departure from Venezuela. He had risen from defeat and chaos to represent unity, cohesion, and creative impulse. He had won acclaim as the first among the liberators to think in hemisphere terms. He had proved repeatedly that he could be brilliant at marshalling raw recruits to win battles. Humble men responded heroically to his faith and vision in a cause they did not understand. His marches and counter-marches, his unorthodox maneuvers, caught superior Spanish forces off guard again and again.

In the short view of history the 1813 campaign becomes one among many episodes in the struggle against Spanish colonialism. In the long view, Bolívar at Barranca becomes a modern version of the *conquistadores*. Those intrepid leaders, separated from their home government by the Atlantic Ocean, were thrown upon their own resources. Their rapid subjugation of two continents was a victory for private venture. Bolívar was not separated from the state, rather, the state had collapsed. Faced with this predicament he drew upon his own resources in much the same manner as Cortés and Pizarro had done three centuries earlier. The successes of his first major campaign were personal triumphs. Ultimate victory in northern South America would also be first of all a Bolivarian achievement, just as the independence of southern South America was due to the determination of José de San Martín. Thus in the early nineteenth century a few determined men stripped Spain of the territory that in the early sixteenth century a dozen equally determined *conquistadores* had won for it.

Liberator and Dictator. In recognition of his having returned western Venezuela to the Patriot fold, the Municipal

Council of Caracas conferred upon Bolívar the title of El Libertador. The action of the Council was both premature and prophetic. Within a year Spanish armies again subjugated the provinces that Bolívar had recently freed, and it would be several years before independence from Spain was permanently won anywhere in the vast area over which Bolívar's armies eventually fought. Still it was as liberator that Bolívar won lasting fame.

In an action recalling the one taken by the Congress of the First Republic in the case of Miranda, the Congress of the Second Republic, on January 2, 1814, voted Bolívar dictatorial powers for both civil and military affairs. Thereafter the liberator-dictator sequence became more or less standardized. This was not surprising. Wherever Bolívar appeared he was so completely in charge that there seemed no alternative to his simultaneous leadership of state and troops. Established institutions having disappeared, people often turned to him because there was no other agency or person who could claim their loyalty. The Spanish reaction cut down the most eminent civilian leaders of the revolution—magistrates, judges, legislators, statesmen—while wars multiplied chiefs and *caudillos* and made the army the primary force, the fundamental basis, and the ultimate guarantor of independence. The result was the ruin of almost all civil influence, the omnipotence of the sword, and the militarization of the mind.[3]

Bolívar had been dictator for only six months when the forces working against the Patriots inundated him. He had invited trouble by having 800 Royalist prisoners massacred at La Guaira, but the Second Republic would almost certainly have fallen in any event. At least a half-dozen considerations guaranteed that. In Europe, Ferdinand VII was restored to the throne in March 1814, following Wellington's defeat of Napoleon's armies. When word of that development reached America, Royalists took heart and erstwhile Patriots switched sides. This psychological lift for the friends of Ferdinand was soon followed by substantial ones in the form of troops and armaments from Spain. Great Britain and the United States, to whose governments Bolívar had sent delegates seeking recognition and protection, continued their hands-off policy. War, vengeance, levies,

---

[3] José M. Samper, *Ensayo sobre las revoluciones políticas y la condición social de las repúblicas colombianas* (Paris, 1861), p. 190.

atrocities, had stripped the insurgents of leaders; and wanton destruction of property, forced loans, and sequestrations had destroyed them economically. As a consequence, Bolívar inherited despair and poverty.

The Masses Involved. During his march from Cúcuta to Caracas, Bolívar had defeated the Royalist armies repeatedly, but he had not destroyed them. As he moved on, the Royalists regrouped and prepared to fight again. But, more important from the military point of view, the *llaneros* (cowboys from the Orinocan flood plains) joined the Royalists. At the beginning neither *llaneros* nor other popular elements had been encouraged to take an active role in the conspiratorial movements, because many Creoles feared that once aroused the *pardos* could not be controlled. Bolívar had been willing to take that risk because he sensed that freedom could not be assured so long as the common man remained hostile or even uncommitted to the cause of independence. By 1814 the Liberator had made little headway towards broadening the popular base of the movement, but his later decisive victories were firmly grounded on the support of tough, lawless, hard-riding *llaneros* and peasants of the colored castes, who knew only the basic rudiments of civilization. And while Bolívar won battles with his uncultured and often undisciplined troops, their chiefs won social and economic status and mestizied the political and military elites of the emerging republics of northern South America.

The immediate causes of the collapse of the Second Republic were military defeats administered by the infamous José Tomás Boves. A Spanish outcast who had briefly enlisted with the Patriots, he returned to the Royalist side and tapped the manpower pool of the *llanos*. Probably the most ferocious and barbaric individual to emerge from the wars, Boves loosed his hordes, composed almost entirely of *pardos,* to ravage and loot the Patriots. Boves' troops made the war to the death a reality.

No longer able to maintain order and threatened with arrest by some of his restless lieutenants, Bolívar determined to abandon Caracas. With what remained of his badly mauled army, on July 6, 1814, he headed east, where insurgent forces still retained a foothold on the mainland. He was accompanied by 20,000 civilians who chose to flee rather than face the wrath of Boves. Only a few hundred ever returned to Caracas. Four thousand remained in Caracas rather than flee with Bolívar. Many of them died when Boves occupied the city.

Spain on the Offensive. For three years after his forced withdrawal from Caracas, Bolívar suffered one setback after another. By the time that he reached eastern Venezuela his army was completely shattered. His officers went into exile or melted into the plains to organize guerilla bands. Bolívar fled again to Cartagena. He was named Captain-General of New Granada, from Tunja, then the capital. He occupied Bogotá by force and established a capital there, but he was unable to contain the rivalries that were damaging the independence effort. When Cartagena, which in the past had been his second fatherland, refused him the supplies necessary to subdue the recalcitrant coastal provinces, he chose exile in preference to civil war and left New Granada for Jamaica.

In May 1815, just as Bolívar was traveling to Jamaica, the best-equipped expedition ever to sail from Spain reached Venezuela under the command of General Pablo Morillo. Leaving 5,000 of his more than 10,000 veteran troops as a garrison in Venezuela, Morillo sailed for Cartagena. He took the port and in a matter of months reconquered all of the former viceroyalty. Except for La Plata and bits of Guiana and Mexico, all the Empire was again under Spanish absolutist domination.

Bolívar's faith in America was unshaken. The British, however, were not so confident and denied the Liberator's appeals for aid. Undeterred, Bolívar took passage for Haiti, which had become a refuge for Venezuelan and Colombian patriots. President Alexandre Pétion received Bolívar warmly and gave him assistance in return for his promise to free the slaves in all the territories that he might liberate.

With fewer than 250 men, most of whom were officers, Bolívar set sail for Venezuela in the spring of 1816. He landed on the Island of Margarita and on June 2 issued a proclamation freeing all the slaves who joined the insurgent cause. Two feints at the mainland established that the population was apathetic; past misfortunes had conditioned them to fear Spanish reprisal more than to desire Patriot approval. At Ocumare, between La Guaira and Puerto Cabello, the expedition suffered a military disaster. Bolívar never fully lived down his part in the incident. At worst he displayed gross military incompetence and lack of courage; at best he was guilty of appalling military behavior.[4]

The year 1816 tested Bolívar's capacity for comebacks. Ocumare represented the nadir of his military career. For three months thereafter he wandered about the Caribbean searching for supplies, finally returning in early September to the protection and generosity of Haiti's President Pétion. When he departed from Haiti on September 21, 1816, he was sailing, as it turned out, into a new life. During all of 1817 and most of 1818 his resourcefulness was taxed to the limit, but he held to his objectives and re-established his reputation as a military commander. Beginning in 1819 victories presaged greater victories. In five years his armies would free Colombians, Venezuelans, Ecuadorians, Peruvians, and Bolivians from Spanish control.

The Forces of Change. It was not by accident that Bolívar's fortunes changed when they did. On the contrary, a conjunction of circumstances finally made his goals achievable. First of all he had made a happy choice by heading for the Orinoco River region and establishing his base of operations at Angostura, now Ciudad Bolívar. The Orinoco offered easy means of transportation, its swamps, protection. The Royalists were weaker there than anywhere in Venezuela. Patriot guerilla bands provided nuclei around which a regular army could be built. And Angostura was within relatively easy reach of the *llanos* which Bolívar saw as a major source of manpower.

There were other equally compelling considerations. Arms and supplies began arriving from Europe, thanks to Napoleon's defeat and to speculators working out of London. British troops, seasoned in Peninsula campaigns against the French, volunteered their services. Eventually 2,500 joined the Patriot forces. Others came from Ireland, Germany, France, Italy, and Poland. These veterans of European wars, along with the few Spaniards who deserted to the Patriots, repeatedly showed themselves to be outstanding officers and soldiers. Prime Minister Castlereagh's memorandum of August 20, 1817, was of even greater significance. It served notice that only Spain could apply force to

[4] Masur, who writes, "No event in Bolívar's life became the object of so much bitter criticism as the catastrophe of Ocumare," treats this episode in considerable detail in *Simón Bolívar*, p. 280ff.

bring back its colonies. By refusing to allow Europe to intervene while the issue was still in the balance, Great Britain made
the triumph of the secessionist movements a certainty.

Strange though it may seem, Ferdinand VII also made a major
contribution to the Independence movement. During his exile
and imprisonment he had learned nothing and forgotten nothing.
After he returned to the throne he was entirely blind to the
changes wrought by the revolution in America and he never
made a serious effort to satisfy the demands of the insurgents.
In particular he refused to accept a liberal constitution or to
recognize the autonomy of the Spanish American colonies, on
the grounds that those proposals were incompatible with the
principles of absolutism, in which he believed fanatically. By
1817 his obstinacy had stiffened Creole opposition to Spain
and had wrecked any hope whatever of reconciliation.

The Road to Victory, Boyacá. Bolívar's parade of military
victories began with the Colombian campaign of 1819. Before
that campaign was undertaken the Liberator had called a Congress at Angostura which created the Republic of Gran Colombia
and named Bolívar to lead it. No less important from a military
point of view, the *llaneros,* who had been primarily responsible
for the fall of the Second Republic, had become a vital compo-
nent of the military establishment. Bolívar's personal dynamism
and rhetorical eloquence helped to win over their new *Jefe
Supremo,* José Antonio Páez, but their transfer of allegiance
was also based upon more mundane considerations. Caracas was
now under the control of the Royalists, and the *llaneros* looked
upon the capital an an enemy to be opposed in battle. In this
respect the attitude of the "centaurs of the plains" was not unlike the traditional one of the rural populations of modern Latin
America. Everywhere, in every era, and ordinarily with good
reason, rural peoples in Latin America have expected punishment rather than reward from their national capitals. Furthermore, what wealth remained in Venezuela was now in Royalist
hands. And because war followed by pillaging was then, as it
continued to be for a century, the principal means by which the
lower classes could hope to share in the redistribution of capital,
the *llaneros* looked upon the Royalists as fair game.

With the *llaneros* wearing the armband of the Patriots, Bolívar
was ready once again to turn to offensive warfare. He had learned
something of the cost of combatting disciplined forces and now,

rather than confronting head-on the veteran regiments guarding Caracas, he did the unexpected. He ordered the *llaneros* to carry out a series of lightning campaigns—the kind at which they excelled—to nail down the Royalists in Venezuela, while he engaged in an enormous flank attack on the enemy's Colombian elements. In one of the truly brilliant campaigns of Hemisphere history, he marched his 4,000 troops parallel to the Orinoco and Arauco Rivers and over the Andes to strike at the Royalists holding Colombia. (*See Reading No. 10.*) Both the *llaneros* and the Liberator's forces performed their roles to perfection, and their efforts were completely successful. Under the daring Páez, who was rapidly developing into a first-rate, imaginative officer, the *llaneros* kept the Spanish forces in a constant state of confusion. Bolívar took the enemy completely by surprise when his forces, after a thousand-mile march, swept down from the *cordilleras* onto the highlands of Boyacá. In a major battle fought at the Boyacá Bridge near Tunja, on August 7, 1819, the Patriots and some 500 foreign legionnaires completely crushed a Royalist contingent. The Royalist units in Colombia never recovered from that loss. Although it would require time to drive the remaining Spanish troops into the sea, Spanish power in Colombia was in effect ended forever. Bolívar had liberated his first country.

The Liberator entered Bogotá to a hero's welcome and an invitation to head the new republic's government. He relished the pageantry, and after a proper show of reticence agreed to rule. However, he soon longed for the excitement of the battle-field and prepared to return to Angostura and plot the reconquest of Venezuela. He named Francisco de Paula Santander to head the government in his stead and with his troops headed for his Orinoco base, which he reached in December 1819.

Santander had served ably as an army officer but in contrast to Bolívar thought primarily as a civilian and legalist rather than as a soldier. During the next decade he would represent the institutionalist and the politician. As the war drew to a close Santander remarked, "The armies have given us independence, the laws will give us peace." Bolívar, meanwhile, continued to trust in his troops and used them to counter the legalist.

The Riego Revolt. The far-reaching consequence of victory at Boyacá was a welcome surprise to the independence forces. But fewer than four months later, on January 1, 1820, they were literally handed a "gift" of at least equal significance. On that day in Cádiz, Spain a regiment revolted. It was one of several awaiting embarkation for America, and among the major objectives of the revolutionaries, who were led by Colonel Rafael Riego, was the restoration of the liberal constitution of 1812. Other conspiratorial movements within the armed forces followed. Ferdinand VII lost control of his government temporarily and the departure of the military expedition, which was to have been even larger than the one sent in 1815 under Morillo, was suspended permanently.

In response to the uprisings on the Peninsula, conservative Creole elements in New Spain (Mexico), who had feared class warfare if the viceroyalty separated from the mother country, now declared independence rather than accept the new liberalism. In northern South America, Royalist forces were first demoralized by the liberal-conservative struggle and then divided between partisans of Ferdinand VII and partisans of the Constitution of 1812. This division seriously reduced their effectiveness against the Patriots; meanwhile, the Republican forces were buoyed by the political controversy in Spain and the realization that Spanish armies in America were not to receive the large-scale reinforcements they had anticipated.

With Spain weakened by political dissension, with Spanish liberals undermining the military structure, and with Spanish forces in America splitting into camps reflecting the struggle taking place in Spain, the government in Madrid ordered its generals and viceroys to negotiate with the Patriots, offering them political concessions in return for their allegiance to the Spanish Constitution of 1812. Royalist General Morillo, in carrying out his instructions in northern South America, initially sought to divide the Patriot forces by treating individually with various military-political figures. However, in an unusual show of unity, they lined up behind Bolívar. When the Liberator was approached in July 1820, his position was strong and he was in no hurry to negotiate. Following victory at Boyacá morale had improved everywhere and financial contributions to the war effort had increased. Desertions of Royalist troops augmented the American forces. It had become very clear that the Spanish armies could win battles but could not hold the territory they seized. In Washington, Henry Clay had proposed recognition of Colombia. Great Britain had moved closer to establishing formal diplomatic relations with the Republican leaders.

With the current of battle running in his favor Bolívar could set a higher price for peace than he could have only a few months earlier. Thus when Morillo proposed that the opposing armies agree to an armistice, Bolívar countered with the demand that any negotiations be carried on in the name of sovereign states; in other words he demanded that Spain recognize the independence of its former colonies. For several months the exchange of proposals and counter-proposals dragged on while Morillo maintained that he could not recognize Colombian sovereignty. On November 27, he capitulated and with Bolívar signed an armistice in the name of Spain and "Colombia." They agreed to include provisions regarding the humane treatment of prisoners of war, formally ending the barbarism that had followed the proclamation of the War to the Death six years earlier.

Bolívar was criticized in some quarters for signing a document which in effect recognized Spanish claims to those areas still in Royalist hands. However, the Liberator insisted that he had won a major diplomatic victory. The armistice had tactical merits: it provided a respite for civilians and soldiers alike, and it also gave Bolívar an opportunity to strengthen his forces prior to renewing the struggle.

Carabobo. Any fear that the ultimate consequences of the armistice would work against the Patriots was removed soon after it ended and hostilities were renewed on August 28, 1821. Bolívar had used his time profitably. He had ordered a massing of troops at San Carlos, and when Páez, who had been stationed in the Apure River area, arrived with his cavalry during the second week of June, Bolívar had a total of 6,500 troops. With this, his largest army to date, he marched toward the Plains of Carabobo, which begin slightly to the southwest of the city of Valencia. On July 24, he confronted a Spanish force equal in size to his own and annihilated it. Remnants of the enemy forces held on for a year, but the victory of Carabobo was decisive. It liberated Venezuela two years after Boyacá had freed Colombia.

With Colombia and Venezuela secure, Bolívar turned his attention to the South. He was already deeply involved in the liberation of the vast area stretching from Popayán in southern Colombia all the way to the Puna of central Bolivia. He now determined that an early conclusion to that endeavor was of greatest importance. Two considerations swayed him. First, the area was rich in minerals which, if successfully exploited, could stave off economic disaster once Spain was expelled. Second, San Martín had been campaigning in the neighborhood of Lima for several months, and if the monarchically-oriented Argentine were permitted to go unchecked he could divert Bolívar's drive for glory and his grand plan for a confederation comprising all of Spanish America.

Pichincha. With these thoughts in mind, six months before the battle of Carabobo, Bolívar had ordered his ablest lieutenant, José Antonio Sucre, to outfit and lead an expedition to Guayaquil, Ecuador. The expedition could not have been placed in better hands. Sucre, then twenty-six years old, possessed the qualities that made Bolívar such a brilliant military leader and Santander such an exceptional civilian administrator. Along with those two independence heroes, Sucre made up the outstanding triumvirate to emerge from the liberation movement in northern South America.

Sailing from the Pacific ocean port of Buenaventura with fewer than a thousand officers and men, Sucre reached Guayaquil in May 1821. On the 25th of May, a month before victory at Carabobo, he signed a convention with the *junta,* named in Guayaquil after the successful uprising against Spain the preceding October. According to the convention, the province of Guayaquil placed itself under the protection of New Granada and conferred upon Bolívar the powers which he deemed necessary to preserve its independence. As later events proved, this agreement greatly strengthened Bolívar's hand when he disputed with San Martín the future of the region now comprising Ecuador, Peru and Bolivia.

Sucre's first probe into the Ecuadorian highlands in November 1821 ended in failure, and Royalist resistance in that area discouraged another major advance for several months. In the meantime, important changes elsewhere fortified the Patriots' position. On October 16, 1821 Venezuelan troops had re-occupied the strategic island of Margarita. On November 28, Panama declared its independence. This meant that the Royalist forces on the west coast could not be supplied except by the straits of Magellan, and that passage was defended on either side by Patriot men-of-war along the Argentine and Chilean coasts.

In Ecuador, Sucre marshalled and trained several hundred recruits. Reinforcements sent from Peru by General San Martín were placed under the command of the Bolivian mestizo, Colonel Andrés Santa Cruz, future dictator of Bolivia and of the short-lived Peruvian-Bolivian Confederation. These troops included a large percentage of magnificently trained Argentine veterans who had fought in their homeland, in Chile, and in Peru before joining Sucre in the steaming lowlands of Ecuador. They stiffened the fiber of Sucre's forces and in battle proved themselves the equals of those who had become heroes on the battlefields of Venezuela and Colombia.

Sucre crossed the Andes in February 1822 with approximately 2,600 troops. He then moved north toward Quito, the old colonial capital. On the morning of May 24, a year after he had reached the agreement with the Guayaquil *junta,* Sucre was on the slopes of the volcano Pichincha, overlooking Quito to the east. That afternoon Spanish forces about the size of his own challenged him and he defeated them decisively. As part of the terms of the surrender the Patriots received what was for them huge booty in the form of military hardware. More important, the victory freed Ecuador and set the stage for the liberation of Peru and Bolivia, the next act in the great drama Bolívar was directing.

Bolívar did not play a personal part in any major battle that expelled the Royalists from Ecuador. After Carabobo, he divided his time between Cúcuta and Bogotá with the result that it was mid-December before his troops headed south by way of the Cauca River Valley. That valley proved a nightmare for him. Its torrential streams had few crossings, and the Royalists who held them had to be dislodged man by man. The passes were rugged even by Andean standards and the routes over them were mere pack trails. Worst of all, the inhabitants of the upper valley were probably the arch-Royalists of America, and they willingly cooperated with the defenders of the old Spanish Empire. It took the Liberator two months to fight his way through a hundred-mile stretch south of Popayán, and in the process his original forces of 2,800 men were cut to 1,800 by desertions, disease, and enemy fire. On April 7 he fought an indecisive battle at Bombóná, fifty miles southwest of Pasto. His losses were so great that he had to retreat approximately seventy-five miles north to await reinforcements before moving on Pasto. However, when the Royalists learned of Sucre's victory at Pichincha, their resistance crumbled. Whereas a few days before, Bolívar had had to fight for every foot of ground, his advance now became a triumphal march. He reached Quito on June 15, 1822.

Meeting at Guayaquil. The Ecuadorian provinces were free. The problem now was whether they should form a sovereign nation, or be incorporated into either Colombia or Peru. Bolívar was determined that they become a part of Colombia and he knew that the principal obstacle to the fulfillment of his objective was not local desire for an independent republic, but San Martín's support of Peruvian claims to the area.

Bolívar moved swiftly to tie Ecuador to Gran Colombia. Leaving Sucre to control Quito, Bolívar headed for Guayaquil with his battle-hardened Colombian battalions. Profiting from the prestige that Sucre had won at Pichincha, Bolívar soon had the *guayaquileños* clamoring for incorporation into Colombia and for the Liberator to rule them. He took advantage of the wave of popularity to declare himself dictator.

Still, the final test would come only when San Martín, who had announced his intention of visiting Guayaquil, should confront the Liberator. The Argentine arrived on July 25th. Bolívar welcomed him to "Colombian" soil. San Martín felt that there were sound historical and economic reasons why Guayaquil should be attached to Peru and was taken aback by Bolívar's bluntness and *fait accompli*. San Martín could have claimed that the contribution of his forces to the liberation of Quito entitled Peru to a voice in the area's destiny. However, he had no intention of being a party to any dispute that might set Patriot to fighting Patriot or postpone the liberation of the entire continent.

The two giants of the Independence movement met at intervals throughout July 26th and 27th. We do not know precisely what questions, other than that of Guayaquil, were raised or what answers given. No third party heard the exchanges and neither of the principals ever fully revealed what took place.[5] If they had done so immediately after the meeting their revelations probably would have hurt the Patriot effort because the two leaders apparently disagreed on several major points. They clashed, it appears, over the recurrent monarchy vs. republican issue, Bolívar's opposition to the monarchical system having been fortified by developments in Mexico, where the Creole General Augustín Iturbide had been named emperor. The Liberator probably refused to supply San Martín with the number of Colombian troops he believed that he needed to defeat the Royalists in Peru. Bolívar presumably justified his action on the ground that his men were needed in Colombia, but it is possible that he withheld them because he would not derive glory from San Martín's successes.

When his attempts to obtain troops failed, the Argentine apparently proposed that he serve under Bolívar. The Liberator demurred, either because he knew that he could never be sure of the loyalty of the Argentine troops under San Martín's command, or because he already knew, as sooner or later others would come to know, that only he held the power to defeat the Royalists. When that reality was appreciated he would free Peru on his own terms.

Frustrated by Bolívar's refusal to yield on any point, San Martín broke off the meeting. He then returned to Lima a discouraged man, renounced his administrative post, and within a matter of weeks prepared to go into exile.

The meeting of Guayaquil did not produce a victor and a vanquished. San Martín's self-abnegation has won him much well-deserved respect. Bolívar behaved the only way he could have. He held all the cards and he was never one to underbid his hand. Furthermore, on this occasion his judgment was sound.

The Rough Road to Victory in Peru. The Liberator immediately increased his contacts with Peru but it was a year before he went there himself. He was in no hurry to fill the vacuum created by San Martín's departure. Over the short term the prospects for victory in Peru did not appear promising. Bolívar was physically exhausted and there were signs that his

[5] Bolívar, *Selected Writings,* I, 312-317, contains a pro-Bolívar account of the meeting.

health was breaking under the strain of constant activity. To the north, his political creation, Gran Colombia, offered all kinds of political problems. At times it appeared that remnants of the Spanish along the Caribbean coast might fight their way out of the enclaves into which the Patriots had driven them. Pasto, which had bitterly resisted Bolívar, rose in rebellion, and General Sucre moved in to quell the uprising.

In Bogotá Santander, in defense of constitutionalism and in defiance of his chief, insisted that Colombian involvement in Peru must have legislative approval. This taxed Bolívar's patience, but law was on Santander's side and, furthermore, it was he who actually guided through the Congress the legislation that legalized the sending of Colombian forces into Peru. It should not be forgotten that Peruvian independence was won first of all by Colombian troops and that Santander more than anyone else was responsible for raising those troops and keeping them in the field. Although his methods often differed from Bolívar's, Santander was equally dedicated to freedom.

Bolívar was uncertain about Colombia but he had no doubts about Peru. He knew that country was in a state of chaos. In Lima members of the triumvirate, who had been named following San Martín's resignation, fought among themselves for personal advantage. Many of the Creole aristocracy, recalling their privileges and the glory that was Lima's (City of the Kings) under the viceroys, remained steadfastly Royalist. Until the end there were probably more Peruvian Creoles in the Royalist armies than in the Patriot forces. Many of those who posed as Patriots thought in terms of what independence would do for them or at most for that small part of America they knew personally. In a premature display of misdirected nationalism, the Peruvian Congress divided over accepting aid from Colombia.

The military picture was equally discouraging. Peruvian troops were no match for the enemy. They were poorly trained and badly treated and the irresponsible conduct of their civil and military leaders did little to instill in them enthusiasm for or appreciation of independence. With San Martín gone and the Buenos Aires government searching for an accommodation with Spain, morale among the Argentine veterans declined to the point where mutiny within their ranks became an ever-present threat. The Chilean government recalled some of its troops from Peru, and Bolívar felt that the Santiago regime generally failed to live up to its agreements with him.

This chaotic civil-military situation went on for several months after the Liberator's arrival in Lima on September 1, 1823. He had been in the country only two months when he had to take to the field to prevent former President José de la Riva Agüero from going over to the Royalists with 3,000 troops under his command. The following February disloyal troops surrendered the port of Callao, forcing the Patriots to evacuate Lima. During the same month several high officials, including President Torre Tagle, deserted to the Royalists. And during March at least two officers defected to the Royalists with their troops.

But if the immediate future was dark, the longer view was bright. On June 19, 1822 the United States, by officially receiving a Colombian agent, became the first non-Latin American nation to recognize one of the new republics. A year and a half later, on December 2, 1823, the President of the United States sent to Congress a message embodying the substance of the Monroe Doctrine. Great Britain's navy continued to stand between America and those who would help Spain to recoup her losses. These measures on the part of the United States and Great Britain convinced Bolívar that time was running out for the Spaniards. Divisions within the ranks of the Spanish commanders in Peru following Ferdinand's return to supreme control in late 1823 helped to confirm that view. In military terms, once the defeat of Spain became "inevitable" the Patriots could gamble, secure in the knowledge that to lose a battle did not mean to lose the war. This gave them a freedom of action that they had never before enjoyed. Finally, Bolívar knew that if the state of his health forced him to slow his pace he had in Sucre, the hero of Pichincha, a brilliant lieutenant who could be trusted to bear the brunt of organizing, supplying, and leading the liberating forces.

With time on his side, but aware that he could expect little from the Peruvians, Bolívar worked to circumvent them. On September 10, 1823, ten days after reaching Lima, he won from a divided Congress the title of Supreme Military Commander. Exactly five months later, the government invested him with all the military and civil powers needed "to save the republic." In other words, it made him a dictator, a role he knew well by then. In the meantime he placed an ever-growing dependence upon his Colombian military contingents, as he built his armies around those who had proved themselves at Boyacá, Carabobo, and Pichincha. Knowing that they were too few to do the job, Bolívar pleaded with Santander to send with all haste five or six thousand more equipped troops. In return he promised to free Peru.

Junín. The first pay-off for his efforts in maneuvering came on August 6, 1824, at Junín, situated northeast of Lima. When Lima became impossibly chaotic, Bolívar transferred his headquarters to Trujillo and from there ordered Sucre to move the Patriot soldiers inland across the first range of the Andes in preparation for battle. Bolívar rejoined his troops before the crossing was complete and decided to advance immediately upon the Spanish who were weakened when Viceroy José de la Serna, a Constitutionalist, sent troops into upper Peru (Bolivia) to subdue General Pedro Antonio de Olañata, who favored Ferdinand's assumption of absolutist powers. The Patriot armies, increased to over 8,000 in part by the arrival of reinforcements from Colombia, engaged the Spaniards near Lake Junín. In a battle that lasted only an hour and that was fought entirely by the cavalry divisions, the Patriots won a stunning victory and put the Spaniards into headlong flight. Victory at Junín prepared the way for a greater one at Ayacucho.

Following Junín, Bolívar returned to Lima in the expectation that the Royalists would attack the Patriot forces preparing to lay seige to Callao. That threat never materialized. Instead, Viceroy La Serna brought nearly all of the Spanish forces together at Cuzco and prepared for a showdown. Sucre accepted the challenge although he had fewer than 6,000 troops to more than 9,000 for the Royalists.

Ayacucho. On December 9, 1824, near Ayacucho, halfway between Lima and Cuzco, at an elevation of 11,000 feet, Sucre sent his troops into battle. In a short, violent contest the Royalists were decisively defeated and Viceroy La Serna was taken prisoner. Before hostilities had begun individuals from the two armies had stepped forward to exchange farewells with friends. After the fighting had ceased, the Spaniards were offered a generous armistice. Emotions had subsided greatly since the ravages of men like Boves whom Bolívar sought to counter by his proclamation of The War to the Death.

When word of Ayacucho reached him in Lima, Bolívar danced with joy, crying, "Victory! Victory! Victory!" Well he might have. Peru was the pivot of what remained of Spanish power in South America and that power had been completely and definitively crushed, as was soon proved when Patriot forces marched into mineral-rich Bolivia without fighting a major battle. Ayacucho not only ended organized military resistance to independence, it also ended Spanish political control on the Spanish American mainland.

Ayacucho vindicated the judgment of those small minorities who a decade and a half earlier had held that Spanish America should and could be free. It created a lasting monument to those hundreds of thousands who had died throughout the Hemisphere fighting a valiant and resourceful enemy. It justified the faith that Venezuelans and Colombians and later Ecuadorians and Peruvians had placed in Bolívar the soldier. It guaranteed, if further guarantees were needed, that Bolivar was in truth The Liberator that his countrymen had declared him to be eleven years earlier.

Between Cartagena and Ayacucho, Bolívar proved a thousand times over that he was a born military leader and a great warrior who acted more from instinct than from method. Even before Ayacucho he was being hailed throughout Latin America, the United States, and Western Europe as a military genius and revolutionary leader. Had his temperament permitted, he might have rested on his hard-won laurels, but it would not. The new nations must be ruled and they must be trained to live with themselves and the world. That would not be easy, and Bolívar knew it. As early as 1821 he had written "I fear peace more than war," [6] but this did not deter him from attempting to mold Latin America's postwar political destiny.

He moved immediately from the battlefield to the arena of international politics. There he soon learned that if nationalism would forge the peace, internationalism must protect it. He found that internationalism and nationalism were in constant conflict. In Bolívar, as in the case of so many internationalists, that conflict was never resolved.

[6] Bolívar, *Cartas,* II, 348-349.

CHAPTER 5

Bolívar as International Idealist and National Pragmatist

Internationalists throughout the world claim Bolívar as one of their heroes. To many of them, especially those in this hemisphere, he is the spiritual father of Pan-Americanism, the precursor of the League of Nations, and a prophet of the United Nations. Meanwhile, this generation of Venezuelans, as did two earlier ones, honors him as the Father of their country. It is fitting that he is recognized by both groups. In his own mind he undoubtedly had a dual loyalty. When he was filled with optimism and his imagination soared, he tended to consider himself a Spanish American and the entire hemisphere a stage on which to play out his role. When he was exhausted or depressed and longed for tranquility, his thoughts often turned to Caracas and Venezuela. In priority I believe Bolívar was an American first and a Venezuelan second. But the discussion which follows does not attempt to answer that question or to determine whether internationalists or nationalists have prior claim to Bolívar. What is attempted is an explanation of what Bolívar's internationalism and nationalism amounted to.

The Search for Unity. During and immediately following the Wars of Independence, internationalism—a term which strictly speaking is not applicable to Spanish America until after the former colonies became "nations"—developed from two basic sources. They were, first, the cultural affinity of the inhabitants of the various regions and, second, the need for a defensive Spanish American political alliance in order that the colonies might emancipate themselves from Spain and better protect their liberty against inroads from the outside. Without in any way intending to gloss over its importance, unity on the basis of cultural affinity can be disposed of rather quickly. It was essentially Creolism which had gained limited acceptance among a few intellectuals and political propagandists in the eighteenth century, and later enjoyed considerable currency among the privileged elements after Napoleon overran the peninsula. (*See Chapter 2.*)

The case for a common culture was no more sustainable during the Independence Era than it is today. A large part of the total population of the empire did not use Spanish as their first language. The disparities between the mestizo-plains-livestock culture of Argentina and the Indian-mountain-dirt-farming culture of Ecuador were at least as great then as they are now.

Still the cultural homogeneity argument had a crisis appeal in 1810, as it has today. Everywhere the great and not so great invoked it in their efforts to rally their forces and enlist the support of their neighbors. In the Cartagena manifesto, Bolívar called on Colombians not to be "insensible to the cries of your brothers" [the Venezuelans]. After the fall of the second Venezuelan Republic, Bolívar returned to Colombia where in an address before General Rafael Urdaneta's troops he stated, "I am but a soldier, come to offer my services to this sister nation. Our Fatherland is America. . . ." Four years later he wrote to Juan Martín Pueyrredón, the Supreme Director of the United Provinces of Río de la Plata, "There should be but one country for all Americans, since we have been perfectly united in every other way." [1]

The appeal to unity, the promise that through union Hispanic America's cultural destiny would be fulfilled, lent itself to oratory that in some circles fell on understanding ears, but in the final analysis international cooperation based on the hard realities of politics in war counted most. All the prominent figures of the Independence movement at one point or another recognized this. Bolivar talked of a common culture but he drove hard bargains with politicians and military figures in Caracas, Bogotá, Guayaquil, Lima, and La Paz, to get the kind of cooperation he needed. Also, he readily went outside the Hispanic world to solicit aid and assistance in French-Negro Haiti, Protestant North America, and trade-minded Anglo-Saxon Britain. His victorious armies were the fruits of international cooperation but, except for their officers, they were hardly Hispanic in character. His North European veterans and his Negro slaves, un-

[1] Bolívar, *Selected Writings,* I, 159-161.

lettered Indian peasants, and mestizo herdsmen from a half-dozen future republics knew little or nothing of the cultural concepts embodied in Creolism. If his Hispanic American contingents had anything in common it was a desire for freedom, freedom from the rigid social restrictions imposed by their Creole masters.

Bolívar and Internationalism. Bolívar's internationalism went through three overlapping periods before emerging nationalism and personalism scuttled any chances of serious cooperation among the new states. During the first period, the Liberator, thinking primarily in military terms, was convinced that the entire continent was an indivisible theater of revolution. This conviction guided him through more than a decade of military campaigning. During the second and third periods he was first of all a statesman who envisaged the creation of powerful new republics that would voluntarily come together to protect their independence and well being. His thinking during the second period caused him to call the Congress of Panama, held in 1826, which ended on an unproductive note. During the third period he accepted the fact that he would have to scale down his objectives. This led him to propose a Confederation of the Andes, composed of Venezuela, Colombia, Ecuador, Peru, and Bolivia.

The first stage of Bolívar's internationalism was part and parcel of his idea of emancipation. (*See Chapter 4.*) The concept of Hispanic American solidarity did not originate with him. The Precursor, Miranda, had called attention to it on several occasions and had received responses from individuals in Mexico, Central America, and Chile expressing agreement with his view. In 1810 the Chileans Juan Martínez de Rozas and Juan Egaña set forth a plan of organization for the Spanish possessions in America and, when the *cabildos* of Buenos Aires, Caracas and Bogotá first considered breaking with Spain, they had exchanged communications considering the possibility of mutual assistance.

Although the concept of a united Hispanic American front against Spain first germinated in the minds of others, Bolívar more than any other individual gave it substance. The entire continent was home and battlefield to him. After Boyacá, General Páez urged him to return to Venezuela and save it. Bolívar replied, "As you say, it is now time to save heroic Venezuela forever, and I add that now is the time to save South America." [2] Actually he was preparing to do both by ordering Sucre south while he crossed the Andes to Venezuela and victory at Carabobo.

With Colombia and Venezuela free and united, Bolívar was restless to get on with his task of nation-building. Quito was the next obvious theater for action and he moved on that stage as naturally and surely as he later made his entries into Lima and La Paz. If domestic strife had not been so intense that international cooperation by 1825 had become more and more difficult, Bolívar probably would not have stopped his international brigades at the borders of Bolivia. We reach this conclusion because even as his world tottered, he continued to think of himself as a soldier in the service of the continent. At one point in 1825 he decided that he could perform the greatest good by becoming a kind of super military Commander-in-Chief of an international army charged with policing the new states. He elaborated this in a letter to Santander, dated November 11, 1825, and sent from Chuquisaca. It read in part:

> . . . you must make every effort to prevent Colombian glory from remaining incomplete, in order that I may become the arbiter (*regulador*) of the destinies of South America. . . . I cannot take part in the domestic affairs of Colombia, since at any moment I might find myself involved with one faction or another; whereas, on the outside at the head of a great army, I am beyond the reach of danger; consequently, I can threaten the seditious elements with a formidable force. . . . Caesar threatened Rome from Gaul; I, from Bolivia, threaten every conspirator in America and thus I keep every republic alive.

Bolívar could hardly have carried his internationalism further.

The Panama Congress. The now famous Panama Congress, generally acknowledged to be the forerunner of all the Congresses in which the Latin Americans have sought adequate representation of their interests, was held between June 22 and July 15, 1826. The Congress itself, although not the idea, was strictly the brainchild of Bolívar and it was a logical political projection of his thinking. He issued the invitations to the Con-

[2] Vicente Lecuna, "Campaña de Boyacá," in *Boletín de la Academia Nacional de la Historia* [Caracas], XXIII, No. 92 (Oct., 1940), p. 612.

gress in anticipation of the total defeat of Spain. The invitations were actually extended under date of December 7, 1824, two days before Ayacucho.

The decision to call the Congress did not come easily. For a decade and a half Bolívar had alternately favored a league of Hispanic American states and a single nation. As a young diplomat in London in 1810 he had foreseen the several Spanish colonies first becoming individual states and then uniting in a powerful and permanent confederation. Three years later, as Dictator of the Second Venezuelan republic, he had discarded the idea of a League in favor of a "colossus" American government, as a way of avoiding the bloody spectacles that Europe periodically re-enacted and of adding a third force to the balance of power in the Western world. By the time that he was in communication with the Gentlemen of Jamaica (1815) he once again pleaded for a confederation, whose importance would "exceed that of the Congress of Corinth for the Greeks." However, when he wrote to the Supreme Director of the United Provinces of Río de la Plata in 1818 he had returned to the one-nation concept.[3] As the wars drew to a close, Bolívar realistically accepted what he had known a decade earlier: that the area's climatic differences and geographic diversities, its inhabitants' dissimilar characteristics and conflicting interests argued against the creation and survival of a single nation. It was only after he had definitely accepted that fact that he determined to try for the most suitable alternative, a Congress of Panama, with a view to paving the way for a lasting society of sovereign states.

When the Liberator sent out the invitations to the Congress in December 1824, he had in mind something more and, at the same time, something far less than a Pan-American League. His thinking went beyond a Pan-American Union in providing for a link between the Hispanic world and Great Britain and fell far short of true Pan-American proportions because he did not intend to invite Paraguay, Brazil, Haiti, or the United States of America. His determination to include Great Britain was in accord with his convictions that if the emerging nations could

[3] See above this chapter. For a different interpretation of Bolívar's thinking at this time, consult Raimundo Rivas, "Bolívar as Internationalist," in *Bulletin of the Pan-American Union*, LXIV (Dec., 1930), 1278.

reach a political and military agreement with England, the British would assume "a kind of moral protectorate or cultural leadership over Spanish America." (*See Reading No. 11.*) He originally excluded Paraguay because it had fallen under the harsh dictatorship of José Gaspar Rodríguez de Francia, and Brazil because he suspected it of representing the interests of the Holy Alliance and also because it was intervening in the internal affairs of La Plata. He ruled out Haiti because of its non-Iberian origins and also because it had already entered a period of such extreme anarchy that it had come to epitomize for the Liberator the worst in social behavior. In May 1825, Bolívar admonished Santander not to liberate Cuba because to do so would be to create another Haiti. He did not include the United States for two reasons: he feared that strong ties with that republic would tend to alienate Great Britain, and he believed that the northern republic would inevitably intervene in the affairs of the new states to the disadvantage of the entire Hispanic American world. In 1829 Bolívar informed the British *chargé d'affaires* in Bogotá that the United States "seemed destined by providence to plague America with torments in the name of freedom. . . ." [4]

Between the time that Bolívar first pressed for the Congress and the delegates actually convened in Panama, the membership underwent important changes. La Plata declined to attend. The decision of the leaders in Buenos Aires rested on three considerations. They distrusted Bolívar's personal ambitions. They feared that a successful Congress would attempt to constitute "a Supreme or Sublime Authority on the continent under the control of Colombia." They objected to Bolívar's decision to create Bolivia out of territory to which Argentina, as the heir of the old viceroyalty, had certain legitimate claims. Chile, caught up in a power struggle between Federalists and Centralists, accepted the invitation to attend the Congress but in the end did not send delegates. Sucre, as actual head of the Bolivian government, invited Bolívar to name that country's delegates but the appointments were made quite late and Bolivia was not represented at the Congress. Meanwhile, additional invitations were extended. Bolívar invited Paraguay, but Dictator Francia declined. In Bogotá, Santander forcefully recommended and Bolívar somewhat

4 Bolívar, *Selected Writings*, II, 732.

grudgingly agreed that Brazil and the United States should be invited. After some delay invitations were sent to both countries and they accepted, but for different reasons neither was officially represented at the session. The upshot was that plenipotentiaries from only Gran Colombia, the Central American Confederation, Peru, and Mexico, plus an official observer from Great Britain and an unofficial representative from the Netherlands, finally met in the city of Panama.

Initially, important accomplishments were expected from the Congress. The preliminary exchanges, especially those between Gran Colombia and Peru and the instructions to the delegates of the various countries, dealt in a positive manner with just about every conceivable subject that might have served the interests of the new states. As a minimum it was anticipated that the Congress would lay the foundations for an amphictyonic body (a league of good neighbors), which would arbitrate differences between member states and serve as a great bulwark against further interference in the hemisphere by the conservative powers of Europe. But, as the departure of the delegates was postponed again and again and officials at home became increasingly preoccupied with domestic issues, enthusiasm for the Congress subsided. On reaching the Isthmus, delegates from Peru and Mexico quickly revealed the changed feelings of their superiors by recommending that the sessions be terminated as speedily as possible. And in the rush to complete their assignment, the representatives ignored many of the proposals which, if adopted, would have given a hemispheric character to the meetings. When they adjourned after three weeks of meetings they had agreed upon only four quite unimaginative conventions embodying five basic principles. They were (a) the creation of a permanent army and navy, financed by fixed contributions from each republic and material assistance in case of attack by a foreign power (a confidential agreement relating to the organization and disposition of the forces was also made); (b) friendly arbitration of disputes; (c) extension of the rights of citizenship in one republic to citizens of other American countries; (d) renunciation of the slave trade; and (e) guarantees of the integrity of the participating nations. Only Colombia finally ratified the agreements.

The achievements of the Congress were indeed unimpressive.

But Bolívar was being overly pessimistic when he compared it to "that mad Greek who from his rock tried to direct the course of ships sailing by." Actually the Congress was a success in a number of respects. It established that there was an underlying need for continental unity in peacetime as well as in war. It provided the first opportunity for a number of new nations to express opinions on matters of common concern. It was the first of a series of congresses out of which emerged the Organization of American States, the Central American Common Market, and the Latin American Free Trade Association. That the hemisphere nations, at least publicly, continue to hold out hopes for a positive contribution from those agencies, despite the fact that they are constantly restricted in their activities by the same kinds of petty personalism and nationalism that reduced the effectiveness of the Panama Congress, suggests that the attempt at cooperation in 1826 should not be considered so much a failure of Bolívar's international policy as a credit to his vision.

The Andean Union. As it turned out, the Liberator attained his highest level of international statesmanship in establishing the original guidelines for the Congress of Panama. Even before its sessions began, he foresaw the outcome and began a retreat away from continentalism in favor of a much more modest proposal, the Andean Union or Andean Confederation.[5]

Had Bolívar had his way, the Andean Union would have been comprised of Gran Colombia, Peru, and Bolivia. Each nation would have had its own government, but in matters pertaining to the Confederation, all would have been subject to a higher authority represented by a life president. Bolívar would have been the first person to hold that office.

In considering the Liberator as an internationalist, the proposed Andean Union is important in two particulars. First, it suggests that Bolívar had despaired of stability for Hispanic America. In order to avoid the conflicts that already existed and could be anticipated in the future, he was prepared to isolate from the rest of America those people whom he had led to freedom. Second, in turning to the Andean Confederation, Bolívar in effect admitted that he no longer held any hope that the people of all of Hispanic America would call upon him to lead them. If the Union had been formed and had survived, it would have

[5] *Ibid.,* II, 633-634.

been so large and strong that the weaker states on its fringes
would have endangered their sovereignty by associating themselves with it or by choosing as their leader the individual who
headed the Confederation.

The proposed Confederation attracted flurries of attention
until late 1827 as developments occurred which seemed to be
strengthening Bolívar's hand. In response to his expressed wish
that all members of the union adopt the Bolivian Code of 1826,
the Government Council of Peru not only took that step but
named him President of Peru for life. Bolivia, under Sucre's
guidance, decreed federation with Peru and Gran Colombia.
Bolívar freely publicized his belief that the Colombian government would support his plan.

Chile, Argentina, Brazil, the Central American Confederation,
and Mexico, all watched these developments with varying degrees of apprehension but they need not have. Nationalism
rather than internationalism, division rather than union—these
were the waves of the future and there was nothing that Bolívar
could do to stop them. He threatened, he pleaded, he reminded
national leaders and military commanders of their debt to him,
but to no avail. The union never had a chance of being accepted, except by the use of force, if for no other reason than
that the Colombians under Santander would have nothing to do
with it.

Bolívar never recovered the prestige the rejection of his proposal cost him. Still, one cannot realistically lament his failure
in this instance. To be perhaps less than generous to him, we
cannot be sure whether he promoted the union because he believed it would serve the best interest of the people or because
he could not bear the thought of surrendering "his nations" to
the leadership of others. But whether or not his intentions were
honorable is not so relevant as is the fact that Bolivia, Peru, and
Gran Colombia, from which Venezuela and Ecuador would
soon separate, simply were not ready for union. Bolívar was
their most important commonality. If they had formed a Confederation it would have been because of the Liberator, whose
influence still towered over that of anyone else despite the fact
that by 1828 many of his enemies were attacking him from
the relative security of high public offices. That being the case,
it would seem to follow that with Bolívar's death the federation

would have sundered and the individual nations would have embarked upon their separate courses, a tendency they exhibit yet today, nearly a century and a half later.

Bolívar and Nationalism. In building monuments to Bolívar the Internationalist, Bolívar the Nationalist is often overlooked. The Liberator surely would have preferred it that way. He believed, as do many today, that international blocs rather than individual nations promise the most acceptable solutions to the major problems confronting the Hispanic American world. He liked to think of himself as a daring innovator, exploring the frontiers of knowledge, capturing ideas with which he could predict the future. Were he alive today this predilection for the vanguard would commit him to internationalism. Still the evidence argues that to ignore nationalism is to misunderstand much of Bolívar's life's work. He was, after all, responsible for the creation of five nations that have persisted from his day to ours. And his entire public life was intimately and constantly linked to nationalism, sometimes by choice and other times by the exigencies of politics.

Before pinning a nationalist label on Bolívar, it should be clear that the label can be meaningful only if it is understood to represent the early nineteenth-century variety of that ideology. When the Liberator lived, nationalism as a fundamental concept was still in its infancy and Paris was its nursery. In western Europe, where it had reached its most advanced stage of development, it bore only a family resemblance to the noisy, vibrant ideology that it has become in our time. Early nineteenth-century Nationalists in Europe did not go beyond calling for a society with essentially liberal objectives. At the core of their thinking was the Fatherland, a politically sovereign entity with defined boundaries, flag, anthem, customs, festivals, and heroes. Over and above these was the assumed right of the state to demand and receive the services of its citizens in times of emergencies and to judge those actions which were or appeared to be treasonable.

In Hispanic America, meanwhile, there were prior to the Independence movement only a scattered few informed individuals who ever considered the implications of nationalism's practical application to their own situations. Creolism, one of the key justifications for separation from Spain, was continental rather

than national in scope. When most members of the leading
groups thought in exclusivist terms, their ideas were ill-defined
and almost always on the peripheries of their thinking. Not until
the independence struggles drew to a close, leaving regions exhausted and their resources depleted, did the political-military
elites fall back upon what we today consider essentially nationalistic arguments and then only those of a primarily patriotic or
political nature.

On the basis of his words and actions Bolívar could have
been a good Nationalist in early nineteenth-century France or
Great Britain. He never questioned his power to demand military service from citizens or to punish those whose actions he
considered detrimental to the state. Up to the point where
nationalists in Hispanic America began to veer towards an
intolerant nativism, he was in nearly all respects one with them.
He assumed that the different regions would have their own
flags, seals, and coinage; that the condor and llama would replace the Spanish lion and double-headed eagle. His Cartagena
Manifesto and his War to the Death proclamation, by inviting
hatred of Spain and love of homeland, played upon pride and
passion just as surely as did the original hymns written to rally
support for the new governments.

The Liberator did not question that the new states would
have their own saints and feast days, and he considered religion a personal matter. However, like nearly all early nationalist leaders he did not question the power of civilian
officials to regulate the Roman Catholic Church. The legislation he sponsored in Gran Colombia, Peru, and Bolivia left no
doubt that he was determined to strengthen nationalist institutions at the expense of religious institutions. His Bolivian
charter—which he considered the model of excellence in government for Hispanic America—stopped short of proposing a
national church. It did, however, grant the nation ultimate
authority over the Church in Bolivia by reserving to the nation the sole power to select all Church officials from archbishop
to parish priest.

In the fashion of many nationalists and patriots then and
now, the Liberator felt an emotional attachment to one community, in his case Venezuela and more especially Caracas.
Even after he came to symbolize continentalism he continued to
belong integrally to Venezuela. In September 1825, when at the

height of his glory, he wrote to General Páez, "My heart is always in Caracas: There I received life, there I ought to surrender it: And my *caraqueños* will always be my first countrymen." Later when xenophobic nationalists were taking the lead in destroying his dreams, Venezuela continued to be his "beloved Fatherland." [6] "My beloved Venezuela is what I adore above all things," he wrote his relative, the Marquis de Toro. And only a few months before his death, when Venezuela had already seceded from Gran Colombia and was setting itself up as an independent republic, Bolívar related to his friend Dr. José Angel Alamo, "Venezuela is the idol of my heart and Caracas is my Patria." [7]

The Liberator's ambition to lead a confederation of Hispanic American states forced him to be a nationalist. He could not claim for himself a supranational role and at the same time oppose the nationalist character of the governments erected in the areas he freed from Spain. However, even if his political ambitions had not made him a nationalist, his understanding of conditions throughout the continent probably would have. In the Jamaica Letter he stated that the formation of several nation-states was the only acceptable alternative to complete fragmentation of the empire. Furthermore, he believed that the new nations would profit more from the colonial experience if their old imperial administrative or juridical entities were preserved. As it turned out, the borders of the new states followed in a rough manner the boundaries of the colonial districts. In South America, Peru, Argentina, and Colombia were the centers of former viceroyalties; Chile and Venezuela of captain-generalcies; Bolivia of an *audiencia;* Ecuador of a presidency; and Uruguay of a military district. Paraguay was a special case. There the effects of the Jesuit mission organization and prolonged physical isolation from the major imperial centers produced a spirit of unity which was the overriding consideration in the separation of Paraguay from Argentina, with which it had been linked under Spanish rule.

Anti-nationalism. Unlike the xenophobes and petty politicians who sought to make the nation-state a supreme and final entity, Bolívar knew that to build a "national spirit" anywhere

[6] Guillermo Ruíz Rivas, *Simón Bolívar más allá del mito,* 2 vols. (Bogotá, 1964), II, 295-296.
[7] Augusto Mijares, *El Libertador* (Caracas, 1964), p. 4.

in Spanish America would require consummate political skill. Spanish nationalism did not provide a good example; it had been Regionalist or Federalist. The most enlightened minorities in the former colonies could not be depended upon to furnish responsible guidance because during the war years, in their efforts to imitate Europe they had increasingly disassociated themselves from the American political reality. No area had an art or a literature that would help promote a feeling of national unity. Rugged terrain and climatic extremes on the one hand and grossly inadequate transportation and communication facilities on the other divided and isolated neighboring areas, and often encouraged antipathy among them. The masses, impoverished and lacking both education and training in citizenship, were concerned primarily with local matters. Their allegiances focused on smaller, not larger, political units.

In 1830 nationalists in general had not pushed their case beyond the limits suggested above. In Italy, however, Mazzini was already formulating a defense for nationality based on a common language, and a decade later Norway began to develop the linguistic and literary expression which it later used to justify separation from Sweden. Throughout western Europe nationalists were, to an ever greater degree, associating national well-being with various kinds of economic preferences. In view of these developments it is reasonable to ask where Spanish Americans, and particularly Bolívar, would have stood in regard to them.

Hispanic American nationalists could not exploit the language issue because it simply did not exist. The wars were fought by and for the Creoles, and from the first it was assumed that following independence from Spain, power would revert to Spanish-speaking Creoles and those "people of color" who had thoroughly adopted Creole values. Hence, persons in positions of responsibility during the Independence Era did not feel a serious obligation to undertake the long process of teaching Spanish to millions of Indians or initiating measures to overcome the much more complex problems of ethnic and political integration upon which full nationhood rests.

Bolívar was far more concerned than all but a very few figures of his era about the condition of the masses. But his interest was as a social reformer and political pragmatist rather than as a nationalist. As a liberal he had a sincere and abiding desire to improve the welfare of the Indian. As a reformer he freed his own Negro slaves as early as 1811. While he was still fighting to gain a foothold on the mainland he declared slaves freed in the areas he temporarily held. At Angostura, he asked a reluctant Congress to abolish slavery, and in one of the few instances that an upper-class Creole suggested the need for racial mixing he implored, "Our blood is different, let us mix it in order to unite it." [8]

Ethnic Integration. As a pragmatist, the Liberator did not let his own social views override practical political considerations. To avoid alienating the powerful slaveholding elements, he approved the Cúcuta Charter of 1821 although it did not go beyond declaring free the children henceforth born of slaves in Gran Colombia. If throughout the last half decade of the wars he successfully sustained his position that slaves who bore arms in Patriot armies should be granted their freedom, it was often for reasons which were neither reformist nor nationalist. He needed soldiers habituated to privation and to fighting for themselves, and Negro slaves qualified on both of these counts. In Venezuela he had seen the free population dying and slaves surviving and he worried that if those conditions were permitted to continue slaves would eventually dare to rebel against their masters and produce another Haitian debacle. With this latter possibility in mind he bluntly insisted that if slaves were required to fight for their freedom on the battlefield, their dangerous number would be diminished.

The Liberator's willingness to see the percentage of slaves in the total population reduced, if necessary by death in battle, was consistent with his conviction that the unassimilated, dissatisfied popular elements constituted the greatest single obstacle to the future welfare and development of the new nations. For him the "people of color" were ungovernable. Their centuries of servitude, profound ignorance, and lack of lasting values would cause them, for many years to come, to take "license for liberty,

[8] Augusto Mijares, "La evolución política de Venezuela (1810-1960)," in Fundación Mendoza, *Venezuela independiente, 1810-1960* (Caracas, 1962), p. 52.

treachery for patriotism, and vengeance for justice. . . ." [9] Consequently when the popular masses, especially the *pardos* in Venezuela, took advantage of the war-time weakening of colonial caste barriers to demand both legal and real equality with the upper classes, Bolívar reacted by actively opposing their integration into the national polity. He fought those who for selfish ends wished to politicize the masses, and various constitutions which he approved in effect disenfranchised the "people of color" by making literacy and ownership of property qualifications for voting.

Thus the masses under the early nationalists ended up very near where they had been under the imperialists. No one, including Bolívar, was able or willing to challenge traditional arrangements. The first national constitutions gave "the people of color" certain legal equalities, but the Creoles promptly countered that move by substituting mythical racial inequalities. The mestizos, Indians, and Negroes were, in general, unmindful of their rights and responsibilities as citizens and the elites did not propose to teach them. Social divisiveness had served the interests of Hapsburgs and Bourbons, now it would be made to serve the interest of the Creoles. They had no intention of transforming a society of castes into a society of classes, in making one nation, one people, or—to use an expression widely employed by nationalists currently—one family. Men might be created equal in the sight of God, but they were not equal in the eyes of the Creoles.

Economic Nationalism.   At least two considerations ruled out any possibility that Bolívar and his contemporaries might follow the lead of budding European economic nationalists. First, the new states had nothing but economic privileges to offer Great Britain in return for its protection. Second, they realized that public revenues and local investment capital were in such short supply that the emerging nations could not on their own account hope to pump new life into their disrupted economies and consequently would have to depend upon private foreign capital.

Great Britain exacted a high price for the protection that it gave Hispanic America, and no one paid that price more willingly than Bolívar. To the last for him Great Britain represented security, investment capital and commercial and in-

[9] Bolívar, *Selected Writings,* I, 176.

dustrial ability, and those things counted more than the apparent dangers that small states faced in their relations with large nations. The Liberator was remarkably constant in his confidence that the British held the key to political and economic happiness. As early as 1814 in a statement on English policy, he held that British trading vessels plying between northern South America and a Europe free of Napoleon would be the foundations for the "prosperity of our commerce and agriculture." [10] A year later in a plea for British military assistance, he promised his prospective sponsors a bright economic future made brighter by British technicians. "The mountains of New Granada are of gold and silver. A small number of [British] mineralogists could discover more mines than those of all Peru and New Spain. What immense expectations that small part of the New World holds for British industry." To whet further the British appetite, Panama and Nicaragua could be ceded to His Majesty's government, which would build canals that would make the Isthmus the entrepôt of world commerce and "permanently establish British commercial supremacy." [11]

By 1825 when national debts had become a greater worry than the Spanish armies, Bolívar turned to the sale of mining rights as a way of meeting public obligations. With that source of revenue in mind he first decreed all neglected and abandoned mines in Bolivia the rightful property of the government, and then sold the mines for 2.5 million pesos. His satisfaction with the outcome of that venture prompted him to suggest that Colombia and Peru do the same thing. Colombia, he argued, should take over all unworked mines and sell them to an English company. "I believe we could realize a few million by resorting to such devices, as the moment is favorable for mining transactions," he wrote.[12] He recommended to Peru that it sell to England all its mines, lands, and properties, and other assets, to cover the national debt of not fewer than 20 million pesos.[13]

Whether or not the new administrators were well advised to conclude that foreign borrowing was necessary to meet ordinary expenses and promote economic growth is both debatable and for this study irrelevant. There were, however, several considera-

[10] *Ibid.*, I, 970.
[11] *Ibid.*, I, 98-99.
[12] *Ibid.*, II, 529.
[13] *Ibid.*, II, 545.

tions which are not debatable and are relevant. First, the new
republics did rush to borrow from abroad before determining
their minimum needs. Second, Great Britain, going through a
speculative boom of great proportions, did little to discourage
its citizens from making financially unsound loans and from
creating companies that promptly collapsed, thereby adversely
affecting Hispanic America's economic image in Europe. Third,
the funds derived from foreign borrowing were for the most
part squandered in paying salaries of superfluous civilian and
military bureaucrats, rather than in developing ports and roads,
promoting agriculture and industry, or expanding educational
systems. Fourth, when the new governments failed to meet their
payments on interest and principal they completely destroyed
their credit standing and it was in most cases nearly a half-
century before they could again borrow in Europe, and then
only on highly unfavorable terms.

However much one may regret the outcome of Hispanic
America's initial introduction to foreign borrowing, the lessons
of the subsequent century and a quarter of international finance
teach that Bolívar and his contemporaries are hardly to be condemned for their mistakes. As will be recalled, they had had
little administrative experience. They were leaders when new
nations were still novelties and the problems of such societies
were as little understood as they are today. International finance
was equally novel. When the officials of Hispanic America went
abroad to borrow and British investors made the loans, both
groups were serving as guinea pigs for one of the most important
—and controversial—developments of the modern world. They
could not know the ramifications of large-scale flow of capital
from economically strong to economically depressed nations.
We do not know them today. Also, the nationalist leaders of
1825 cannot be faulted for their misuse of funds when so many
of their counterparts today in Africa, Asia, and the Middle
East, with the best counsel of their former mother countries
available to them, still allocate their physical and human resources so uneconomically. In this regard it is interesting, if
not necessarily fruitful, to speculate on what the course of
Hispanic America's development would have been had Spain
come to the assistance of its former colonies instead of forcing
them to maintain armies to ward off its threats of re-conquest,
and to search abroad for capital and skills.

CHAPTER 6

Bolívar as Political Theorist

Bolívar's political thought was inevitably a response to crisis. From 1813 to 1824 it developed to meet the exigencies of war and the demands of Creoles for republican government. From 1824 until his death in 1830 it was refined as an attempt to reconcile fratricidal factions, to avert civil war, and to counter threats of invasion from Spain and the Holy Alliance. The state of crisis was constant, and Bolívar's analysis of it and his methods of dealing with it constitute the continuity of his political thinking. Bolívar's priorities were unity, control, stability, and security, roughly in that order. Unity was the consolidation of Creole support of the war effort; control, the containment and direction of the shaky Federalist-Centralist alliances that resulted; stability, the maintenance of that equilibrium; and security, the assurance of Creole ascendancy.

He feared dictatorship less than the anarchy of the masses. He asked that executive decision-making be made efficient enough and free enough to function forcefully. His enemies accused him of talking democratically and acting despotically. He countered by saying that he was innovating, attempting to find a new middle way between monarchy and republicanism, a new kind of government for a new people. He insisted that the new government be able to purge license from liberty as well as to assure that authority would not become tyranny. And always his commitment to independence and to strong central government remained constant.

What changed were the means by which he thought unity, order, and continuity in government could be achieved. In defense of independence he proposed at various times confederation, inter-American alliance, and league with Britain. In the early years he advocated a complete break with the Spanish past. Later, when peace came, he tended to restore the bases of Spanish order: imperial centralization; the Catholic Church; repression of "dangerous" theories from abroad; methods of getting revenue. What changed most of all was the role he envisaged for himself in the new society: sometimes dictator;

sometimes an itinerant Caesar, keeping order within a great confederation; sometimes wise giver of laws; and rarely, a simple citizen, resting in retirement.

What we know of Bolívar's political development comes primarily from four documents in which he set forth his political creed. The first was a call to arms, the Cartagena Manifesto of 1812. The second was the Jamaica Letter of 1815. The third was his recommendation for a Constitution for Colombia which he proposed at Angostura in 1819. The last was his Constitution for Bolivia of 1826, a new government for a new republic, and one which he believed was suited for all of Spanish South America. Letters to Sucre, to Santander, and to his Irish aide, Daniel O'Leary, give perspective to the observations of foreign officials and diplomats. Bolívar's theoretical proposals tell us more than his practical accomplishments, for when the Liberator was in power, he acted as a military pacifier whose political solutions dealt only with the most immediate of problems.

The Cartagena Manifesto. In the Cartagena Manifesto Bolívar pleaded for unity to win the war: a simple Centralist government, a single and vigorous authority. (*See Reading No. 11.*) Most of all, he advocated force. Only force could "liberate peoples who are ignorant of their rights." Only force could neutralize "the internal factions which in reality were the fatal poison" that had laid Venezuela in its tomb. Only force could annihilate the "criminal clemency" that acquitted sedition and conspiracy in the name of human rights and was repaid by treason. Like Rousseau, Bolívar insisted that in the name of the general good, men should be forced to be free. On this point he never changed his mind. The bitterness of his later years came from the realization that it could not be done.

The Cartagena Manifesto proclaimed three political convictions that Bolívar maintained throughout his career. The first was that federalism was a form of government unsuited to Spanish America. In 1813 he called federalism a vicious political idea. In 1821 he referred to it as "a Greek edifice . . . on the brink of a crater." In 1829 he concluded brusquely, "I think it would be better for South America to adopt the Koran rather than the United States' form of government, although the latter is the best in the world." [1]

[1] Bolívar, *Selected Writings,* I, 45, 268; II, 738.

Bolívar realized that because their conversion to republicanism was more an emotional than an intellectual process, Spanish American Federalists proposed to deny their past and give authority to provinces. This was an innovation that simply had no precedent. Spanish imperial dominion had depended upon incommunicado parochialism. Both administratively and economically each colony was joined directly to the Crown. Intercolonial exchanges were discouraged. In addition, since no serious effort was made to develop roads, Spanish America, as it approached the end of the colonial period, was a galaxy of enclaves. Isolation fostered provincialism. Cities, like xenophobic nationalists of our day, saw their neighbors as either rivals or enemies. Lacking was a basis for allegiances which would place the aggregated interests of society above narrow exclusivism.

Bolívar noted that the Spanish bureaucratic system had deprived Creoles of experience in the "roles of legislator, minister of Treasury, diplomat, general, and every other position of authority." And he might have added that almost none of them was known beyond his own city or village. He correctly foresaw that at least initially Congressional representatives would tend to place regional and partisan objectives above the general welfare. Although, after a time, they might rise above local interests, they would still lack the expert knowledge required to develop national planning. Thus legislative action would at best be intermittent just when the former colonies desperately needed firm and consistent direction.

So Bolívar's second conviction justified the first. He believed that a wholly representative government was unsuited to Spanish Americans because they lacked "civic virtue," and to him that meant more than just the lack of a parliamentary tradition. "Civic virtue" was that Athenian ideal by which slaves and servants and wage earners were refused citizenship because they could not devote their full time and energies to public service. Bolívar interpreted it in the orthodox Enlightenment fashion. He followed Montesquieu in believing that it had become a characteristic unique to English-speaking peoples. Latin peoples must re-learn it. It was on the grounds of civic virtue that Bolívar later defended a specific legislative chamber, the Censors, whose sole purpose would be to train professional political leaders and to assure the development of good citizens. Similarly in the

Bolivian Constitution of 1826 he disfranchised laborers, illiterates, debtors, criminals, drunkards, gamblers, beggars, and corrupt politicians. The concept of civic virtue was pervasive in Spanish America during that period. It was easily transformed into pious moralism as in the case of the Chilean Constitution of 1823, which prohibited atheists from residing in the country and prescribed Easter communion for all children over the age of ten.

Sometimes Bolívar held politicians primarily responsible for creating a climate unfavorable to the development of civic virtue. At other times he held the colonial past accountable. In 1826 he wrote,

> All our antecedents are enveloped in the black cloak of crime. We are the abominable offspring of those raging beasts that came to America to waste her blood and to breed with their victims before sacrificing them. Later, the illegitimate offspring of these unions commingled with the offspring of slaves transplanted from Africa. With such racial mixtures and such a moral history, can we place laws above heroes and principles above men? [2]

When he blamed the politicians, he thought constitutional checks on their activity could solve the problem. But when he condemned the past, he concluded that Spanish Americans could never be free until they altered their very nature. It was at those times that he recalled Montesquieu: a people corrupted by slavery needed conquerors, not liberators.

Bolívar's third political conviction of the Cartagena Manifesto was that only a strong central government could win the war and construct a lasting peace. Then, as now, the equation was made that centralization equals progress. But the "common good" in the nineteenth century was defined as institutional well-being and individual freedom, while in the twentieth century it is concerned with institutional efficiency and individual well-being.

Nineteenth-century centralists could not use economic justifications, partly because the common man was excluded from political participation and partly because leaders were either economically illiterate or committed to Adam Smith's teachings that economic development would occur in proportion to the extent that the government did *not* meddle with it. Economic questions were thus defined as existing outside the realm of

[2] *Ibid.,* II, 624.

political action. Like other political leaders of his time, Bolívar was more concerned with external credit rating than he was with internal economic development. The "shame of bankruptcy," not terms of trade, preoccupied him.

The Jamaica Letter. The Jamaica Letter of 1815 contains very little specific description of political structure. (*See Reading No. 12.*) It is evident that at this early date Bolívar was thinking in terms of a life executive, a hereditary Senate (like the French counterpart of the House of Lords which Napoleon and Benjamin Constant revived in 1815), a strong central government, and some kind of political apprenticeship for citizens. His primary model was the same as Montesquieu's: British parliamentary monarchy.

Even though he borrowed heavily from the political fashions of his day, Bolívar would never have admitted that he was an imitator. He always thought of himself as a political innovator. His tutor, Simón Rodríguez, described him as the kind of man who preferred thinking to reading. When he did read, he read to criticize. His plans represented his own interpretation of the ideas of others, and to the extent that he made them his own, his plans were original. "*Imitate* and adopt, *adapt* and create. . . . General Bolívar does not imitate; whatever evil he does, he [alone] may justly be held responsible. . . ." [3]

As early as 1812 and as late as 1828, Bolívar was determined to introduce the principles of British constitutionalism to South America. When he imitated Britain, he adopted Montesquieu, for not only did *The Spirit of the Laws* convince him that it was the best of all possible governments: from the very beginning Bolívar saw reality in the same paradoxical dualisms as Montesquieu did.[4]

The perception they shared was this: any political system, they believed, threatened a horrible alternative: either the tyranny of a despot or the tyranny of a mob. Montesquieu warned that a constitution aimed at guaranteeing the independence of individuals must result in oppression. Bolívar cited the example of

---

[3] Simón Rodríguez, *Escritos de Simón Rodríguez,* comp. Pedro Grases, 3 vols. (Caracas, 1954), I, 200.
[4] For what the Liberator knew of Montesquieu see Simón Bolívar, *Escritos del Libertador* (Caracas, 1964), I, 254, 259, 339, 341-342, 381, 408, 426-427.

the Venezuelan Republic, submerged after having tried to follow
the Federalist example of the United States. Both Bolívar and
Montesquieu believed that the people were incapable of ruling
themselves, but that they must be given the right to choose their
representatives. That is, they believed in a representative but not
a popular government. Both put their trust in a divided legislature
to guarantee that distinguished men could check the licentious-
ness of the people. In *The Spirit of the Laws* Montesquieu wrote
that the best government was "that which best agrees with the
humor of the people in whose favor it is established." In the
Jamaica Letter Bolívar echoed, "Do not adopt the best system
of government, but the one that is most likely to succeed." To
determine what exactly the "humor of the people" might be,
Montesquieu considered land, occupation, religion, commerce,
manners, customs, and ideals. Bolívar, in reviewing the state
of the "revolution" in 1815, followed his model precisely and
characterized each area of Spanish America in terms of its
geographic location, wealth, population, and character.

Because Bolívar always asked for authority in the name of
order, his political analysis invariably emphasized chaos, anarchy,
and factionalism. Right or wrong, this persistent pessimism was
shared by those leaders in other areas who ultimately consolidated their nations. Francia demanded that his Paraguayans
live in peace and silence so that the ideal of national independence could be realized. As early as 1822, Diego Portales
of Chile wrote that he was seeking a strong centralized government, neither a monarchy nor a democracy, whose leaders
would provide the people with models of civic virtue. Bolívar,
like builders of new nations then and now, distrusted the institutions created by Federalists as inadequate to contain the
surge of energy released by a wartime society in flux. He, like
them, insisted on political tutelage. To greater or lesser degrees
he viewed dissent as disruptive and sought to silence it. Finally,
he demanded great executive authority. Nowhere in Spanish
America was a new nation stabilized by either federalism or
truly divided powers.

The Congress of Angostura. Bolívar presented his first
developed theory of government to the Congress of Angostura
on February 15, 1819, when Northern South America was
only half-free. (*See Reading No. 13.*) He stood before the

congressmen as a military Commander-in-Chief, backed by his army, dependent upon no faction, sanctioned by no social group. Once again his words were directed at England. Still seeking arms, supplies, and men from abroad as well as the prestige of international recognition, he was required at the same time to quell the doubts of lawyers who suspected that he would impose a military dictatorship on Colombia, his new creation.

To wean the constitutionalists away from federalism, he affirmed republicanism and the Rights of Man: liberty, property, security, and resistance to oppression. To win the admirers of the United States, he asked that the Venezuelan judiciary, modeled on that of the United States, be retained. But in the words of Abbé de Pradt he warned that the example of the United States, so tempting because of their "remarkable prosperity" and "full and absolute enjoyment of sovereignty, independence, and freedom" was inappropriate to an area which had suffered hundreds of years of Spanish domination. To assure the support of the one well-defined power group he knew would back him, he asked Congress to approve his Order of Liberators and to execute his decree that veterans be compensated from confiscated Loyalist land and property. To maintain and supplement his army, or perhaps to fulfill his promise to Haitian President Alexandre Pétion, he asked for the abolition of slavery. By not proclaiming religious toleration, he won support from orthodox Catholics who interpreted it as a sanction for the status quo. Yet because he did not definitively establish the Church, both anticlericals and powerful Protestant nations in Europe could assume that religious toleration existed in fact.

To moderate the popular will, he advocated limited suffrage and indirect elections. To instruct the masses in civic virtue, he proposed a Chamber of Censors, a "holy alliance of morality" to watch over youth and to impose moral penalties for actions which violated either the Constitution or the sense of public decency. Bolívar's critics have blasted this third legislative Chamber as a sort of lay inquisition, as perhaps it might have been in action. But in theory it was the product of French Enlightenment, the "civil religion" advocated by Rousseau, the Athenian Aereopagus recalled by Montesquieu.

The "very soul" of the new republic was to be a hereditary Senate, selected at first from the Order of Liberators, with bishops as honorary members. In the second generation, the sons of the Liberators would be professionalized "from earliest youth." The Congress of Angostura, voting on this proposal, found the prospect of a new military aristocracy distasteful and changed the tenure of senators to life.

To limit public authority Bolívar again chose the British example. The strong executive would be triply checked, by responsible ministers, by the Senate, and by the power of the purse in an elected lower house.

The Liberator asked the Congress the rhetorical question, how can we prevent "the remnants of our past fetters from becoming liberty-destroying weapons?" His solution anticipated the one seized upon by the distinguished Argentine Generation of 1837. It was: become something else. By tutelage, become Anglo-Saxon. Forge the national spirit to a moral power.

Bolívar was proposing that a government be based on experience rather than rhetoric. Yet when in 1821 it came time to promulgate a constitution for Colombia that the New Granadans could approve, the Congress of Cúcuta rejected the Angostura proposals. Although most of the delegates endorsed Bolívar personally, they weakened executive powers, created a popular bicameral legislature with eight- and four-year terms, and ignored the Chamber of Censors. Then, giving him full military powers, they elected him President.

Soldier-Statesman Dichotomy. Bolívar was a man of action and a notoriously poor administrator. When he hesitated to accept the presidency, he told the Congress of Cúcuta, "I am a soldier by necessity and also by choice. . . . A Government office is a torture chamber for me." [5] There is little reason to suspect him of hypocrisy. He finally accepted, determined that Santander as Vice-President should play the role of "indispensable man" and exercise full authority. That arrangement would leave Bolívar free to fulfill his military destiny as Liberator.

Disturbed that the new republic which had been his goal for ten years was unprotected by the moderating checks of his Angostura constitution, he indulged himself in pessimism throughout the year 1821. In Venezuela all was chaos. Cities like Valencia he called "demonopolis." Nothing could be done because, he said, the good men had disappeared and the bad had multi-

[5] Bolívar, *Selected Writings,* I, 285.

plied. Behind him were the *llaneros,* proud, ignorant, hostile, a volcano about to erupt. Before him were the learned men of New Granada, who theorized about federalism and who thought that citizens were well-bred people like themselves. But Colombians were not just Creoles, whose theories changed with every *tertulia.* They were Indians along the Orinoco, cattlemen on the Apure, Maracaibo sailors, Magdalena rivermen, bandits, the "savage hordes of Africa and America," the army. If the *llaneros* did not destroy the nation, Bolívar prophesied, the tranquil philosophers of legalistic Colombia would. In 1826 Santander corroborated his view. (*See Reading No. 14.*)

Bolívar had little faith in legislative processes and little conviction that they would serve the best interests of the emerging nations. However right he may have been in his pessimistic prediction—and history bears his judgment out in numerous instances—that view, especially in conjunction with his preference for personal action over laws and institutions, was inconsistent with his professed commitment to republicanism. His attitude towards legislators probably explains in large part his inability to identify with the offices granted to him. Political office was important to him only insofar as it gave him power which could be directly translated into order and stability. He left to others the manipulating, the negotiating, and the bargaining which are the trademarks of the accomplished politician. He was a lawgiver rather than a lawmaker.

Conscious that he was playing a definitive role, he trusted to intuition and his own personal prestige. It was just this characteristic which infuriated Santander. When Bolívar chided him for delaying the cause of independence in Peru, Santander, provoked, retorted:

> I rule Colombia, not Peru. The laws given me to rule this republic have nothing to do with Peru, and their character does not change just because Colombia's president commands an army on foreign soil. . . . Either there are laws or there are not. If there are none, why do we deceive people with phantoms? And if there are, they must be kept and obeyed.[6]

On the other hand, Bolívar never went quite so far in denying the efficacy of legislation as did the man credited with stabilizing

[6] Francisco de Paula Santander, *Cartas de Santander,* ed. Vicente Lecuna, 3 vols. (Caracas, 1942), I, 290.

Chile under a rule of law, Diego Portales. He also saw his countrymen as part barbarians and the rest fools, and in 1834 he wrote:

> . . . what the devil are Constitutions and papers good for if they are incapable of remedying a known evil? . . . Damn the law if it cannot let the government proceed with a free hand at the opportune moment.[7]

The Bolivian Constitution. There was in the character of Bolívar that unique paradox which arises when a man of the sword, devoted to intellectual pursuits, commits his energies to the *word* as a universal panacea. This is what happened in 1826. When the Liberator conceived the Bolivian Constitution as *the* political answer to Spanish America's problems, he became a victim of the same fallacy that he had so derisively condemned in Federalist lawgivers: proposing Utopian political answers to problems which were essentially social and economic.

Bolívar thought that his constitution for Bolivia was a new method by which a new Hispanic America could reconcile the differences between army and people, democracy and aristocracy, monarchy and republic. He believed that it provided for a firm, stable government without exacting a price of either freedom or equality. When it was finished, he wrote to influential friends in Colombia that he could discover no other representative system of government that offered so vigorous an executive or so much popular freedom and direct participation of citizens in sovereignty.

> In it are combined all the advantages of federalism, all the firmness of centralized government, all the stability of monarchical regimes. By means of it, all interests are intertwined, and all rights and guarantees are assured.[8]

Bolívar was not simply applauding his own genius. What had happened was that just when he was framing the new constitution, Páez and his fellow officers in Venezuela had offered Bolívar a crown. What enthralled him was that the Bolivian Constitution, as he saw it, enabled him to reject a crown and so to escape the opprobrium of Monarchist ambitions while at the same time assuring those who had tempted him to be Napoleon

---

[7] Ricardo Donoso, *Las ideas políticas en Chile* (Mexico, 1946), p. 111.

[8] Bolívar, *Selected Writings*, II, 627.

that he could give them what they wanted. This writer is persuaded that since Bolívar enjoyed the prestige of a monarch and had no legitimate heir, he would have no motive to betray his lifelong commitment to centralism for a superfluous crown.

Whether or not Bolívar ever approved the project of monarchy as a form of government in America is not, however, so clear. In the Jamaica Letter he declared that in his view monarchy would be impractical and impossible and that Americans would prefer republics to kingdoms. However, he was well aware that other Americans did not agree with him. He rightly predicted that the dominant Mexican military-oligarchy would institute a political system that would degenerate into an absolute monarchy, which it did under Iturbide. In 1820 when triumphant liberals in Spain sent out agents to ask for the adherence of Spanish America to the restored constitutional monarchy, groups in Mexico, Peru, Buenos Aires, and Chile, all attempted in one way or another to solicit the service of a Spanish or foreign prince. Only Bolívar and Paraguay's Francia (who flatly refused to negotiate) insisted on independent republicanism.

However, Carlos Villanueva, Salvador de Madariaga and other professional historians have used different evidence to paste a monarchical label on the Liberator.[9] They relied primarily upon the testimony of European officials with whom Bolívar talked, especially British agents in 1825 and 1829. Without more convincing evidence than is now available, it is preferable to conclude that Bolívar's conversations reflected less his true beliefs and more a defensive diplomacy. Bolívar was convinced that some sort of political and military alliance with His Majesty's Government was essential to defend American independence against the reactionary forces of Europe. This alone would have kept him from categorically denouncing any policy that Britain might suggest. At least three additional considerations argue against any monarchical scheming on Bolívar's part. When dealing with British agents he continued to emphasize that he would never accept a crown for himself. As early as 1815 and as late as 1829 he warned that an imposed monarchy probably would not work: no foreign prince would serve

---

[9] See Carlos A. Villanueva, *La monarquía en América: Bolívar y el General San Martín* (Paris, 1912); and Salvador de Madariaga, *Bolívar* (New York, 1952), especially chapters XXV and XXVI.

nations so ridden with debt, anarchy, and poverty; patriot generals would not condone anyone who barred them from authority, and finally, the masses would rise up against a new aristocracy. Because Bolívar believed that Britain's designs on America involved only commercial privileges and a way to counter the international power of the Holy Alliance, he could easily maintain that the British would not insist on a monarchy if those interests were being served by republics. This is precisely what his Bolivian constitution was contrived to do.

The "heart and soul" of the Bolivian Constitution was the executive, an elected president with life tenure who could name his successor. (*See Reading No. 15.*) The tenure was derived from precedents: Alexandre Pétion's life term as President of Haiti and Napoleon's aborted reign in France. The concept of vice-presidential succession and ministerial function Bolívar took from the example of the United States.[10]

It is evident that in his proposal for the Constitution of Bolivia in 1826, the Liberator did not think that he was dealing in theory at all. He thought he had solved urgent and pressing problems in the best compromise possible. He had institutionalized personalism; he had curbed the power of the mob; he had pacified the Monarchists without betraying the republicans. He thought he had provided a system of political tutelage not only in the Senate and the Censors, but also by allowing all citizens to begin their electoral experience by joining in small groups (of ten), to elect men they knew to decide problems with which they were familiar. He thought he had divided authority so as to check and balance power. What he had actually done was to create a government of conflict which would have to operate in the absence of defined interest groups. There were no political parties in Bolivia. There were not even any well-defined social entities or economic interests.

The Bolivian Constitution pleased no one. Sucre, the only leader who ever attempted to act under its authority, damned it roundly. Humboldt dismissed ·it as an inexplicable madness. Scholars have concluded that it united all the defects of all po-

---

[10] John Adams had been Vice-President; Jefferson, Madison, and Monroe, Secretaries of State; John Quincy Adams, elected in 1824, had served as both Secretary of State and Vice-President.

litical systems. Víctor Andrés Belaúnde has observed that it took life tenure from absolutism, the demogoguery of electoral assemblies from democracy, and absolute financial centralization from unitarianism. It combined the worst of centralism with the worst of federalism. British constitutionalism was scrapped in favor of Napoleonic despotism or democratic imperialism. In Angostura, the heart of the system had been a permanent collective institution; in Bolivia it was a single individual. Gerhard Masur observes that Bolívar blundered not in creating an elective kingship like that of the Papacy or the Holy Roman Empire, but in establishing the heir-apparent vice-presidency; in imposing the Constitution on Peru when he knew he could not remain there; and in trying to unite Colombia under it just when the nation was breaking apart.[11]

The Bolivian Constitution failed to function as the masterplan for Latin American political development that Bolívar had intended. Even in Bolivia it was quickly abrogated. However, many of its provisions materialized throughout the hemisphere as characteristics of a new extra-legal political phenomenon, *caudillismo*. When national governments failed to rule and administer provinces, liberators or ex-guerilla leaders, civilian prefects or governors invested themselves with supreme authority in local areas. Isolation, personalism, and the overwhelming desire of landowners for peace bolstered the authority of these *caudillos*. When constitutions failed, force prevailed. In some areas strong *caudillos* took advantage of the failure of urban intellectuals to provide peace and order. By aggregating authority from lesser loyal chiefs and employing funds often provided by foreign investors, some *caudillos* became presidents.

The Caudillos. *Caudillos* resembled the Liberator in several ways. They, too, counted on the combination of personal influence and paid bayonets to obtain the consent of governed and governors. Like Bolívar, they saw the economic future of their countries as raw material producers. When they encouraged foreign trade, however, it was mainly to get at the customs revenues which were the basis of national income. Bolívar never

---

[11] Masur, *op. cit.*, pp. 567-578; also see Víctor Andrés Belaúnde. *Bolívar and the Political Thought of the Spanish American Revolutions* (Baltimore, 1938), pp. 233, 257-258.

tolerated that kind of embezzlement. Because they, like Bolívar, felt that they had guaranteed nationhood, they could not conceive of the nation functioning without them. Their followers were loyal citizens; their rivals were enemies of the nation. The *caudillos* maintained the values, prejudices, and preoccupations of the old society to which Bolívar had been born. They participated in the same socio-economic consensus. They projected upon a people who had lost their institutional identity a new and vigorous personality.

As Bolívar saw *caudillos* gain power, he came to depend more and more on the military to preserve the unity he had dreamed of and less on the promulgation of his cure-all constitution. But he discovered, as other leaders would, that the military was unreliable. Before Bolívar died, some of his most trusted staff members had forsaken him for the *caudillos* he abhorred.

The *caudillos* gave certain provisions of the Bolivian Constitution final adaptation to reality, but other features were not realized at all. The Chamber of Censors never functioned to "safeguard morality, the arts, education and the press." Bolívar had defended secularization of moral sanctions on the grounds that religion had lost most of its power. However, when he realized that either he was wrong or that legislators would not institute the Censors, he turned to Church authorities for support. In 1828 he struck a blow at anticlerical liberalism by proscribing the works of Jeremy Bentham from the curricula of *colegios* and universities. He further attempted to rehabilitate the Church by asking the Archbishop of Bogotá to serve on his advisory council, by restoring chaplains to military service, and by annulling an 1821 law which had abolished convents cloistering fewer than eight people. He also outlawed secret societies, specifically Masons, just at a time when he agreed to restore Dominican and Franciscan foundations in Mérida and Maracaibo. Not the least of the opposition that faced him as his life drew to a close was fostered by liberals who felt he had betrayed them. The *caudillos* who succeeded Bolívar followed his lead and depended on the Catholic Church as the only institutional link which was directly connected to individuals, to sustain the social order. Other provisions of the constitution scrapped without dissent were the vice-president as executive successor and the Chamber of Electors. The "independent judiciary" was maintained on paper, but in practice it meted out justice on the basis of social status.

Students of the early nineteenth century have rightly emphasized theory and neglected practice because what Bolívar did when he was in power was mainly to plan and propose, effect more legislation, propound more theory. For example, Bolívar could define social problems as the desire of *pardos* for social and political equality. He could predict the result as doom: their obsession would lead first to *pardocracy* (rule of the darker-skinned elements) and then, as it had in Haiti, to the extermination of the privileged class. But he could effect no solution other than to pay his troops and bureaucracies regularly.

He attempted to stimulate interest in education by using clerical revenues to found military academies and *colegios*. Impressed as early as 1810 with the new educational theories of Joseph Lancaster, Bolívar personally financed the Englishman's trip to Caracas as educational consultant and in Peru proposed to establish Lancastrian one-room schoolhouses, where, as Andrés Bello later said, the half-taught would teach the untaught. Concerned with humanitarian welfare services, both Bolívar and Sucre tried with quite limited success to provide for orphans, the aged, and the indigent by confiscating Church properties and assigning land, rents, and buildings for their care.

A major problem which preoccupied liberals all over Spanish America in the nineteenth century was the plight and future of Indians. Bolívar's theoretical solution was the same as that of Benito Juárez: give them a stake in society in the form of small independent properties. Divide Indian communities into individual parcels and create a nation of private-enterprise yeomen. Educate Indian leaders by giving them scholarships. End the segregation of Indians by permitting all classes of people to live in their towns. In Andean South America the word "Indian" was suppressed and replaced officially by the word "native" (*indígena*).

However, by 1828, the Liberator had become convinced that the Indians' lot had worsened since independence. He then restored tribute and communal ownership and exempted Indians from military service. His confederate Paéz, later entertained the idea of re-establishing missions to care for Indian vagrants. Once again the new leaders reverted to the old Spanish methods of social control.[12]

When Bolívar looked back on his career and on the course of the revolution, he saw only failure. The entire New World was an "abyss of abominations": assassinations, plunder of public funds, the Federalist furor of town set against town and province against province. Force, faction, and bribery determined everything. Nowhere did legal elections take place; nowhere were treaties or constitutions more than scraps of paper. In despair he concluded that the price of war had exceeded its benefits. Those who waged it had wasted their time, wrecked their own illusions, and worsened the condition of the people. Spanish America had been better off as a colony, Bolívar suggested, for at least Americans then had possessed certain rights and enjoyed some tangible progress.[13]

Bolívar had liberated colonies, but he was unable to stabilize even one nation. He never set his talents resolutely in a single direction for a specific future. He began as a radical revolutionary and ended as a restorer of the old Spanish ways of keeping order. He began his public life as a symbol of Creole determination and republicanism; progressed from Jacobin to general, and ended as an ostracized dictator. He always worked to create a strong central government but never succeeded in defining its scope: Colombia, all of South America, the northern part, or just Venezuela. His political analyses were always more brilliant than his proposals. Willing to form armies from all levels of society, Bolívar was never able to contain the social ferment that he himself had created. Independence was his single consistent goal. His determination to make continental solidarity the basis for emergence into world power, and his attempt to find a "third world" way to resolve the ideological alternatives of his day, all find echoes in today's young Latin American reformers. It is Bolívar's challenge to innovate, not his failure to do so, that has relevance to the quest for Spanish American Independence as it continues today.

[12] Juan Friede, "La legislación indígena en la Gran Colombia," *Boletín de historia y antigüedades* (Bogotá, 1949), XXXVI, 286-298; José Antonio Páez, *Autobiografía del general José Antonio Páez*, 3rd ed., 2 vols. (New York, 1878), II, 159-161, 344.
[13] Bolívar, *Selected Writings*, II, 741-747.

CHAPTER 7

The Consolidation of Creole Conservatism

Bolívar during a lifetime of public service fulfilled many roles. He epitomized the struggle against colonial rule. He personified sacrifice. He stood above the cleavages of society and integrated conflicting interests. He represented unity. He nourished the pride of his people by commanding international respect.

These varied roles gave the Liberator moments of great exhilaration, but they did not give him happiness. He was truly happy only when contemplating his next part in the great drama that he was directing and in which he always assigned himself the lead. From his arrival in Cartagena in October 1812, until total military victory at Ayacucho in December 1824, each time that he acted his part well, he undertook a more demanding one. Consequently, when the Peruvian Congress, after considerable goading from the Liberator, adopted the Bolivian constitution and named him president for life, Bolívar had good reason to regard this new role as yet another on his way to becoming the great moderator of the Hispanic world. He had envisaged this when he called for the Panama Congress, and later the somewhat more modest Federation of the Andes.

As it turned out, Bolívar never played that last role. Times and interests changed rapidly as international wars gave way to domestic strifes. The Liberator soon lost much of his appeal to the galleries. A generally weak supporting cast sensed what was happening and rushed on stage to steal scenes from him. As a rule they acted their parts poorly, but well enough to keep the Liberator from proving whether or not he could be as good a trouper in the costume of a civilian administrator as he had been in that of the battle hero.

Decline. When Peru approved the Bolivian Charter in August 1826, and granted Bolívar lifetime presidential powers under it, the Liberator had his last moments of glory. They were brief. Within a month he was called to Gran Colombia, where his position was deteriorating, and where his proposed Federation of the Andes was being held up to public derision. By the time that he reached Popayán in southern Colombia, Bolívar

knew beyond any doubt that the Federation no longer had a
chance of success, and he told General Santa Cruz in Lima as
much, urging him to discard the plan in favor of one which
would serve Peru's national interests.

Bolívar's recommendation to Santa Cruz was the last constructive influence that the living Bolívar exercised over Peru.
Once he departed Lima, the aristocrats, many of whom had
never felt a deep commitment to independence, withdrew their
active support from him. This created a power hiatus and
prompted his enemies to declare themselves in rebellion against
his regime. Within weeks the Peruvian military had overthrown
Bolívar's representatives, many of whom were Colombians and
Venezuelans, and seized control of the government. Thereupon
they stripped Bolívar of the powers bestowed upon him only
four months earlier. Peru lapsed into a prolonged period of
anarchy, tyranny, and corruption that eventually cost it much of
its national territory and self-respect.

Regionalism Takes Root. A major shock awaited Bolívar
when he reached Bogotá in November. He had anticipated that
he would have to moderate differences between Vice-President
Santander in Colombia and José Páez, who had become the principal spokesman for Venezuelan nationalism; but he was un-
prepared for the degree of independence that Santander showed.
The Vice-President had taken advantage of Bolívar's absence in
Peru to build himself an effective political machine. Now he
used the influence his following gave him to sustain his views
against Bolívar's. The Liberator had accepted Santander's legal-
ism, but he could not abide his independence. Public declarations of friendship and mutual respect did not conceal the fact
that the two men were on a collision course. Bolívar's followers
would have had him resolve the issue by assuming dictatorial
powers, but he refused. Instead he set out for Venezuela where
he widened the gap of misunderstanding between himself and
Santander by publicly embracing the separatist Páez in return for
his keeping Venezuela within Gran Colombia.

Having brought Páez back into the fold, Bolívar probably
should have retraced his steps to Colombia to defend his interests, but instead he chose to assume extra-constitutional powers
and to indulge his affection for Caracas. For six months he was
again the unrestrained leader, reforming taxes, promising schools,

and proposing legislation which he said would protect the poor without burdening the rich. Most significant, perhaps, he liberally gave out promotions to his wartime comrades, thereby seeming to reaffirm his faith in the military as the strong right arm of administrative regimes in new states.

Bolívar returned to Bogotá in September 1827, with the express purpose of restoring his power position. It was too late. His removal of Santander as vice-president brought charges that the Liberator was seeking to establish either a dictatorship or a monarchy with himself as its head. He called together a constituent convention which opened at Ocaña in April 1828. The delegates refused to accept the Bolivian Constitution and Bolívar was forced to withdraw his representatives. On June 24, 1828, he established an outright dictatorship. With Santander under arrest and amid rumors of monarchical plots, an attempt was made upon the Liberator's life on September 25, 1828. He was losing ground elsewhere. A month earlier, contingents of Peruvian troops had forced Sucre's resignation as vice-president of Bolivia. Peruvian forces had invaded Quito, and Generals Sucre and Juan José Flores had turned them back when Bolívar reached Ecuador, where his health took a definite turn for the worse. Thereafter his illnesses were a constant factor in his political fortunes.

Sick and discouraged, Bolívar returned to Bogotá in January 1830. A few of his military colleagues were prepared to prop up any regime that had him at its head. Bolívar appreciated the gesture but he knew that he could not survive for long in the dangerous crosscurrents of Colombian politics. His civilian support by then had all but disappeared. The downfall of Gran Colombia had become a certainty. In December Páez had definitively withdrawn Venezuela from the confederation, and in the south General Flores was busy laying the ground for a secessionist movement. On March 13, Ecuador declared its independence. On June 4, Sucre was murdered.

Bolívar learned of Ecuador's secession and Sucre's death while in self-imposed exile on the Caribbean coast of Colombia. On March 1, 1830 he had surrendered his executive powers to the Council of Ministers after first naming General Caicedo as that body's president. On that occasion there had been no clamor, as there had been on many previous ones, for him to renounce his decision to withdraw from public life. He dallied in Bogotá, perhaps hoping against hope that a favorable turn of events would again seem to make him indispensable. Nothing happened except that his influence continued to dwindle. (*See Reading No. 16.*) Finally on May 8, he left for the coast, expecting to sail for France. Before he reached Cartagena, where he had begun his rise to power, he became too ill to undertake an ocean voyage. On December 1 he made the short trip to the port city of Santa Marta. A week later he went to the home of a Peninsular Spaniard some three miles distant, where he died on December 17, 1830.

Faith in Political Answers. Bolívar's enemies, and there were many, hailed his death as the birth of a new era. He had been for them the source of all political evil. With government freed from his excesses, law would supplant personalism. The Liberator's followers, a diminishing group, despaired that society had lost its one unifying force, the one individual big enough to rise above politics. Both the anti- and the pro-Bolivarian forces exposed a basic fallacy in their thinking in attributing so much importance to the passing of an individual who had not as a civilian established his political or administrative skills, far less his capacity for sustained attention to social and economic issues. What they were saying, in effect, was that the problems of their nations were essentially political in nature and that if the right political mix could be found, social, economic, and military matters would somehow resolve themselves. The profound faith in political answers, not the death of Bolívar, was the tragedy of Hispanic America in 1830. (*See Reading No. 17.*)

The wars had been a shattering experience for the popular elements who comprised 85 per cent of the total population. Military service had been deeply unpopular with many Indian groups. Whole villages had migrated to escape recruiting officers. Impoverished and untutored, most Indians probably would have chosen a refuge beyond the fringes of civilization, there to sacrifice promises of progress for apparent security. But they were not asked to choose. They were needed for labor, to bear arms, and on occasion to cast ballots. These requirements dictated that the Indians be located on *haciendas* or in Indian villages, to be present when called upon, to await "grace" that could be bestowed by any privileged or powerful individual and, in the meantime, to endure the legacies of a rigid caste system: paternalism, oppression, and servilism.

Unlike the Indian who sought obscurity, the mestizos and Negro freedmen were turbulent in their demands for greater participation. Without the assurance that family and communal organization often gave the Indian, the mixed castes exaggerated their individualism and made a mania of the heroic. They compensated for a lack of established norms by making virtues of the vices of a primitive past. When they figured in society, it was as a problem and not as an ideal.

The privileged elements had permanent standards but they did not seek to correlate them with prevailing realities. Especially in the rural areas but also to a considerable degree in the cities, they were by nature dispersive and anarchical to the determinant of social solidarity. Inequality was as dear to their hearts as liberty itself. As a consequence they refused to submit themselves to the leveling processes of democracy.

European Models. The culture they defended was largely derivative. They attached high prestige to the imitation of European models and frowned upon autochthonous expression. In the first few years after independence, England gave the tone to society in dress, style, furniture, food, parties. Soon the French began to introduce their habits and customs, and they came to be preferred.[1]

The privileged groups were not socially constructive. They brought no pressures to combat degeneration and injustice. They would not support one code by which the actions of all could be judged. In fact, while nearly every member of every privileged group wished law to be enforced, he wished no less that an exception should be made in his own particular case.

The Middle Sectors. A thin intermediate layer of intellectuals and professionals separated the elites from the popular masses. Ethnically and culturally those middle groups were far closer to the upper classes than they were to the "people of color." Some of them had been trained in Europe, but the vast majority was largely self-taught or the products of local secondary schools and institutions of higher learning. They lived in

[1] José María Luis Mora, *Méjico y sus revoluciones,* 3 vols. (Paris, 1836), I, 147-151.

the cities because they preferred it that way, and also because they were not welcomed by the rural oligarchs.

Like the elites, the intellectuals and professionals drew heavily upon Europe. From there they learned the lessons of the Enlightenment that made them concerned about the masses, antipathetic to the heritage left by Spain, and in favor of law and precedent. However, economic considerations drove them into the arms of the elites who were not enlightened and who benefited from perpetuating the past. The aristocrats and the oligarchically-oriented Catholic Church were the principal buyers of professional skills, art, and literature, including the newspapers; they also controlled the governments and hence the bureaucracies to which the intellectuals and professionals flocked when they were in political favor. As functionaries the middle groups had almost no freedom of action. They were implementors, and they performed their unoriginal responsibilities with great unoriginality. Their humanistic training had given them slight exposure to the art of government. By temperament they were poorly qualified for the tedium of administration and management. Society would have been worse off without them, but it was not as yet significantly better off because of them.

Town and Country. The gulf between the inhabitants of the interior and the residents of the major population centers added to the social divisiveness. Provincial society was bound to the past, that of the cities to the future. Social practices throughout the hinterlands continued very much as they had before independence began, while the cities made a fetish of turning their backs upon the past. In the interior the evening stroll in the plaza, billiards, cock-fighting, cards, games involving horsemanship, afforded the inhabitants nearly all the pleasures not provided by the family unit; the cities imported the latest cultural fads from Europe. The interior was suspicious of secular education; the cities worshipped it, without, however, doing very much to promote it. Provincials took their religion seriously and without question. They did not hesitate to label as enemies of the Church those residents of the cities who paraded their divided loyalties and secular beliefs. In the rigid societies of the provincial towns everyone knew his place, while in the metropolitan areas many were scrambling to improve their position. There was a singular lack of diversified interest groups in rural areas, partly because the existence of such groups would have brought to the countryside the social and political turmoil of the cities, and the rural elites possessed more than enough political and military power to prevent that from happening.

The Catholic Church. The Catholic Church provided the glue that kept these disorganized societies from becoming completely unstuck. It was the final interpreter of the social value system. It practically monopolized education. That it performed these roles in 1830 despite two decades of institutional setbacks, bore witness to its massive influence upon Hispanic American culture.

At the moment of independence the Church had been an ally of the State, serving the secular needs of the Crown and the spiritual needs of the deeply devout, undemanding masses. Throughout the struggles, the Church hierarchy had remained faithful to the Crown. This decision did not affect its relationship with the unthinking masses, in part because the lower clergy often fostered social protest. It did make the Church the principal target of the liberal elements. They attacked the institution for its worldliness and its clergy for their duplicity, but except for a few extremists there was no desire to destroy the Church as a religious institution. They knew, as Bolívar knew, that for all their well-founded complaints against the Church, it was the only sure anchor in the unsettled waters on which the new societies were tossing. Because the Church knew what the liberals knew, and also because it was certain in the knowledge that its future was more dependent on the devoutness of the rich and the fanaticism of the poor than on legal statutes, it bent only slightly, when at all, to the will of anything as ephemeral as a civilian political regime.

Unresolved Economic Problems. If politics proved ineffectual as a transformer of society, neither could it resolve Hispanic America's economic issues. The new nations achieved their independence under highly unfavorable conditions. Much of their wealth had been destroyed. Part of it had gone to Spain and the Caribbean. Much of what remained belonged to the Church. The requisition of animals, levies of men, and the destruction of buildings, fields, and herds had burdened the rich and poor alike. Mines were inundated, their antiquated equipment in disrepair. The sparse population clustered in economic enclaves, separated from one another by deserts, mountains, uplands, and jungles that challenged the creation of viable economies. A deep regard for private property and the power and influence of the Catholic Church prevented reforms from basically altering the inherited colonial structure. Unfavorable as conditions were, they were not so bad as to tax the ingenuity to survive.

In France the cry of "liberty, equality, and fraternity" had signalled the collapse of feudalism. In Hispanic America it affirmed self-sufficient colonial power symbolized by the *hacienda*. That institution was more than a farm or plantation; it was a society under private auspices. It dominated the lives of all attached to it and spread its retarding influence to the surrounding countryside. The workers accepted servility in return for protection and the possible benevolence of the master. The *hacienda* lived by itself and for itself in the traditional immobility of a patriarchal form of government. Money played almost no role because the overwhelming aim of production was sustenance. The *hacendados* prized the prestige and security that went with land more than the profits that might come from it.

The power and influence of the landed aristocracy contributed to an investment mentality that discouraged balanced development. Those who in some way acquired surplus capital—through the government or the military, for example—invested in farms and dwellings rather than commerce and industry. A corollary of this investment habit was that rentals from real estate were to be preferred to profits from commercial activities.

The influence of the British and the memory of the stifling effects of Spanish mercantilism caused the new nations, except Paraguay, to adopt *laissez-faire* economic policies. As reasonable as those policies seemed, they caused more problems than they solved. The new states became dependent for public revenues upon custom duties tied to erratic international mineral and luxury markets. More important, *laissez-faire* economics did not produce a domestic commercial class that would have had a strong interest in responsible, orderly government. The failure to develop a commercial class occurred first of all because the wars drove out most of the Spaniards who had dominated commerce. Then speculators in Europe, the Caribbean Islands, and the United States took over control of trade in military supplies, nearly all of which, except food and basic textiles, had to be imported. Finally, with free trade came free-wheeling merchants whose skills and contacts abroad and with the *caudillos* gave them an unsurmountable advantage over local competition.

Free trade had no less an effect upon industry. Foreign traders flooded the new republics with cheap manufactured goods. The long-range consequences of this were several. Local artisans producing with primitive methods at high costs were driven out of business. Thus, the one group that might have accumulated capital and provided a base for a profit-minded domestic element was destroyed. The hinterlands, especially in Argentina, where many of the artisans carried on their trades, were forced to return to rudimentary agriculture which reinforced the conditions of *caudillo* rule.

Liberty and Despotism. Politics did not solve Hispanic America's political problems in 1830: it exacerbated them. The people were adrift. More than anything else they needed political peace. Instead they got political warfare on a grand scale. With the monarch gone and Church discredited, they required a person whom all could trust or an institution to which all could swear allegiance. The liberators, who had destroyed the old regime without liquidating it, were unable to create a design that produced either. Because of this failure and also because politicians failed to harmonize theory and practice, and privileged elements refused to couple liberty with law, politics became a game played in personal rather than national terms.

Democracy, with no American tradition to appeal to, was nearly smothered before it was born. It survived, but it was so poorly nurtured that it turned out to be little more than an adornment of oligarchically-controlled peasant states.

Scattered members of the privileged elements refused to accept their political responsibilities, but a great many were quite ready to assume more responsibility than their fitness warranted. The reticent bought protection. The willing divided themselves into two basic groups, one favoring revolution, the other counter-revolution. From their extremist positions they conducted a constant intraclass struggle for power, but never permitted a power vacuum to form into which the masses might rush. Their chronic battles and conspiracies were largely irrelevant to the great part of the nation because the structure and conditions of government were little affected by the outcome of their political antics.

The ideational leadership of those who preferred "Liberty" centered in the cities, where politics was a natural corollary of limited opportunities in other spheres. Ideological guidelines for the contending elements came from the countryside and the Church, with oligarch and bishop offering each other mutual support in defense of privilege.

The contest for power might have developed into a healthy one had it been possible to keep the military out of the fray. That proved impossible on two scores. First, politicians insisted on involving the armed forces. This expedience was usually resorted to by the representatives of the landed aristocrats and the Church, but there were also those who "out of love of liberty invoked the use of force." Second, ambitious men in uniform beginning with the greater and lesser liberators—Bolívar, Páez, Flores, Gamarra, Santa Cruz, Iturbide, to name only a few— used the armed forces, which had grown to maturity during the Wars of Independence, as starting blocks from which to make their dash for presidential chairs.

Once the military was injected into politics, force was quickly elevated to a political fundamental and violence was rationalized for each new situation. Abrupt changes in government became regular and recurring phenomena. As soon as the armed forces established their decision-making ability there was no containing them. Using the Coup as their principal political instrument, armed forces officers, commanding ranks filled with grossly uncultured peasants brought in by forced conscription or induced to join up by the opportunities to rob and pillage with immunity, became the final political arbitrators. Neither progress nor the status quo was as important to them as the power to regulate both.

Force also produced civilian *caudillos,* some of whom sought power to satisfy their private ambitions, others because they thought they were needed to defend the system. None was truly revolutionary. The civilian *caudillos* were personalists with predatory egotisms, who aspired to the place left by the *conquistadores.* They understood their people well. There was a dramatic side to their regimes which they supplied and to which the people succumbed.

The Politics of Personalism. *Caudillos* did not share power, they maximized it. They could be autocrats because there was not a bourgeoisie strong enough to serve as an effective counterbalance to their ambition. They were temperamentally incapable of training successors. Their removal from office by death or "uprising" almost always produced an interlude of disorder. As a result everything tended to be transitory and discontinuous.

Political parties fared poorly in the presence of either military or civilian *caudillos*. They did not need organizations because they did not campaign in the usual sense of that term. When they had party platforms it was to satisfy a formality. The fact that executive power tended to be the only power in government further reduced the relevance of political parties. Legislatures existed primarily to give a certain subtlety to the determination of the *Jefe*. Legislative debate was a privilege of those who formed the executive's rubber-stamp. Since control in effect made argument incontrovertible, there was no reason for opposition parties to exist once an election was decided.

The national pattern of politics, with all of its personalism, drama, and crudities, was repeated in the provinces and municipalities. It was natural that this should have occurred. Under Spain the great landholders of the interiors had been left largely to their own resources as long as they fulfilled the loosely defined military obligations of the system in which they lived and recognized the ultimate authority of the Crown. This relationship produced a self-reliant, domineering individual who unilaterally determined what was best for himself and for those around him. Under the most favorable circumstances the new governments were not in a position to challenge traditional provincial practices. They faced the same crippling problem of communication that Spain had and they lacked sufficient numbers of competent bureaucrats to create the image of the State as "Protector." The end result was that anyone who separated himself from the local leadership faced the possibility of retribution at a later date. Under the worst of conditions the national governments often had to delegate authority to local strong men, hence giving their informal control an aura of legality.

Ideas and Ideals. By 1830 the people of Hispanic America had learned that there is nothing so hard as the apprenticeship for freedom. Caught and carried along in the whirlwind of revolution of their time, they freed themselves from Spain; but, conditioned to obey, they did not know what to do with liberty when they achieved it. The same ideals that in France produced a social transformation, in their hands yielded a vocabulary and inappropriate political forms. Doctrines that in Anglo-America created unity, in Hispanic America created disunity. The colonies went to war against Spain in order to become like the West, but when they won their independence, they were rejected by the West, or at least remained the most anonymous entity within the West. It could not be said of them, as it has been said of the new nations of Africa, the Middle East, and Asia, that because they joined the community of independent societies the world could no longer be the same. There was nothing new to export from Hispanic America's revolt against Spain.

Prospects for the future could hardly have been dimmer when Bolívar in 1830 lamented, "Those who served the Revolution have plowed the sea." [2] Anarchy was everywhere. Nations seemed to be dissolving into chaos. But with the benefit of historical hindsight, we know that he was wrong. For however deep they have mired themselves in muddy politics, the people of Hispanic America have retained the humane ideal that their leaders originally set out to win. Today the underprivileged share, at times unconsciously, ideals that only the highly privileged entertained a century and a quarter ago. Today, as in Bolívar's time, legislators take the best from all over the civilized world and codify it into laws that become statements of aspiration. By law, education is universal and free, social welfare a public obligation. Respect for the individual continues to be so vitally important that punishment by death for civil crimes has become for all practical purposes a social anachronism. In the midst of social suffering, economic uncertainty, and military authoritarianism, the people of Hispanic America affirm afresh each day in the United Nations their faith in universalism; in inter-American organizations their faith in continentalism; and in national governments their faith in themselves. Bolívar, man of ideas and ideals, could have hoped for more, but he could have received less.

[2] José Antonio Páez, *op. cit.,* I, 475, quotes the full text of Bolívar's letter of November 9, 1830.

Part II

SELECTED READINGS

"Don Quijote Bolívar"*

The personalized philosophical essay is a genre of writing in which Spaniards and Spanish Americans excel. Of the many humanists who have sought to capture the essence of the Liberator, none has succeeded more brilliantly than Miguel de Unamuno. Philosopher, novelist, pensador, *proto-Existentialist, and Professor of Greek, Unamuno was one of the most distinguished of Spain's stellar literary generation of 1898.*

Bolívar was master of the art of war, not an expert . . . in military science; he was a guerilla fighter rather than a soldier . . . he was theatrical and emphatic, naturally and unaffectedly as his race, our race is, but he was not a pedant. Bolívar was a man, all man; a whole and true man. . . . Bolívar was of the ilk of Don Quixote, he of the large, black and drooping moustache. . . .

There is no doubt that his teacher, don Simón Rodríguez, plutarchized him by rousseauing him. . . .

He made war, one might say, alone, by himself, without a general staff, like Don Quixote. Humanity followed him—humanity not merely an army—[and that humanity] was his Sancho. . . .

Who does not recall that phrase of Bolívar's, uttered when he was practically dying: "The three greatest fools (*majaderos*) of history have been Jesus Christ, Don Quixote—and I!" . . .

Bolívar had several affairs, or rather amours; he did not lack a touch of Don Juan. It is enough to recall Josefina, Anita Lenoir, Manuelita Sáenz, the niña of Potosí. . . . But the memory of that eighteen-year-old love [his wife] became his Dulcinea del Toboso, his glory.

* Miguel de Unamuno, "Don Quijote Bolívar," in *Simón Bolívar libertador de la América del Sur; por los más grandes escritores americanos,* translated by Doris M. Ladd (Madrid: Renacimiento, 1914), pp. i-iv, vii-xi, xiii-xv.

And then his Amadis, Napoleon. For the fascination that Napoleon exercised over Bolívar is undeniable. . . . Never did
Bolívar resemble Napoleon more than when he made an effort
not to imitate him. It was like Chateaubriand with Rousseau. . . .

[It was] the Quixotic love of glory, ambition, true ambition,
not covetousness, not the vanity of the pedant, not the desire to
win fleeting applause like a buffoon, but rather the lofty Quixotic
ambition to leave a lasting and honorable fame [that] moved
him. . . .

In spite of terrible confrontations with reality, he soon returned, as did Don Quixote, to his life-giving and liberating madness. . . .

What was his achievement? What was his attainment? . . .

In the proclamation of July 29, 1824, the fourteenth year of
Independence, he addressed his soldiers . . . "Peru and all
America await peace, the daughter of your victory; and even
liberal Europe views you with fascination, because the freedom
of the New World is the hope of the Universe!" The hope of
liberty for the whole world! . . .

The minister of Napoleon III wrote truthfully that at that
time Bolívar's name was circulating among the people of Europe
—even in Spain—as a synonym for Liberty. With the name of
Bolívar on their lips . . . the revolutionaries took Paris in 1830.

And has not Bolívar, in liberating South America from Spanish domination, contributed to the future, complete liberation of
Spain?

Much has been spoken of the anti-Hispanism of Bolívar, judging from those phrases of inflamed rhetoric which civil wars inspire. . . . But who can take all that *ferocious despotism, cruel
Spaniards, bands of Tartars* seriously . . . ? Rhetoric, rhetoric,
rhetoric! And even more rhetorical when Bolívar, the pure de-
scendant of Spaniards, of Basque origin, speaks to us of having
broken the chains which Pizarro had riveted on the sons of
Manco-Capac!

Bolívar's most noble rival . . . the Spanish General Pablo
Morillo, said of him: "He has traits and qualities from his noble Spanish origins which make him very superior [even] when
he is surrounded." And doubtlessly much superior to those . . .

upon whose sons Pizarro riveted chains, that same Pizarro who was more Bolívar's brother than the Inca.

Bolívar complained that the war in America had killed so many Spaniards: "because it is they . . . who ought to populate and civilize our deserts. . . ."

Another time he included in a document these or similar words: "We must not confuse the Spanish Government with the Spaniards. We are making war against the one, not the others." And was it not Bolívar, in whose veins ran Quixotic blood, who wrote: "It is our ambition to offer the Spaniards a second Fatherland, but a proud one, not [one] oppressed by chains?" . . .

Nothing appears more Spanish to me than when one speaks ill or seems to speak ill of Spain—in Spanish! No. Don Quixote could never speak ill of Spain, though he may have defamed the Spaniards.

Bolívar's very style was Quixotic, somewhat emphatic, very Spanish . . . but with an evident influence of the French writers of the end of the eighteenth century. Who has not paused before the sentences of his speeches and proclamations? Urging, at the beginning of the revolution, that independence be declared, he asked: "So great projects should be prepared in tranquility! Three hundred years of tranquility, weren't they enough? Do you want still another three hundred?" And elsewhere! . . . "We were blind; blows have opened our eyes! Soldiers! Hundreds of victories will prolong your lives to the end of the world!" And a hundred similar phrases.

Stoned and robbed by Ginés de Pasamonte and the other galley-slaves whom he had tried to liberate in the Sierra Morena, Don Quixote, somewhat sorrowfully, said: "to do good to villains is to cast water into the sea." Something similar occurred to Bolívar. . . . Insulted, villified, abused, ostracized by the same peoples he had tried to liberate, he exclaimed: "I have ploughed the sea."

What was Bolívar's religion? Here is the most obscure problem of his life. His religion was his work, was his Quixotism.

A son of the eighteenth century, he *thought* of religion as they *thought* of it then; but how did he feel it? . . . we are told that Voltaire was the Liberator's favorite author. . . . And like a good Voltairian he distinguished between the man and the citizen. He, as a citizen, went to mass to set a good example, but he carried a volume of the *Biblioteca Americana* with him to read and he did not cross himself. . . . "I am a philosopher for myself or for some few friends and a priest for the populace," he said with the only pedantry that I have discovered in him. And it is only when he was speaking of religion because his Voltairianism was pedantry. . . . "Long live the God of Colombia!" he said from his Bogotá headquarters on March 8, 1820. . . . In the God of the Fatherland he had found his religion. For God is not the god of individuals, but of peoples; the God of battles is the God of Fatherlands.

[Because] Christianity was worn out at the end of the eighteenth century and the beginning of the nineteenth, [because it was] a Christianity very much influenced by Encyclopedic rationalism and no less cold and dry, it could not satisfy a soul like Bolívar's. And furthermore, for the Liberator, action was thought. . . . But it does not concern us how he *thought* of religion but rather how he *felt* it, how he felt the Quixotic religion of the God of Colombia.

Bolívar, man of ideas and of ideals, was clearly aware of his lofty Quixotic mission, of his function as liberator. . . . "My duty is always to unsheathe my sword for justice and to fight wherever there are enslaved peoples to defend." . . .

On his prophetic visions, on the opening of the Panama Canal, on International Arbitration, on American Public Law, on what he said about the future of the peoples of the New World and on democracy, I shall not comment here. . . .

It is enough to say that some of those nations which Bolívar began to forge, some of those nations which sprang forth from the blow of his sword and from his impassioned incantation are still seeking their souls. . . .

Portrait of Bolívar*

Carlos A. Villanueva's monumental multivolume study of monarchy in America was based on extensive research in the secret diplomatic archives of Venezuela, Colombia, Spain, France, and England. Although disapproving of Bolívar's political ambitions, Villanueva, as this selection shôws, admired Bolívar the man.

Bolívar's favorite goddess was Venus, on whose altars he offered the most beautiful flowers of his soul. Among women, Colonel Hamilton tells us, he enjoyed the reputation *d'un garçon de bonne fortune.* In his youth he had a passion for gambling; but the years corrected this. . . . He was abstemious. He did not know the value of money. He read a great deal; he worked more. He slept little. He adored dancing. He was smooth in his social relationships and extremely affable with women although as a man of war, he had choleric disputes with men, his "crises of bile," as he called them; still, he knew how to dominate. Of an extremely nervous temperament, his voice at times assumed a harsh, even violent tone. He was quick to reach decisions and even quicker in carrying them out. . . . He was a good horseman. . . . With a will of iron he decreed the war to the death and executed it with cold conviction. But this does not permit one to call him bloodthirsty or cruel; he used reprisal to make his cause triumph. . . . He was an intellectual . . . though in his youth he was not studious. . . . His writings reveal persistent reading in French and a carelessness with his mother tongue. In him literary, political, and philosophical influences—from English, French and Spanish authors—joined and formed a truly original character, though . . . the classic Spaniard predominated. He was a Catholic Christian, but anticlerical. . . . He followed the episodes of the French revolu-

* Carlos A. Villanueva, *La monarquía en América,* 2 vols., translated by Doris M. Ladd (Paris: Librería Ollendorff, 1912), I, 281-283. The volume from which this excerpt is taken is entitled "Bolívar y el General San Martín."

tion scrupulously, and many of his actions were inspired by them; his romanticism came from reading Chateaubriand, and his proclamations had a Napoleonic style. He is French rather than English, for he had nothing but the adaptation he made from British constitutional principles and the respect which the seriousness of that great people inspired in him. It is false that he hated Spain; he could not have, for one never hates his mother. . . . Neither did he hate France; on the contrary, he loved it because it was his intellectual mother. He cried out against France because it allied with Spain to submerge and destroy him. . . .

With all his defects and weaknesses he was the greatest American of the nineteenth century, whether as soldier, statesman, diplomat or administrator. He was, it is true, ambitious: ambitious for glory and power, but if he had not been, he would not have become the Liberator of a world, nor would he have fixed the standard of Caracas on the heights of Potosí.

His greatest glory, in our opinion, is in not having assumed the crown of Emperor of the Andes or Emperor of Colombia, which his lieutenants in Caracas, Bogotá, Quito, Lima, and Chuquisaca, and chancellors in London and Paris . . . offered him. There is no doubt that circumstances caused him to dream of it and to seek it out; nor that circumstances gave it to him; but it is no less certain that when he was about to grasp it, he backed away frightened, whether because of scruples, [or] fear that his lieutenants would drive him to the fate of Iturbide, [or] his remaining true to his public declarations, or because he dreaded that the liberals would call him usurper, tyrant, and an opportunist.

A Letter to American Spaniards*

In the eighteenth century only a few lone voices spoke for America and against Spain. One such truly revolutionary protest poured from the pen of an exiled Peruvian Jesuit, the abbot Juan Pablo Viscardo (1748-1798). In 1799 this explosive tract *was published in French under a false Philadelphia publication citation. In 1801 it appeared in Spanish. By 1803 the letter was circulating freely in Venezuela. Miranda used it to justify his abortive intervention in Coro in 1806. In 1809 the Precursor persuaded James Mill to analyze it in the* Edinburgh Review.

The approach of the fourth century of the establishment of our ancestors in the new world is an extremely notable occurrence, worthy of our attention. The discovery of so great a part of the earth is and always will be the most memorable event in the annals of the human race. For us, its inhabitants, and for our descendants, it is an object of even more importance. The new world is our *patria,* its history is ours. . . .

Our history for three centuries . . . might be reduced to these four words: *ingratitude, injustice, servitude,* and *desolation.* . . .

When our ancestors removed themselves so far from their native land, renouncing not only the nourishment but also the civil protection that belonged to them there and which could not reach them at such a distance, they set out at their own expense, . . . fatigue, and . . . risk to find a new means of subsistence. The great success which crowned the efforts of the conquistadors gave them, it would appear, a right, which though it was

* Juan Pablo Viscardo, *Carta derijida[sic] a los españoles americanos* (London, 1801). Reproduced in facsimile from the Archivo General de Indias as a final appendix, in Spanish and in French, in Miguel Batllori, S.I., *El Abate Viscardo: historia y mito de la intervención de los jesuítas en la independencia,* translated by Doris M. Ladd (Caracas: Instituto Panamericano de Geografía e Historia, 1953), pp. vii-xxi, lxvii-lxxxvii. Reprinted with permission of the editor, Fr. Miguel Batllori, S.I.

not the most just, was at least a better one than the old *godos*
of Spain had, to take for themselves the fruit of their valor and
their labor. . . .

Although these legitimate hopes were frustrated, [we] their
descendants and those of other Spaniards who came later to
America . . . have respected, conserved, and loved . . . the
attachment of our forefathers for their first *patria*. Guided by
blind enthusiasm, we have not considered that so much fealty to
a country which is foreign to us, to which we owe nothing, is
cruelly treasonous to the country of our birth. . . . [Nor have
we considered] that our veneration for the affection [that] our
parents [showed] for their first *patria* is the most decisive proof
of the preference that we owe to ours. Everything that we have
lavished on Spain has been usurped from us and our children;
our simplicity was such that we have let ourselves be chained
with irons, which unless we break in time, will offer us no other
recourse than to support this ignominious slavery patiently. . . .

Every law that opposes the universal well-being of those for
whom it is made is an act of tyranny; to demand compliance is
to force into slavery; a law which is directly intended to destroy
the bases of the prosperity of a people would be an unspeakable
monstrosity. . . .

Since men first began to organize themselves into society for
their greater welfare, we are the only ones [whose] government
obliges us to buy what we need at the highest prices and to sell
our products at the lowest prices. So that this outrage might
succeed completely, they have isolated us, as in a city under
siege, [by closing off] the means by which other nations could
supply us, at moderate rates and by equitable exchanges, with
the things we need. The taxes of government, the fees of min-
istries, the avarice of merchants, all authorized to exert in con-
cert . . . the most unrestrained monopoly. . . .

For the honor of humanity and of our nation, it is better to
pass over in silence the horrors and violence of that other monopoly (known in Peru as *repartimientos*) which *corregidores*
and *alcaldes mayores* unjustly exact to the despair and ruin of
the unfortunate Indians and *Mestizos*. Is it not a marvel that
with enough gold and silver to almost satiate the universe, we
barely possess the wherewithal to cover our nakedness? What
purposes do so many fertile lands serve if, besides lacking the

instruments to work them, it is useless for us to produce anything more than for our consumption? . . .

Although in court, in the army, [and] in the tribunals, the
monarchy bestows riches and honors upon foreigners of all nations, we alone are declared unworthy of them, even in our own
country, and incapable of filling positions which technically belong to us exclusively. . . .

. . . Montesquieu, that sublime genius, has said, "The Indies
and Spain are two powers beneath one command; but the Indies
are the principal and Spain the accessory. . . ."

A powerful navy, ready to bring upon us all the horrors of
destruction, is another means by which our past reticence has
fostered tyranny. . . . The decree of 8 July 1787 ordered *that
the revenues from the Indies* (except for tobacco) *furnish
enough funds to pay half or a third of the enormous expenses
that the royal navy requires.*

Our establishments . . . even in their infancy were open to
invasion: and now [that] our [own] forces are greater, it is clear
that the expansion of troops and of the navy is for us an expense
as enormous as it is useless for our defense. . . .

Let us admit . . . to being a different people: let us renounce
the ridiculous system of *union* and of *equality* with our tyrant
masters; let us renounce a government which [because of its]
remoteness cannot provide for us even a part of the advantages
which all men should expect of the society of which they are
members; this government which far from fulfilling its indispensable obligation to protect the liberty and security of our persons, persists in destroying them and instead of making an effort
to make us happy, heaps all kinds of calamities upon us. Since
the rights and duties of government and of subjects are recipro-
cal, Spain has reneged first: she has broken all the weak links
which would have united us and kept us close.

Nature has separated us from Spain by immense seas. A son
who found himself at such a distance from his father would
doubtless be a dolt if he expected his father to solve his smallest
problems. The son is emancipated by natural law. . . .

Distance . . . proclaims our natural independence. . . .

The diverse regions of Europe which the Crown of Spain has
been obliged to renounce, such as the Kingdom of Portugal . . .
and the famous Republic of the United Provinces [the Nether-

lands], which escaped its yoke of iron, demonstrate to us that a continent infinitely greater than Spain, richer, more powerful, more populous, ought not depend on that kingdom. . . .

The valor with which the English Colonies of America fought for liberty, which they now gloriously enjoy, covers our indolence with shame. . . . Add [to that] the pledge of the Courts of Spain and France to sustain the cause of the American Englishmen. That valor indicts our apathy. . . .

The moment has arrived: let us seize it with all . . . gratitude, and . . . for the little effort we make, wise liberty, heaven's precious gift, accompanied by all the virtues and followed by prosperity will begin its reign [in] the new world, and tyranny will be immediately destroyed. . . .

This glorious triumph . . . will cost humanity little. The frailty of the only enemy interested in opposing it will not be permitted to employ overt force without accelerating its [own] ruin. . . . Besides, our cause is so just, so favorable to the human race, that it is impossible to find among other nations a single one which would burden itself with the infamy of combatting us. . . . The wise and virtuous Spaniard, who grieves in silence under the oppression of his fatherland will applaud our endeavor. The national glory of an immense empire will be reborn, transformed into a refuge for all . . . Spaniards . . . who have always been here, can breathe freely beneath the laws of reason and justice. . . .

How many [other men from all nations], fleeing from oppression or from misery, will come to enrich us with their industry, with their knowledge, and to revitalize our debilitated population! In this way America shall reunite the ends of the earth, and its inhabitants will be bound together by a common interest into one single GREAT FAMILY OF BROTHERS.

Creolism*

The Bourbon reforms of the eighteenth century heightened already existing antagonisms between Spaniards born on the Peninsula and those born in America. In this selection Alexander von Humboldt examines the conditions under which many Creoles developed a feeling of common identity as "Americans." He also calls attention to the differences in attitudes between those Creoles residing in urban centers and those living in rural areas.

Amongst the inhabitants of pure origin the whites would occupy the second place, considering them only in the relation of number. They are divided into whites born in Europe, and descendants of Europeans born in the Spanish colonies of America or in the Asiatic islands. The former bear the name of *Chapetones* or *Gachupines,* and the second that of *Criollos.* The natives of the Canary islands, who go under the general denomination of *Islenos* (islanders), and who are *gerans* of the plantations, are considered as Europeans. The Spanish laws allow the same rights to all whites; but those who have the execution of the laws endeavor to destroy an equality which shocks the European pride. The government, suspicious of the Creoles, bestows the great places exclusively on the natives of Old Spain. For some years back they have disposed at Madrid even of the most trifling employments in the administration of the customs and the tobacco revenue. At an epoch when every thing tended to a uniform relaxation in the springs of the state, the system of venality made an alarming progress. For the most part it was by no means a suspicious and distrustful policy; it was pecuniary interest alone which bestowed all employments on Europeans. The result has been a jealous and perpetual hatred between the Chapetons and the Creoles. The most miserable European, without education, and without intellectual cultivation, thinks himself superior to the whites born in the new continent. He knows

* Alexander von Humboldt, *Political Essay on the Kingdom of New Spain,* 4 vols., translated by John Black (New York, 1811), I, 153, 154, 158.

that, protected by his countrymen, and favoured by chances common enough in a country where fortunes are as rapidly acquired as they are lost, he may one day reach places to which the access is almost interdicted to the natives, even to those of them distinguished for their talents, knowledge and moral qualities. The natives prefer the denomination of *Americans* to that of Creoles. Since the peace of Versailles, and, in particular, since the year 1789, we frequently hear proudly declared, "I am not a *Spaniard,* I am an *American!*" words which betray the workings of a long resentment. In the eye of law every white Creole is a Spaniard; but the abuse of the laws, the false measures of the colonial government, the example of the United States of America, and the influence of the opinions of the age, have relaxed the ties which formerly united more closely the Spanish Creoles to the European Spaniards. A wise administration may reestablish harmony, calm their passions and resentments, and yet preserve for a long time the union among the members of one and the same great family scattered over Europe and America, from the Patagonian coast to the north of California. . . .

The Spanish laws prohibit all entry into the American possessions to every European not born in the peninsula. The words European and Spaniard are become synonymous in Mexico and Peru. The inhabitants of the remote provinces have therefore a difficulty in conceiving that there can be Europeans who do not speak their language; and they consider this ignorance as a mark of low extraction, because, everywhere around them, all, except the very lowest class of the people, speak Spanish. Better acquainted with the history of the sixteenth century than with that of our own times, they imagine that Spain continues to possess a decided preponderance over the rest of Europe. To them the peninsula appears the very centre of European civilization. It is otherwise with the Americans of the capital. Those of them who are acquainted with the French or English literature fall easily into a contrary extreme; and have still a more unfavourable opinion of the mother country than the French had at a time when communication was less frequent between Spain and the rest of Europe. They prefer strangers from other countries to the Spaniards; and they flatter themselves with the idea that intellectual cultivation has made more rapid progress in the colonies than in the peninsula.

Why Spanish America
Was Reluctant to Revolt*

Until the Napoleonic invasion of Spain, the Creole elites in America, almost without exception, docilely accepted Spanish domination. Even after "radical" elements began to gain the upper hand in 1810 and the colonies moved toward complete independence, many aristocratic Creole families continued loyal to the mother country. In this selection the great Alexander von Humboldt gives us his view of why many Creoles reacted as they did.

It seems to excite surprise in Europe, that the Spaniards of the mother country, of whom we have remarked the small number, have made during ages so long and so firm a resistance. Men forget, that the European party in all the colonies is necessarily augmented by a great mass of the natives. Family interests, the desire of uninterrupted tranquility, the fear of engaging in an enterprize that might fail, prevent these latter from embracing the cause of independence, or aspiring to establish a local and representative government, though dependent on the mother country. Some shrink from violent measures, and flatter themselves, that a gradual reform may render the colonial system less oppressive. They see in revolutions only the loss of their slaves, the spoliation of the clergy, and the introduction of religious toleration, which they believe to be incompatible with the purity of the established worship. Others belong to the small number of families, which, either from hereditary opulence, or having been long settled in the colonies, exercise a real municipal aristocracy. They would rather be deprived of certain rights, than share them with all; they would prefer even a foreign yoke

* Alexander von Humboldt, *Personal Narrative of Travels to the Equinoctial Regions of the New Continent, During the Years 1799-1804,* translated by Helen Maria Williams (2nd ed.; London, 1822), III, 329-41.

to the exercise of authority by the Americans of an inferior
cast; they abhor every constitution founded on equality of
rights; and above all, they dread the loss of those decorations
and titles, which they have with so much difficulty acquired,
and which, as we have observed above, compose so essential a
part of their domestic happiness. Others again, and their number
is very considerable, live in the country on the produce of their
lands; and enjoy that liberty, which, in a country where there is
only a scattered population, is obtained even under the most
oppressive governments. Aspiring to no places themselves, they
see them with indifference filled by men, whose power can never
reach them, and whose names are to them almost unknown.
They would no doubt prefer a national government, and complete liberty of commerce, to the ancient state of the colonies;
but this desire does not sufficiently subdue the love of ease, and
the habits of an indolent life, to impel them to long and painful
sacrifices.

In characterizing these different tendencies of political opinion in the colonies, from the various intercourse I have had with
all classes of the inhabitants, I have developed the causes of the
long and peaceful dominion of the mother country over America. The calm has been the result of habit, of the preponderance
of a few leading families, and above all of the equilibrium established between the hostile forces. But security founded on
disunion must be shaken, whenever a large body of men, for-
getting their individual animosities, shall be united by a sentiment of common interest; when that sentiment, once awakened,
is strengthened by resistance; and when the progress of knowledge, and change of manners, shall diminish the influence of
habit and ancient ideas.

Bolívar Tells How He Came
to Be a Revolutionary*

From April 1, 1828 to May 29, 1829, Bolívar resided in Buca-maranga (Colombia) while awaiting the results of the Convention of Ocaña. A young French officer, Peru de Lacroix, who had fought for Napoleon, kept a diary of a dinner conversation. In this selection the Liberator discusses the influences that the death of his wife and glories of Napoleon had in making him a radical.

". . . I was not yet eighteen when I married in Madrid, and I became a widower in [1803] . . .[1] I loved my wife very much, and her death made me swear not to marry again; I have kept my word. Notice how things go; if I had not been widowed, perhaps my life would have been different: I would neither be General Bolívar nor the Liberator, although I agree that my genius was not intended to be mayor of San Mateo."

"Neither Colombia nor Peru," I replied, "nor all of South America would be free if you had not led the noble and immense task of their independence."

"I wouldn't say that," proceeded His Excellency, "for I was not the sole author of the revolution and during the revolutionary crisis and the long conflict between the Spanish troops and the patriots, some caudillo would have appeared if I had not presented myself and if my luck had not impeded the rise of others. . . . Let us leave the superstitious to believe that providence sent me or destined me to redeem Colombia . . . circumstances, my talent, my character, my passions are what put me on my way; my ambition, my constancy, and the ardor of my

* Louis Peru de Lacroix, *Diario de Bucaramanga,* ed. Nicolas E. Navarro, translated by Doris M. Ladd (Caracas: Ediciones del Ministerio de Educación Nacional, Dirección de Cultura, 1949), pp. 62-65.
[1] Simón Bolívar was born July 24, 1783 and was married May 26, 1802. His wife died on January 22, 1803.

imagination made me continue and have sustained me. Listen to this: an orphan and rich at the age of sixteen, I went to Europe after having visited Mexico and Havana: it was then, in Madrid, I fell in love and married the niece of the old Marquis del Toro, Teresa Toro y Alaiza: I returned from Europe to Caracas in 1801 with my wife and I assure you that at the time my head was only filled with the mists of the most ardent love, and not with political ideas, for they had not yet touched my imagination. [Then] my wife died and I, desolated with that premature and unexpected loss, returned to Spain and from Madrid I went to France and then to Italy. At that time I was already taking some interest in public affairs, politics interested me. . . . I saw the coronation of Napoleon in Paris, in the last month of 1804: that . . . magnificent ceremony filled me with enthusiasm but less because of its pomp than for the sentiments of love that an immense public manifested to the French hero; that general effusion of all hearts, that free and spontaneous popular movement, stimulated by the glories, the heroic feats of Napoleon, made victorious by more than a million individuals seemed to me to be, for the one who would receive such sentiments . . . the ultimate desire of the ultimate ambition of man. The crown that Napoleon placed on his head I considered a miserable Gothic thing; what seemed great to me was the universal acclaim and the interest which his person inspired. This, I confess, made me think of the slavery of my country and the glory that would befit the one who would liberate it; but, how far I was from imagining that such fortune was awaiting me . . . ! Without the death of my wife I would not have made my second voyage to Europe, and it is probable that in Caracas or San Mateo the ideas that came to me in my travels would not have been born and in America I would not have gained the experience or made that study of the world, of men, and of the things which have served me so well throughout my public career. The death of my wife put me on the road to politics very early; it made me follow the chariot of Mars instead of following the plow of Ceres. . . .

The Miranda Incident—1812*

Bolívar was instrumental in handing Miranda over to the Spaniards on July 31, 1812. His harshest critics, among them the Spanish historian Salvador de Madariaga and the Argentine Bartolomé Mitre, condemn his action unreservedly. Of those sympathetic to Bolívar, Gerhard Masur presents perhaps the most dispassionate discussion of the event.

What had estranged the two men so completely within the space of a few short weeks . . . ? It seems likely that what divided the two men was the problem of Spaniards living in America. Bolívar was all for having them expelled in short order, while Miranda, himself the son 'of a Spaniard, supported their right to remain. Actually, the expulsion of the Spaniards, who were for the most part merchants, might have been disastrous for the already weakened economy of the country and Miranda was in the right, while Bolívar wished to apply radical tactics without foreseeing the consequences. This lack of foresight was characteristic of his early phase as politician and soldier, a characteristic only overcome through bitter experience.

The estrangement between Miranda and Bolívar had yet another cause. Miranda distrusted the Creole aristocracy, while Bolívar was its representative. Miranda possessed a cool, methodical mind matured in the cold and sober atmosphere of the eighteenth century, but Bolívar was a young, passionate romantic, a true son of the nineteenth century. Miranda detested Bolívar's theatrical manner and inclination to show off, although he himself was afflicted with the same disease. . . . He called Bolívar a "dangerous youth." But it was not only this contempt of the mature man for the neophyte and military dilettante which was working within Miranda, but also fear of the younger man's coming greatness; and envy on the part of the adventurer for

* Gerhard Masur, *Simón Bolívar* (Albuquerque: University of New Mexico Press, 1948), pp. 128-129, 144-148. Reprinted with the permission of the University of New Mexico Press. Footnotes in original not included.

131

the man of genius. For his part Bolívar saw in Miranda a rival whose abilities he was beginning to doubt but who was barring his way to power. And beyond all political differences, tensions existed between the *Precursor* and the *Libertador* that emanated not from the realm of ideas, but from the fires of passion. . . .

Only he [Bolívar] with the faith to move mountains could cherish any hope of victory for independence. Most of the western regions had been taken by Monteverde, and those provinces not yet in his hands were in a state of disintegration, while the areas in the east, which should have been supplying Caracas with food and reinforcements, were seething beneath uncontrolled rebellion. The counter-revolution had triumphed. Even in the capital, factions engaged continually in hand-to-hand scuffles with the authorities. Anarchy was rife. Miranda watched from the sidelines as his army disintegrated. Whole groups—up to a hundred men with arms and ammunition—deserted. Officers mutinied, then fought alongside the enemy. Miranda, faced with resigning, and thus possibly saving the cause of revolution, or with surrendering to the enemy for better or worse, chose the latter. The military situation was desperate, and the economic conditions of the country hopeless. At best Venezuela could expect a long-drawn-out civil war from which the lower classes, the mestizos and Negroes, would be the beneficiaries. Miranda had, a long time before, made the statement that he would prefer his country to remain another hundred years beneath Spanish oppression than be transformed into an arena for crime. He capitulated.

Above all it must be remembered that the nature of the man was that of an adventurer who took himself more seriously than he did an assignment entrusted him. It was himself that he wished to save. . . .

During lengthy negotiations, . . . when proposals and counterproposals were [being] exchanged between the two headquarters, Miranda left Victoria for La Guayra in order to charter a ship to ensure his flight. Here was proof inconvertible that he had relinquished the cause of the Republic for his own.

The entire country was left at the mercy of Monteverde under the conditions of surrender. Only the inhabitants of territories not yet conquered were protected from persecution and expropriation. Those of the colored population that might be of some use to the conquerors were promised indulgence and the abolition of degrading laws under which they had lived in colonial days. Apart from these exceptions, Venezuelans were to be governed by the rules and regulations to be established by the Spanish Parliament for all of South America. . . .

Two separate sources testify that at this time Miranda was concerned with making himself financially secure. One report states that he accepted eleven thousand ounces of gold offered him by the Spaniards, while the other dealt with a check drawn in his favor by his friend, the Marquis de Casa León. Whether true or not, these dealings do not sound implausible, though it cannot be said that Miranda sold out his country to the Spaniards. He did unquestionably have his eye cocked for the main chance.

Having arrived in Caracas on July 26, Miranda made his report to the City Council on the surrender, without, however, specifying at all the manner in which it had occurred. The thought of his flight possessed him. His papers and belongings had already been sent to La Guayra where the *Sapphire*—the ship on which Bolívar had returned from London—lay at anchor. Miranda himself arrived at the port on July 30, and besides the twenty-two thousand pesos given him out of the state treasury, he took along one thousand ounces of gold. The captain of the *Sapphire* begged him to board the ship immediately, but the General, in preferring to spend the night in La Guayra, signed his own death warrant. . . .

Bolívar, accompanied by a number of other officers, fled to La Guayra on July 30. His indignation against Miranda was boundless. No one knew the conditions of the armistice. When Miranda met for the last time with the leaders of the Patriots at dinner, on July 30, he was pressed for an explanation. But they received answers not only irate but insulting. The report circulating that the General had ordered no one to leave the port other than himself increased the anger at the secrecy surrounding the capitulation. Information concerning the large sums of money stowed aboard the *Sapphire* soon leaked out, and it became evident without further room for doubt, that Miranda had first sold his country down the river and was now preparing to betray those officers willing to continue the fight. Had Miranda believed in the sincerity of the Spaniards and expected the stipulated conditions would be fulfilled, he would have found no reason to flee. And if he did not believe this, he was obviously a traitor.

When Miranda had withdrawn from the company of his dinner companions, the officers proceeded to hold consultation. In addition to Bolívar, there were taking part in this war council the Commandant of La Guayra, Las Casas; Miguel Peña the political delegate; and six or seven high ranking officers. The decision was taken to place Miranda under arrest. Some wished merely to enforce his remaining in the country, while others, Bolívar among them, wished to shoot him as a traitor. The patriots entered Miranda's room before dawn. He thought at first they came to wake him, but on discovering their purpose, asked them to wait. In a few moments he appeared fully dressed and completely composed. His imperturbability never left him, and when Bolívar harshly announced him to be under arrest he did not deign to reply. He took a lantern from the hand of one of his aides, and holding it up to the faces of the conspirators, accused them instead: "Noise, noise, and more noise! That is all these people can make!" He uttered no further word and was brought in silence to Fort San Carlos.

Whatever plans the Patriots may have made, Monteverde left them no time for execution. By July 31 he had already sent an emissary to La Guayra demanding the port's closing and insisting that the non-fulfillment of this order would entail cancellation of all previous pacts. In his desire to win the favor of the conqueror, Las Casas, the commandant, followed the order, and the Venezuelan flag flying on the fort was replaced by the Spanish colors. Miranda was handed over to the Spaniards.

Little in Bolívar's life gave his critics as much food for discussion as his attitude and conduct towards Miranda. Had a man who himself had suffered defeat, whose miscalculations caused the loss of Puerto Cabello, any right to sit in judgment? Had not this man also left his country three times during the fateful years between 1814 and 1818? Bolívar would have answered thus: "I, too, was unhappy as a soldier. But I never surrendered. Never did money or possessions mean anything to me. Never have I lowered the flag of victory. . . ." Bolívar was actually proud of his action against Miranda and boasted of it. . . . There is yet another reason for the tragic ending of the relationship between the two men—perhaps the most cogent. Miranda had at no time been willing to make personal sacrifices, and whether corruptible or not, had not achieved anything it is possible to construe as great in terms of history. Miranda had remained throughout his life a freebooter for whom nothing was as important as his own person. Miranda failed because his personal ambitions were greater than his abilities.

The conquering Spaniards were uninterested in the causes of the Patriots' anger against Miranda. They saw in him the originator of the movement for independence, and therefore they seized him. He remained in the fortress at La Guayra until 1814, when he was taken to the Prison of Four Towers in Cádiz. He died there on July 16, 1816.

READING NO. 8

America Petitions the Cortes of Cádiz*

From 1810 to 1814 Spain was ruled by a liberal legislature in which representatives from the New World colonies participated. This is Herbert I. Priestley's summary of what the American delegates demanded and how the Cortes responded.

The American delegates to the Cortes on December 16 [1810] presented to it for consideration the aspirations of the people of Spanish America, as they understood them. Their demands were made under eleven points. (1) They demanded equality with Spain in representation in the Cortes for the American realms, on a population basis. This the Cortes rejected, alleging fear of the Indian populations. (2) Their demand that agriculture, manufacturing, and the mechanical trades should be freed from all restrictions, was accepted without debate. But their proposals (3) that commerce should be absolutely free, whether carried in Spanish or foreign bottoms, (4) that free trade should be granted

* Herbert Ingram Priestley, *The Mexican Nation: A History* (New York: The Macmillan Company, 1923), pp. 227-228. Reprinted with the permission of Mrs. Elizabeth P. Morby.

between America and Asia as well, and (5) that all restrictions of this kind should be immediately abolished, all brought forth the warmest discussion, as a result of which it was decided to take no action until the advice of the American commercial and governmental bodies could be ascertained. The pretension (6) that all government monopolies should be abolished, with compensation in special duties on all monopolized articles freed, was also postponed, the only lucrative monopoly then being that of tobacco. The suggestion (7) that the working of American quicksilver mines should be made free was adopted without debate, as was the proposal (8) that all Americans, whether Indian or white, were to be given the same political rights as Spaniards. But when it came to granting (9) that at least half the offices in the several kingdoms should be given to natives, postponement was again taken. The same action was taken upon the proposal (10) to create a nominating board to control the equitable distribution of political offices. The eleventh point, which called for the reëstablishment of the Jesuit order, was almost unanimously rejected; many of the American delegates themselves opposed it, though a generation earlier the marquis of Croix had said of the Jesuits, when they were expelled from all Spanish America, that they absolutely controlled the minds and hearts of the Mexican people.

Such were the aims with which the American delegates entered the Cortes which was on March 18, 1812, to enunciate the famous Spanish Constitution of that year, a constitution destined to become a model for most of the revolutionary countries of Europe which set themselves shortly to the undoing of the old powers of absolutism. The salient features of this new constitution may be briefly set forth. It declared: that the sovereignty should henceforth reside in the nation; that Catholicism should be the established religion; that the government should be an hereditary monarchy; that the powers of government should be segregated into functions legislative, executive, and judicial; that representation in the Cortes should be proportionate to population; that municipal offices should be no longer hereditary, but annually elective; that each province should have a chief appointed by the crown and advised by a council, which should control the municipalities; that freedom of the press should prevail.

The War to the Death, 1813*

The War to the Death, one of the most controversial decisions that Bolívar ever made, intensified the savagery and brutality with which the independence struggle was waged in Venezuela.

Trujillo, June 15, 1813.

Venezuelans: An army of your brothers, sent by the Sovereign Congress of New Granada, has come to liberate you. Having expelled the oppressors from the provinces of Mérida and Trujillo, it is now among you.

We are sent to destroy the Spaniards, to protect the Americans, and to reëstablish the republican governments that once formed the Confederation of Venezuela. The states defended by our arms are again governed by their former constitutions and tribunals, in full enjoyment of their liberty and independence, for our mission is designed only to break the chains of servitude which still shackle some of our towns, and not to impose laws or exercise acts of dominion to which the rules of war might entitle us.

Moved by your misfortunes, we have been unable to observe with indifference the afflictions you were forced to experience by the barbarous Spaniards, who have ravished you, plundered you, and brought you death and destruction. They have violated the sacred rights of nations. They have broken the most solemn agreements and treaties. In fact, they have committed every manner of crime, reducing the Republic of Venezuela to the most frightful desolation. Justice therefore demands vengeance, and necessity compels us to exact it. Let the monsters who infest Colombian soil, who have drenched it in blood, be cast out forever; may their punishment be equal to the enormity of their

* Simón Bolívar, *Selected Writings,* compiled by Vicente Lecuna, edited by Harold A. Bierck, Jr., translated by Lewis Bertrand, published by Banco de Venezuela, 2 vols. (New York, 1951), I, 31-32. Reprinted with the permission of Banco de Venezuela. Footnote in original not included.

perfidy, so that we may eradicate the stain of our ignominy and demonstrate to the nations of the world that the sons of America cannot be offended with impunity.

Despite our just resentment toward the iniquitous Spaniards, our magnanimous heart still commands us to open to them for the last time a path to reconciliation and friendship; they are invited to live peacefully among us, if they will abjure their crimes, honestly change their ways, and coöperate with us in destroying the intruding Spanish government and in the reëstablishment of the Republic of Venezuela.

Any Spaniard who does not, by every active and effective means, work against tyranny in behalf of this just cause, will be considered an enemy and punished; as a traitor to the nation, he will inevitably be shot by a firing squad. On the other hand, a general and absolute amnesty is granted to those who come over to our army with or without their arms, as well as to those who render aid to the good citizens who are endeavoring to throw off the yoke of tyranny. Army officers and civil magistrates who proclaim the government of Venezuela and join with us shall retain their posts and positions; in a word, those Spaniards who render outstanding service to the State shall be regarded and treated as Americans.

And you Americans who, by error or treachery, have been lured from the paths of justice, are informed that your brothers, deeply regretting the error of your ways, have pardoned you as we are profoundly convinced that you cannot be truly to blame, for only the blindness and ignorance in which you have been kept up to now by those responsible for your crimes could have induced you to commit them. Fear not the sword that comes to avenge you and to sever the ignoble ties with which your executioners have bound you to their own fate. You are hereby assured, with absolute impunity, of your honor, lives, and property. The single title, "Americans," shall be your safeguard and guarantee. Our arms have come to protect you, and they shall never be raised against a single one of you, our brothers.

This amnesty is extended even to the very traitors who most recently have committed felonious acts, and it shall be so religiously applied that no reason, cause, or pretext will be sufficient to oblige us to violate our offer, however extraordinary and extreme the occasion you may give to provoke our wrath.

Spaniards and Canary Islanders, you will die, though you be neutral, unless you actively espouse the cause of America's liberation. Americans, you will live, even if you have trespassed.

General Headquarters, Trujillo, June 15, 1813. The 3d [year].

SIMÓN BOLÍVAR

READING NO. 10

The Crossing of the Andes to Boyacá*

In June 1819, Bolívar undertook to free Colombia in one of the most dramatic campaigns of the independence struggles, a winter crossing of the Andes. An eyewitness, Daniel O'Leary, describes the arduous campaign. His multivolumed memoirs containing correspondence, narration, and documents, and his position as one of Bolívar's favorite aides, make him, in a sense, the Bernal Díaz of the Wars of Independence.

From Tamé to Pore, capital of Casanare, all the road was flooded: "the terrain where the army had to make its first marches was more like a small sea than dry land," said Santander in his version of this campaign. On the 22nd of June another kind of obstacle was encountered, the gigantic Andes, which were considered impassable in this season. [They] seemed to place an insuperable barrier before the progress of the army. For four days the troops battled with the difficulties of those rugged roads, if craggy precipices merit such a name.

The llaneros contemplated the stupendous heights with wonder and fear, and marvelled that a land so different from theirs could exist. Their surprise grew the more they climbed, with each mountain they climbed; for that which they had taken to be the last summit was but the beginning of another and an-

* Daniel F. O'Leary, *Bolívar y la emancipación de Sur-América.* Translated from the English by his son, Simón B. O'Leary and with a foreword by Rufino Blanco Fombona, translated by Doris M. Ladd (Madrid: Sociedad Española de Librería, 1915), I, 665-671.

other even higher, from whose summits still more mountains stretched on, whose peaks seemed to be lost among the ethereal mists of the firmament. Men of the pampas accustomed to cross torrential rivers, to break wild horses and to conquer fierce bulls, crocodiles, and tigers, with their bare hands, now quailed before the aspect of such strange surroundings. Without hope of being able to overcome such extraordinary difficulties, their horses dead with fatigue, they were convinced that only fools would persevere, through climates which dulled their senses and froze their bodies, and the result was that many deserted.

The mules which were carrying arms and ammunition fell beneath the weight of their burdens; few horses survived the five days of marching, and those that died in the forward division obstructed the road and added to the difficulties of the rear guard. It rained incessantly, day and night, and the cold increased in proportion to the ascent. Cold water, to which the troops were unaccustomed, gave them diarrhea. . . .

After a few days of rest, the army continued its march on the 2nd of July. The royalist detachment, which had been defeated in Paya, retreated to Labranza Grande, a point which controlled the only route considered passable at that season; there was another one, through the marsh of Pisba, but it was so rugged and uneven that it was seldom used even in summer. It was considered impassable by the Spaniards, and for this reason they neglected its defense, precisely the reason Bolívar decided to choose it. . . .

In many places the way was obstructed completely by immense rocks and fallen trees and by declines (desmedros) caused by the continual rains which made the footing dangerous and slippery. The soldiers, who had received four-day rations . . . threw them away and carried only their guns. . . . On this day's journey the few horses that had survived perished.

Late that night the army reached the base of Pisba Marsh and camped there; a horrible night, for it was impossible to keep the fires lit since there were no habitations whatsoever in the area and because the incessant rain accompanied by hail and an unceasing icy wind put out, as soon as they were lit, the campfires which they tried to make in the open air.

Since the troops were almost naked and the majority of them were from the burning llanos of Venezuela, it is easier to imagine their cruel sufferings than to describe them. The following day they crossed the marsh itself, a dismal, inhospitable waste, bare of all vegetation because of its altitude. On that day the effect of the frigid and penetrating cold was fatal for many soldiers; in the line of march many fell suddenly ill and died within a few minutes. Whipping was employed with success in some cases to arouse those who collapsed and a cavalry colonel saved himself in this way. . . .

One hundred men would have sufficed to destroy the patriot army in the crossing of this marsh. . . .

On the sixth [of July] Anzoategui's division arrived at Socha, the first town [reached in] the province of Tunja. . . . The soldiers, on seeing the high crests of the mountains behind them covered with clouds and mists, swore spontaneously to win or die rather than to retreat, for they feared the latter more than the enemy, no matter how formidable they might be. In Socha the army received the solicitous hospitality of the inhabitants of the town and the surrounding countryside. Bread, tobacco, and *chicha,* a drink made with maize and honey, compensated for the pains suffered by the troops. . . .

READING NO. 11

The Cartagena Manifesto*

The "Manifesto" was Bolívar's first eloquent and perceptive expression as a statesman. Published when the revolutionary cause was in the process of disintegration because of force (royalist military victories) and blandishment (the liberal conciliatory terms as expressed in the Spanish Constitution of 1812) it pleads the case for American Independence at any cost. The factors Bolívar so brilliantly enumerated to explain the downfall of the first Venezuelan Republic have become the historical

* Simón Bolívar, *Selected Writings of Bolívar,* 2 vols., compiled by Vicente Lecuna, ed. Harold A. Bierck, Jr., translated by Lewis Bertrand, published by Banco de Venezuela (New York, 1951), I, 18-26. Reprinted with the permission of Banco de Venezeula.

generalizations which reveal the failures of the new nations from
1825 to 1850.

Cartagena de [las] Indias, December 15, 1812.

To spare New Granada the fate of Venezuela and to release
the latter from its suffering are the objects which I have set for
myself in this memorial. Condescend to accept it with indulgence, my Fellow-Citizens, for the sake of such laudable objectives.

I am, Granadans, a son of unhappy Caracas, who miracu-
lously escaped from amidst her physical and political ruins, and,
ever faithful to the liberal and just system proclaimed by my
country, I have come here to follow the banners of independence which so gloriously wave in these states.

Forgive me if I, inspired by patriotic zeal, take the liberty of
addressing you, in order to sketch briefly the causes that brought
Venezuela to its destruction. I flatter myself that the terrible and
exemplary lessons which that defunct Republic has supplied may
induce America to mend her ways and correct her shortcomings
in unity, strength, and energy, which are apparent in her governments.

The most grievous error committed by Venezuela in making
her start on the political stage was, as none can deny, her fatal
adoption of the system of tolerance—a system long condemned
as weak and inadequate by every man of common sense, yet
tenaciously maintained with an unparalleled blindness to the
very end.

The first indication of senseless weakness demonstrated by our
government was manifested in the case of the city of Coro,
which, having refused to recognize the legitimacy of the government, was declared in rebellion and treated as an enemy. The
supreme *junta,* instead of subjugating that undefended city,
which would have surrendered as soon as our maritime forces
had appeared off its harbor, gave it time to fortify itself and
build up a strength so respectable that it later succeeded in subjugating the entire confederation almost as easily as we ourselves
could previously have defeated it. The *junta* based its policy on
poorly understood principles of humanity, which do not authorize governments to use force in order to liberate peoples who are
ignorant of the value of their rights.

The codes consulted by our magistrates were not those which

could teach them the practical science of government but were those devised by certain benevolent visionaries, who, creating fantastic republics in their imaginations, have sought to attain political perfection, assuming the perfectibility of the human race. Thus we were given philosophers for leaders, philanthropy for legislation, dialectic for tactics, and sophists for soldiers. Through such a distortion of principles, the social order was thoroughly shaken, and from that time on the State made giant strides toward its general dissolution, which, indeed, shortly came to pass.

Thence was born an impunity toward crimes against the State. They were shamelessly committed by the malcontents, and particularly by our born and implacable enemies, the European Spaniards, who had schemingly remained in our country in order to keep it in continual turmoil and to foster whatever conspiracies our judges permitted them to organize, by always acquitting them even when their misdeeds were of such enormity as to endanger public welfare.

The doctrine which supported this procedure had its origin in the charitable maxims of a few writers who defend the thesis that no man is vested with the right to deprive another of his life even though he be guilty of the crime of treason. Under the cloak of this pious doctrine, every conspiracy was followed by acquittal; and every acquittal by another conspiracy, which again brought acquittal—all because a liberal government must be characterized by clemency. Criminal clemency, more than anything else, contributed to the destruction of the structure which we had not yet entirely completed!

Next came the firm opposition to raising seasoned, disciplined troops, prepared to take their place on the field of battle and indoctrinated with the desire to defend liberty with success and honor. Instead, innumerable undisciplined militia units were formed. The salaries paid the staff officers of these units exhausted the funds of the national treasury. Agriculture was destroyed because the farmers were torn from their homes; this brought odium upon the Government which had forced them to abandon their families and take up arms.

"Republics," said our statesmen, "have no need for hirelings to maintain their liberty. Every citizen will turn soldier when the enemy attacks us. Greece, Rome, Venice, Genoa, Switzerland, Holland, and recently North America defeated their adversaries without the aid of mercenary troops, who stand always ready to support despotism and subjugate their fellow-citizens."

With such political thinking and inaccurate reasoning, they deceived the simple-minded; but they did not convince the judicious who clearly understood the immense difference between the peoples, times, and customs of those republics and ours. It is true that they did not pay standing armies, but that was because these did not exist in antiquity; the safety and the honor of their states was entrusted to their civic virtues, their austere habits, and their military qualities—traits which we are very far from possessing. As regards the modern nations which have thrown off the yoke of tyranny, it is well known that they have maintained the number of hardened veterans necessary to insure their security. North America, however, being at peace with the world and protected by the sea, has not seen fit, in recent years, to maintain the complement of veteran troops needed to defend her borders and cities.

What followed in Venezuela was bitter evidence of the error of her calculations. The militia that went to meet the enemy, not knowing how to handle arms and unaccustomed to discipline and obedience, was routed at the very beginning of the last campaign, notwithstanding the heroic and extraordinary efforts of their leaders to lead them to victory. This defeat caused general discouragement among soldiers and officers, for it is a military truth that only battle-hardened armies are capable of surmounting the first reverses of a campaign. The novice soldier believes all is lost when he has once been routed. Experience has not proved to him that bravery, skill, and perseverance can mend misfortune.

The subdividing of the province of Caracas, planned, discussed, and sanctioned by the Federal Congress, awakened and fomented bitter rivalry against the capital in the smaller cities and towns. "Which," said congressmen, eager for control of their districts, "was the tyrant among cities and the leech of the State?" In this way the flame of civil war was kindled in Valencia, and, even with the reduction of that city, it was never extinguished. It remained hidden under the surface and spread to the adjacent towns of Coro and Maracaibo. These cities established communications with Valencia, thereby facilitating the entry of the Spaniards, which brought about the fall of Venezuela.

The dissipation of the public taxes for frivolous and harmful purposes, and particularly on salaries for an infinite number of officeholders, secretaries, judges, magistrates, and provincial and federal legislators dealt the Republic a mortal blow, since it was obliged to seek recourse in the dangerous expedient of issuing paper money, with no other guarantee than the probable revenues and backing of the Confederation. This new money, in the eyes of most people, was a direct violation of property rights, because they felt that they were being deprived of objects of intrinsic value in exchange for others of uncertain and even problematical worth. The paper money roused discontent among the otherwise indifferent people of the interior; hence, they called upon the commandant of the Spanish troops to come and free them from a currency which they regarded with a horror greater than slavery.

But what weakened the Venezuelan government most was the federal form it adopted in keeping with the exaggerated precepts of the rights of man; this form by authorizing self-government, disrupts social contracts and reduces nations to anarchy. Such was the true state of the Confederation. Each province governed itself independently; and, following this example, each city demanded like powers, based on the practice of the provinces and on the theory that all men and all peoples are entitled to establish arbitrarily the form of government that pleases them.

The federal system, although the most perfect and the most capable of providing for human happiness in society, is, nevertheless, the most contrary to the interests of our infant states. Generally speaking, our fellow-citizens are not yet able to exercise their rights themselves in the fullest measure, because they lack the political virtues that characterize true republicans—virtues that are not acquired under absolute governments, where the rights and duties of the citizen are not recognized.

Moreover, what country in the world, however well trained and republican it may be, can, amidst internal factions and foreign war, be governed by so complicated and weak a system as the federal? No, this system cannot possibly be maintained during the turbulence of battles and political factions. It is essential that a government mold itself, so to speak, to the nature of the circumstances, the times, and the men that comprise it. If these factors are prosperity and peace, the government should be mild and protecting; but if they are turbulence and disaster, it should be stern and arm itself with a firmness that matches the dangers, without regard for laws or constitutions until happiness and peace have been reëstablished.

Caracas was made to suffer severely by the shortcomings of the Confederation, which, far from aiding it, exhausted its treasury and war supplies. When danger threatened, the Confederation abandoned the city to its fate without assisting it with even a small contingent. The Confederation, moreover, created new difficulties, for the rivalry which developed between the federal and the provincial authorities enabled the enemies to penetrate deep into the heart of the State and to occupy a large part of the province before the question as to whether federal or provincial troops should go out to repel them was settled. This fatal debate resulted in a terrible and costly delay to our armies, for they were routed at San Carlos while awaiting the reinforcements needed for victory.

I believe that, unless we centralize our American governments, our enemies will gain every advantage. We will inevitably be involved in the horrors of civil strife and miserably defeated by that handful of bandits who infest our territories.

The popular elections held by the simple people of the country and by the scheming inhabitants of the city added a further obstacle to our practice of federation, because the former are so ignorant that they cast their votes mechanically and the latter so ambitious that they convert everything into factions. As a result, Venezuela never witnessed a free and proper election and the government was placed in the hands of men who were either inept, immoral, or opposed to the cause of independence. Party spirit determined everything and, consequently, caused us more disorganization than the circumstances themselves. Our division, not Spanish arms, returned us to slavery.

The earthquake of March 26, to be sure, was physically and morally destructive and can properly be termed the immediate cause of Venezuela's ruin; but this event could have happened without producing such fatal results had Caracas been governed at that time by a single authority, who, acting promptly and vigorously, could have repaired the damage without those hindrances and rivalries which retarded the effectiveness of the measures taken and allowed the evil to grow to such proportions that it is beyond remedy.

If Caracas had established the simple government that its political and military situation required, instead of a slow-moving and insubstantial confederation, Venezuela would still exist and enjoy its freedom today!

Following the earthquake, ecclesiastical influences played a very considerable part in the insurgency of the villages and smaller towns, and in bringing enemies into the country, thereby sacrilegiously abusing the sanctity of their office in behalf of the fomenters of civil war. We must, nevertheless, honestly confess that these traitorous priests were encouraged to commit the execrable crimes of which they are justly accused because they enjoyed absolute impunity for their crimes—an impunity which found scandalous support in the Congress. This injustice reached such a point that, following the insurrection of the city of Valencia, the pacification of which cost up perhaps a thousand men, not a single rebel was brought to justice; all retained their lives and many their property.

From the above it follows that among the causes that brought about Venezuela's downfall the nature of its Constitution ranks first, which, I repeat, was as contrary to Venezuela's interests as it was favorable to those of her adversaries; second, the spirit of misanthropy which possessed our governing officials; third, the opposition to the establishment of a military force which could save the Republic and repulse the Spanish attacks; fourth, the earthquake, accompanied by a fanaticism that used this occurrence to its best advantage; and, last, the internal factions which in reality were the fatal poison that laid the country in its tomb.

These instances of error and misfortune will not be entirely without benefit to the peoples of South America who aspire to achieve liberty and independence.

New Granada has seen Venezuela succumb and should therefore avoid the pitfalls that destroyed the latter. To this end, I submit, as a measure indispensable for the security of New Granada, the reconquest of Caracas. At first sight this project will appear farfetched, costly, perhaps impracticable; but, examined closely, with foresight and careful reflection, it is as impossible to deny its necessity as to fail to put it into execution once it is proved advisable.

The first factor which offers itself in support of this operation is the fundamental cause of the destruction of Caracas, which was simply the contempt with which that city regarded the existence of an enemy who appeared of little account but who, taken in his true light, was not so at all.

Coro certainly could not have competed with Caracas, if intrinsic strength had been the deciding factor; but, in the realm of human vicissitudes, it is not always physical preponderance that governs. If superiority of moral power determines political balance, the government of Venezuela should, for this reason, have wiped out an enemy, who, while seemingly weak, was backed by the province of Maracaibo and by all those provinces which obeyed the Regency, by gold, and by the coöperation of our eternal enemies, the Europeans who reside among us. Further, Coro was supported by the clerical party, always devoted to its companion and aid, despotism; and she had, above all, the never-ending support of every ignorant and superstitious person within the limits of our states. Thus, no sooner did one traitorous official submit to the enemy, than the political machinery was upset, and all the unparalleled patriotic efforts exerted by the defenders of Caracas proved insufficient to prevent the fall of an edifice already tottering from the blow that it had received from one single man.

Applying the example of Venezuela to New Granada and putting it in the form of a ratio, we find that Coro is to Caracas as Caracas is to all America; consequently, the danger which threatens this country is in proportion to the foregoing ratio. With Spain in possession of the territory of Venezuela, she can easily draw upon it for men, provisions, and munitions of war, and her armies, under the direction of leaders who have had experience against those great masters of warfare, the French, can move inland from the provinces of Barinas and Maracaibo to the farthest confines of South America.

Spain today has a great number of daring and ambitious general officers, long accustomed to danger and to privations, who long to come here and seek an empire to replace that which they have just lost.

It is probable that following the downfall of the Peninsula there will be a tremendous emigration of men of all classes, particularly of cardinals, archbishops, bishops, canons, and revolutionary clerics, all capable not only of subverting our incipient, faltering states, but of encompassing the entire new world in frightful anarchy. The religious influence, the rule of civil and military domination, and all the prestige they can bring to bear upon the human spirit will be additional instruments which they will use in subjugating these countries.

Nothing will stand in the way of Spanish emigration. It is conceivable that England will cover the escape of a group whose departure would partially weaken the forces of Bonaparte in Spain and tend to increase and add new life to their own party in America. Neither France nor North America will be able to prevent this movement, and our attempts would be even more futile, for none of us has a navy worthy of the name.

These émigrés will assuredly find a friendly welcome in Venezuelan ports, since they come to reinforce the oppressors of that country; and those ports will provide them with the means with which to undertake the conquest of the independent states.

They will raise fifteen or twenty thousand men, whom their leaders, officers, sergeants, corporals, and veteran soldiers will rapidly drill and discipline. This army will be followed by another yet more terrible, of ministers, ambassadors, councilors, magistrates, all the ecclesiastical hierarchy and the grandees of Spain, whose trade is deceit and intrigue, and all bearing imposing titles designed to dazzle the multitude. And, descending like a torrent, they will overrun the land tearing Colombia's tree of liberty down to its very roots. The troops will fight on the field, but this army will battle us from their desks, using seduction and fanaticism for arms.

Thus, to fend off these calamities, we have no other recourse than rapidly to pacify our rebellious provinces, before turning our arms upon our enemies. In this manner soldiers and officers worthy to be called the bulwarks of their country can be developed.

Everything conspires to make us adopt this measure. In addition to the urgent necessity of closing the gates against the enemy, there are other reasons which force us to take the offensive, reasons so overwhelming that it would be a military error and a political blunder not to do so. We have been invaded, and consequently we are obliged to hurl the enemy back across the border. Moreover, it is a principle of the art of war that every defensive action is harmful and ruinous for those who wage it, as it weakens them without hope of recovery. Hostilities in enemy territory, however, are always advantageous by reason of the good that results from the enemy's misfortunes; thus on no account should we employ the defensive.

We must also consider the present condition of the enemy, who is in a very critical position. The majority of his creole soldiers have deserted at a time when he is obliged to garrison the patriot cities of Caracas, Puerto Cabello, La Guayra, Barcelona, Cumaná, and Margarita, where he keeps his stores. He does not dare to leave these towns unguarded for fear of a general insurrection the moment he departs. Thus it would not be impossible for our troops to reach the gates of Caracas without engaging in a single open battle.

It is a certainty that, as soon as we enter Venezuela, we will be joined by thousands of valiant patriots, who anxiously await our coming in order to throw off the yoke of their tyrants and unite their efforts with ours in the defense of liberty.

The nature of the present campaign affords us the advantage of approaching Maracaibo by way of Santa Marta, and Barinas by way of Cúcuta.

Let us, therefore, avail ourselves of a time so propitious, lest the reinforcements, which might at any moment arrive from Spain, completely alter the aspect of affairs; and lest we lose, perhaps forever, the welcome opportunity to insure the destiny of these states.

The honor of New Granada imperiously demands that she teach these audacious invaders a lesson, by pursuing them to their last entrenchments. Her good name depends upon her taking over the task of marching into Venezuela to free that cradle of Colombian independence, its martyrs, and the deserving people of Caracas, whose cries are addressed only to their beloved compatriots, the Granadans, whose arrival, as their redeemers, they await with despairing impatience. Let us hasten to break the chains of those victims who groan in the dungeons, ever hopeful of rescue. Make not a mockery of their trust. Be not insensible to the cries of your brothers. Fly to avenge the dead, to give life to the dying, to bring freedom to the oppressed and liberty to all.

SIMÓN BOLÍVAR

The Jamaica Letter, September 6, 1815*

The "Jamaica Letter," also commonly referred to as "The Letter to the Gentleman of Jamaica," was written to stimulate British interest in the cause of independence. The "Letter" is a powerful combination of propaganda and Creole resentment and an extraordinarily precise political prediction. Bolívar focused attention not on the failures of the present but on the promise of the future. Spain, he said, was an "aged serpent"— though he neglected to point out that its coils were still strong enough to embrace all of Spanish America except La Plata.

Kingston, Jamaica, September 6, 1815.

My dear Sir:

I hasten to reply to the letter of the 29th ultimo which you had the honor of sending me and which I received with the greatest satisfaction.

Sensible though I am of the interest you desire to take in the fate of my country, and of your commiseration with her for the tortures she has suffered from the time of her discovery until the present at the hands of her destroyers, the Spaniards, I am no less sensible of the obligation which your solicitous inquiries about the principal objects of American policy place upon me. Thus, I find myself in conflict between the desire to reciprocate your confidence, which honors me, and the difficulty of rewarding it, for lack of documents and books and because of my own limited knowledge of a land so vast, so varied, and so little known as the New World.

In my opinion it is impossible to answer the questions that you have so kindly posed. Baron von Humboldt himself, with his encyclopedic theoretical and practical knowledge, could hardly do so properly, because, although some of the facts about

* Simón Bolívar, *Selected Writings of Bolívar*, 2 vols., compiled by Vicente Lecuna, ed. Harold A. Bierck, Jr., translated by Lewis Bertrand, published by Banco de Venezuela (New York, 1951), I, 103-122. Reprinted with the permission of Banco de Venezuela. Footnotes in original not included.

America and her development are known, I dare say the better part are shrouded in mystery. Accordingly, only conjectures that are more or less approximate can be made, especially with regard to her future and the true plans of the Americans, inasmuch as our continent has within it potentialities for every facet of development revealed in the history of nations, by reason of its physical characteristics and because of the hazards of war and the uncertainties of politics.

As I feel obligated to give due consideration to your esteemed letter and to the philanthropic intentions prompting it, I am impelled to write you these words, wherein you will certainly not find the brilliant thoughts you seek but rather a candid statement of my ideas.

"Three centuries ago," you say, "began the atrocities committed by the Spaniards on this great hemisphere of Columbus." Our age has rejected these atrocities as mythical, because they appear to be beyond the human capacity for evil. Modern critics would never credit them were it not for the many and frequent documents testifying to these horrible truths. The humane Bishop of Chiapas, that apostle of America, Las Casas, has left to posterity a brief description of these horrors, extracted from the trial records in Sevilla relating to the cases brought against the *conquistadores,* and containing the testimony of every respectable person then in the New World, together with the charges [*procesos*], which the tyrants made against each other. All this is attested by the foremost historians of that time. Every impartial person has admitted the zeal, sincerity, and high character of that friend of humanity, who so fervently and so steadfastly denounced to his government and to his contemporaries the most horrible acts of sanguinary frenzy.

With what a feeling of gratitude I read that passage in your letter in which you say to me: "I hope that the success which then followed Spanish arms may now turn in favor of their adversaries, the badly oppressed people of South America." I take this hope as a prediction, if it is justice that determines man's contests. Success will crown our efforts, because the destiny of America has been irrevocably decided; the tie that bound her to Spain has been severed. Only a concept maintained that tie and kept the parts of that immense monarchy together. That which formerly bound them now divides them.

The hatred that the Peninsula has inspired in us is greater than the ocean between us. It would be easier to have the two continents meet than to reconcile the spirits of the two countries. The habit of obedience; a community of interest, of understanding, of religion; mutual goodwill; a tender regard for the birthplace and good name of our forefathers; in short, all that gave rise to our hopes, came to us from Spain. As a result there was born a principle of affinity that seemed eternal, notwithstanding the misbehavior of our rulers which weakened that sympathy, or, rather, that bond enforced by the domination of their rule. At present the contrary attitude persists: we are threatened with the fear of death, dishonor, and every harm; there is nothing we have not suffered at the hands of that unnatural step-mother —Spain. The veil has been torn asunder. We have already seen the light, and it is not our desire to be thrust back into darkness. The chains have been broken; we have been freed, and now our enemies seek to enslave us anew. For this reason America fights desperately, and seldom has desperation failed to achieve victory.

Because successes have been partial and spasmodic, we must not lose faith. In some regions the Independents triumph, while in others the tyrants have the advantage. What is the end result? Is not the entire New World in motion, armed for defense? We have but to look around us on this hemisphere to witness a simultaneous struggle at every point.

The war-like state of the La Plata River provinces has purged that territory and led their victorious armies to Upper Perú, arousing Arequipa and worrying the royalists in Lima. Nearly one million inhabitants there now enjoy liberty.

The territory of Chile, populated by 800,000 souls, is fighting the enemy who is seeking her subjugation; but to no avail, because those who long ago put an end to the conquests of this enemy, the free and indomitable Araucanians, are their neighbors and compatriots. Their sublime example is proof to those fighting in Chile that a people who love independence will eventually achieve it.

The viceroyalty of Perú, whose population approaches a million and a half inhabitants, without doubt suffers the greatest subjection and is obliged to make the most sacrifices for the royal cause; and, although the thought of coöperating with that part of America may be vain, the fact remains that it is not tranquil, nor is it capable of restraining the torrent that threatens most of its provinces.

New Granada, which is, so to speak, the heart of America, obeys a general government, save for the territory of Quito which is held only with the greatest difficulty by its enemies, as it is strongly devoted to the country's cause; and the provinces of Panamá and Santa Marta endure, not without suffering, the tyranny of their masters. Two and a half million people inhabit New Granada and are actually defending that territory against the Spanish army under General Morillo, who will probably suffer defeat at the impregnable fortress of Cartagena. But should he take that city, it will be at the price of heavy casualties, and he will then lack sufficient forces to subdue the unrestrained and brave inhabitants of the interior.

With respect to heroic and hapless Venezuela, events there have moved so rapidly and the devastation has been such that it is reduced to frightful desolation and almost absolute indigence, although it was once among the fairest regions that are the pride of America. Its tyrants govern a desert, and they oppress only those unfortunate survivors who, having escaped death, lead a precarious existence. A few women, children, and old men are all that remain. Most of the men have perished rather than be slaves; those who survive continue to fight furiously on the fields and in the inland towns, until they expire or hurl into the sea those who, insatiable in their thirst for blood and crimes, rival those first monsters who wiped out America's primitive race. Nearly a million persons formerly dwelt in Venezuela, and it is no exaggeration to say that one out of four has succumbed either to the land, sword, hunger, plague, flight, or privation, all consequences of the war, save the earthquake.

According to Baron von Humboldt, New Spain, including Guatemala, had 7,800,000 inhabitants in 1808. Since that time, the insurrection, which has shaken virtually all of her provinces, has appreciably reduced that apparently correct figure, for over a million men have perished, as you can see in the report of Mr. Walton, who describes faithfully the bloody crimes committed in that abundant kingdom. There the struggle continues by dint of human and every other type of sacrifice, for the Spaniards spare nothing that might enable them to subdue those who have had the misfortune of being born on this soil, which appears to

be destined to flow with the blood of its offspring. In spite of
everything, the Mexicans will be free. They have embraced the
country's cause, resolved to avenge their forefathers or follow
them to the grave. Already they say with Raynal: The time has
come at last to repay the Spaniards torture for torture and to
drown that race of annihilators in its own blood or in the sea.

The islands of Puerto Rico and Cuba, with a combined population of perhaps 700,000 to 800,000 souls, are the most tranquil
possessions of the Spaniards, because they are not within range
of contact with the Independents. But are not the people of
those islands Americans? Are they not maltreated? Do they not
desire a better life?

This picture represents, on a military map, an area of 2,000
longitudinal and 900 latitudinal leagues at its greatest point,
wherein 16,000,000 Americans either defend their rights or
suffer repression at the hands of Spain, which, although once
the world's greatest empire, is now too weak, with what little is
left her, to rule the new hemisphere or even to maintain herself
in the old. And shall Europe, the civilized, the merchant, the
lover of liberty allow an aged serpent, bent only on satisfying
its venomous rage, devour the fairest part of our globe? What!
Is Europe deaf to the clamor of her own interests? Has she no
eyes to see justice? Has she grown so hardened as to become insensible? The more I ponder these questions, the more I am confused. I am led to think that America's disappearance is desired;
but this is impossible because all Europe is not Spain. What
madness for our enemy to hope to reconquer America when
she has no navy, no funds, and almost no soldiers! Those troops
which she has are scarcely adequate to keep her own people in
a state of forced obedience and to defend herself from her
neighbors. On the other hand, can that nation carry on the exclusive commerce of one-half the world when it lacks manu-
factures, agricultural products, crafts and sciences, and even a
policy? Assume that this mad venture were successful, and
further assume that pacification ensued, would not the sons of
the Americans of today, together with the sons of the European
reconquistadores twenty years hence, conceive the same patriotic
designs that are now being fought for?

Europe could do Spain a service by dissuading her from her
rash obstinacy, thereby at least sparing her the costs she is in-

curring and the blood she is expending. And if she will fix her attention on her own precincts she can build her prosperity and power upon more solid foundations than doubtful conquests, precarious commerce, and forceful exactions from remote and powerful peoples. Europe herself, as a matter of common sense policy, should have prepared and executed the project of American independence, not alone because the world balance of power so necessitated, but also because this is the legitimate and certain means through which Europe can acquire overseas commercial establishments. A Europe which is not moved by the violent passions of vengeance, ambition, and greed, as is Spain, would seem to be entitled, by all the rules of equity, to make clear to Spain where her best interests lie.

All of the writers who have treated this matter agree on this point. Consequently, we have had reason to hope that the civilized nations would hasten to our aid in order that we might achieve that which must prove to be advantageous to both hemispheres. How vain has been this hope! Not only the Europeans but even our brothers of the North have been apathetic bystanders in this struggle which, by its very essence, is the most just, and in its consequences the most noble and vital of any which have been raised in ancient or in modern times. Indeed, can the far-reaching effects of freedom for the hemisphere which Columbus discovered ever be calculated?

"The criminal action of Bonaparte," you say, "in seizing Charles IV and Ferdinand VII, the monarchs of that nation which three centuries ago treacherously imprisoned two rulers of South America, is a most evident sign of divine retribution, and, at the same time, positive proof that God espouses the just cause of the Americans and will grant them independence."

It appears that you allude to Montezuma, the ruler of Mexico, who was imprisoned by Cortés, and, according to Herrera, was by him slain, although Solís states that it was the work of the people; and to Atahualpa, the Inca of Perú, destroyed by Francisco Pizarro and Diego Almagro. The fate of the monarchs of Spain and of America is too different to admit a comparison. The former were treated with dignity and were kept alive, and eventually they recovered their freedom and their throne; whereas the latter suffered unspeakable tortures and the vilest of treatment. Quauhtemotzin [Guatémoc], Montezuma's successor, was treated as an emperor and crowned, but in ridicule and not in honor, so that he might suffer this humiliation before being put to torture. A like treatment was accorded the ruler of Michoacán, Catzontzin; the *zipa* of Bogotá, and all the other *toquis, imas, zipas, ulmenes, caciques,* and other Indian dignitaries who succumbed before Spain's might.

The case of Ferdinand VII more nearly parallels what happened in Chile in 1535 to the *ulmen* of Copiapó, then ruler of that region. The Spaniard Almagro pretended, like Bonaparte, to espouse the cause of the legitimate sovereign; he therefore called the other a usurper, as did Ferdinand in Spain. Almagro appeared to reëstablish the legitimate sovereign in his estates but ended by shackling the hapless *ulmen* and feeding him to the flames without so much as hearing his defense. This is similar to the case of Ferdinand VII and his usurper: Europe's monarchs, however, only suffer exile; the *ulmen* of Chile is barbarously put to death.

"These several months," you add, "I have given much thought to the situation in America and to her hopes for the future. I have a great interest in her development, but I lack adequate information respecting her present state and the aspirations of her people. I greatly desire to know about the politics of each province, also its peoples, and whether they desire a republic or a monarchy; or whether they seek to form one unified republic or a single monarchy? If you could supply me with this information or suggest the sources I might consult, I should deem it a very special favor."

Generous souls always interest themselves in the fate of a people who strive to recover the rights to which the Creator and Nature have entitled them, and one must indeed be wedded to error and passion not to harbor this noble sentiment. You have given thought to my country and are concerned in its behalf, and for your kindness I am warmly grateful.

I have listed the population, which is based on more or less exact data, but which a thousand circumstances render deceiving. This inaccuracy cannot easily be remedied, because most of the inhabitants live in rural areas and are often nomadic; they are farmers, herders, and migrants, lost amidst thick giant forests, solitary plains, and isolated by lakes and mighty streams. Who is capable of compiling complete statistics of a land like this? Moreover, the tribute paid by the Indians, the punishments of the slaves, the first fruits of the harvest [*primicias*], tithes [*diezmas*], and taxes levied on farmers, and other impositions have driven the poor Americans from their homes. This is not to mention the war of extermination that has already taken a toll of nearly an eighth part of the population and frightened another large part away. All in all, the difficulties are insuperable, and the tally is likely to show only half the true count.

It is even more difficult to foresee the future fate of the New World, to set down its political principles, or to prophesy what manner of government it will adopt. Every conjecture relative to America's future is, I feel, pure speculation. When mankind was in its infancy, steeped in uncertainty, ignorance, and error, was it possible to foresee what system it would adopt for its preservation? Who could venture to say that a certain nation would be a republic or a monarchy; this nation great, that nation small? To my way of thinking, such is our own situation. We are a young people. We inhabit a world apart, separated by broad seas. We are young in the ways of almost all the arts and sciences, although, in a certain manner, we are old in the ways of civilized society. I look upon the present state of America as similar to that of Rome after its fall. Each part of Rome adopted a political system conforming to its interest and situation or was led by the individual ambitions of certain chiefs, dynasties, or associations. But this important difference exists: those dispersed parts later reestablished their ancient nations, subject to the changes imposed by circumstances or events. But we scarcely retain a vestige of what once was; we are, moreover, neither Indian nor European, but a species midway between the legitimate proprietors of this country and the Spanish usurpers. In short, though Americans by birth we derive our rights from Europe, and we have to assert these rights against the rights of the natives, and at the same time we must defend ourselves against the invaders. This places us in a most extraordinary and involved situation. Notwithstanding that it is a type of divination to predict the result of the political course which America is pursuing, I shall venture some conjectures which, of course, are colored by my enthusiasm and dictated by rational desires rather than by reasoned calculations.

The rôle of the inhabitants of the American hemisphere has for centuries been purely passive. Politically they were non-existent. We are still in a position lower than slavery, and therefore it is more difficult for us to rise to the enjoyment of freedom. Permit me these transgressions in order to establish the issue. States are slaves because of either the nature or the misuse of their constitutions; a people is therefore enslaved when the government, by its nature or its vices, infringes on and usurps the rights of the citizen or subject. Applying these principles, we find that America was denied not only its freedom but even an active and effective tyranny. Let me explain. Under absolutism there are no recognized limits to the exercise of governmental powers. The will of the great sultan, khan, bey, and other despotic rulers is the supreme law, carried out more or less arbitrarily by the lesser pashas, khans, and satraps of Turkey and Persia, who have an organized system of oppression in which inferiors participate according to the authority vested in them. To them is entrusted the administration of civil, military, political, religious, and tax matters. But, after all is said and done, the rulers of Ispahan are Persians; the viziers of the Grand Turk are Turks; and the sultans of Tartary are Tartars. China does not bring its military leaders and scholars from the land of Genghis Khan, her conqueror, notwithstanding that the Chinese of today are the lineal descendants of those who were reduced to subjection by the ancestors of the present-day Tartars.

How different is our situation! We have been harassed by a conduct which has not only deprived us of our rights but has kept us in a sort of permanent infancy with regard to public affairs. If we could at least have managed our domestic affairs and our internal administration, we could have acquainted ourselves with the processes and mechanics of public affairs. We should also have enjoyed a personal consideration, thereby commanding a certain unconscious respect from the people, which is so necessary to preserve amidst revolutions. That is why I say we have even been deprived of an active tyranny, since we have not been permitted to exercise its functions.

Americans today, and perhaps to a greater extent than ever

before, who live within the Spanish system occupy a position in society no better than that of serfs destined for labor, or at best they have no more status than that of mere consumers. Yet even this status is surrounded with galling restrictions, such as being forbidden to grow European crops, or to store products which are royal monopolies, or to establish factories of a type the Peninsula itself does not possess. To this add the exclusive trading privileges, even in articles of prime necessity, and the barriers between American provinces, designed to prevent all exchange of trade, traffic, and understanding. In short, do you wish to know what our future held?—simply the cultivation of the fields of indigo, grain, coffee, sugar cane, cacao, and cotton; cattle raising on the broad plains; hunting wild game in the jungles; digging in the earth to mine its gold—but even these limitations could never satisfy the greed of Spain.

So negative was our existence that I can find nothing comparable in any other civilized society, examine as I may the entire history of time and the politics of all nations. Is it not an outrage and a violation of human rights to expect a land so splendidly endowed, so vast, rich, and populous, to remain merely passive?

As I have just explained, we were cut off and, as it were, removed from the world in relation to the science of government and administration of the state. We were never viceroys or governors, save in the rarest of instances; seldom archbishops and bishops; diplomats never; as military men, only subordinates; as nobles, without royal privileges. In brief, we were neither magistrates nor financiers and seldom merchants—all in flagrant contradiction to our institutions.

Emperor Charles V made a pact with the discoverers, conquerors, and settlers of America, and this, as Guerra puts it, is our social contract. The monarchs of Spain made a solemn agreement with them, to be carried out on their own account and at their own risk, expressly prohibiting them from drawing on the royal treasury. In return, they were made the lords of the land, entitled to organize the public administration and act as the court of last appeal, together with many other exemptions and privileges that are too numerous to mention. The King committed himself never to alienate the American provinces, inasmuch as he had no jurisdiction but that of sovereign domain.

Thus, for themselves and their descendants, the *conquistadores* possessed what were tantamount to feudal holdings. Yet there are explicit laws respecting employment in civil, ecclesiastical, and taxraising establishments. These laws favor, almost exclusively, the natives of the country who are of Spanish extraction. Thus, by an outright violation of the laws and the existing agreements, those born in America have been despoiled of their constitutional rights as embodied in the code.

From what I have said it is easy to deduce that America was not prepared to secede from the mother country; this secession was suddenly brought about by the effect of the illegal concessions of Bayonne and the unrighteous war which the Regency unjustly and illegally declared on us. Concerning the nature of the Spanish governments, their stringent and hostile decrees, and their long record of desperate behavior, you can find articles of real merit, by Mr. Blanco, in the newspaper *El Español*. Since this aspect of our history is there very well treated, I shall do no more than refer to it.

The Americans have risen rapidly, without previous knowledge of, and, what is more regrettable, without previous experience in public affairs, to enact upon the world stage the eminent rôles of legislator, magistrate, minister of the treasury, diplomat, general, and every position of authority, supreme or subordinate, that comprises the hierarchy of a fully organized state.

When the French invasion, stopped only by the walls of Cádiz, routed the fragile governments of the Peninsula, we were left orphans. Prior to that invasion, we had been left to the mercy of a foreign usurper. Thereafter, the justice due us was dangled before our eyes, raising hopes that only came to nought. Finally, uncertain of our destiny, and facing anarchy for want of a legitimate, just, and liberal government, we threw ourselves headlong into the chaos of revolution. Attention was first given to obtaining domestic security against enemies within our midst, and then it was extended to the procuring of external security. Authorities were set up to replace those we had deposed, empowered to direct the course of our revolution and to take full advantage of the fortunate turn of events; thus we were able to found a constitutional government worthy of our century and adequate to our situation.

The first steps of all the new governments are marked by the establishment of *juntas* of the people. These *juntas* speedily draft rules for the calling of congresses, which produce great changes. Venezuela erected a democratic and federal government, after declaring for the rights of man. A system of checks and balances was established, and general laws were passed granting civil liberties, such as freedom of the press and others. In short, an independent government was created. New Granada uniformly followed the political institutions and reforms introduced by Venezuela, taking as the fundamental basis of her constitution the most elaborate federal system ever to be brought into existence. Recently the powers of the chief executive have been increased, and he has been given all the powers that are properly his. I understand that Buenos Aires and Chile have followed this same line of procedure, but, as the distance is so great and documents are so few and the news reports so unreliable, I shall not attempt even briefly to sketch their progress.

Events in Mexico have been too varied, confused, swift, and unhappy to follow clearly the course of that revolution. We lack, moreover, the necessary documentary information to enable us to form a judgment. The Independents of Mexico, according to our information, began their insurrection in September, 1810, and a year later they erected a central government in Zitacuaro, where a national *junta* was installed under the auspices of Ferdinand VII, in whose name the government was carried on. The events of the war caused this *junta* to move from place to place; and, having undergone such modifications as events have determined, it may still be in existence.

It is reported that a generalissimo or dictator [*sic*] has been appointed and that he is the illustrious General Morelos, though others mention the celebrated General Rayón. It is certain that one or both of these two great men exercise the supreme authority in that country. And recently a constitution has been created as a framework of government. In March, 1812, the government, then residing in Zultepec, submitted a plan for peace and war to the Viceroy of Mexico that had been conceived with the utmost wisdom. It acclaimed the law of nations and established principles that are true and beyond question. The *junta* proposed that the war be fought as between brothers and countrymen; that it need not be more cruel than a war between foreign nations; that the rules of nations and of war, held inviolable even by infidels and barbarians, must be more binding upon Christians, who are, moreover, subject to one sovereign and to the same laws; that prisoners not be treated as guilty of *lèse majesté,* nor those surrendering arms slain, but rather held as hostages for exchange; and that peaceful towns not be put to fire and sword. The *junta* concluded its proposal by warning that if this plan were not accepted rigorous reprisal would be taken. This proposal was received with scorn: no reply was made to the national *junta.* The original communications were publicly burned in the plaza in Mexico City by the executioner, and the Spaniards have continued the war of extermination with their accustomed fury; meanwhile, the Mexicans and the other American nations have refrained from instituting a war to the death respecting Spanish prisoners. Here it can be seen that as a matter of expediency an appearance of allegiance to the King and even to the Constitution of the monarchy has been maintained. The national *junta,* it appears, is absolute in the exercise of the legislative, executive, and judicial powers, and its membership is very limited.

Events in Costa Firme have proved that institutions which are wholly representative are not suited to our character, customs, and present knowledge. In Caracas party spirit arose in the societies, assemblies, and popular elections; these parties led us back into slavery. Thus, while Venezuela has been the American republic with the most advanced political institutions, she has also been the clearest example of the inefficacy of the democratic and federal system for our new-born states. In New Granada, the large number of excess powers held by the provincial governments and the lack of centralization in the general government have reduced that fair country to her present state. For this reason her foes, though weak, have been able to hold out against all odds. As long as our countrymen do not acquire the abilities and political virtues that distinguish our brothers of the north, wholly popular systems, far from working to our advantage, will, I greatly fear, bring about our downfall. Unfortunately, these traits, to the degree in which they are required, do not appear to be within our reach. On the contrary, we are dominated by the vices that one learns under the rule of a nation like Spain, which has only distinguished itself in ferocity, ambition, vindictiveness, and greed.

It is harder, Montesquieu has written, to release a nation from servitude than to enslave a free nation. This truth is proven by the annals of all times, which reveal that most free nations have been put under the yoke, but very few enslaved nations have recovered their liberty. Despite the convictions of history, South Americans have made efforts to obtain liberal, even perfect, institutions, doubtless out of that instinct to aspire to the greatest possible happiness, which, common to all men, is bound to follow in civil societies founded on the principles of justice, liberty, and equality. But are we capable of maintaining in proper balance the difficult charge of a republic? Is it conceivable that a newly emancipated people can soar to the heights of liberty, and, unlike Icarus, neither have its wings melt nor fall into an abyss? Such a marvel is inconceivable and without precedent. There is no reasonable probability to bolster our hopes.

More than anyone, I desire to see America fashioned into the greatest nation in the world, greatest not so much by virtue of her area and wealth as by her freedom and glory. Although I seek perfection for the government of my country, I cannot persuade myself that the New World can, at the moment, be organized as a great republic. Since it is impossible, I dare not desire it; yet much less do I desire to have all America a monarchy because this plan is not only impracticable but also impossible. Wrongs now existing could not be righted, and our emancipation would be fruitless. The American states need the care of paternal governments to heal the sores and wounds of despotism and war. The parent country, for example, might be Mexico, the only country fitted for the position by her intrinsic strength, and without such power there can be no parent country. Let us assume it were to be the Isthmus of Panamá, the most central point of this vast continent. Would not all parts continue in their lethargy and even in their present disorder? For a single government to infuse life into the New World; to put into use all the resources for public prosperity; to improve, educate, and perfect the New World, that government would have to possess the authority of a god, much less the knowledge and virtues of mankind.

The party spirit that today keeps our states in constant agitation would assume still greater proportions were a central power established, for that power—the only force capable of checking this agitation—would be elsewhere. Furthermore, the chief figures of the capitals would not tolerate the preponderance of leaders at the metropolis, for they would regard these leaders as so many tyrants. Their resentments would attain such heights that they would compare the latter to the hated Spaniards. Any such monarchy would be a misshapen colossus that would collapse of its own weight at the slightest disturbance.

Mr. de Pradt has wisely divided America into fifteen or seventeen mutually independent states, governed by as many monarchs. I am in agreement on the first suggestion, as America can well tolerate seventeen nations; as to the second, though it could easily be achieved, it would serve no purpose. Consequently, I do not favor American monarchies. My reasons are these: The well-understood interest of a republic is limited to the matter of its preservation, prosperity, and glory. Republicans, because they do not desire powers which represent a directly contrary viewpoint, have no reason for expanding the boundaries of their nation to the detriment of their own resources, solely for the purpose of having their neighbors share a liberal constitution. They would not acquire rights or secure any advantage by conquering their neighbors, unless they were to make them colonies, conquered territory, or allies, after the example of Rome. But such thought and action are directly contrary to the principles of justice which characterize republican systems; and, what is more, they are in direct opposition to the interests of their citizens, because a state, too large of itself or together with its dependencies, ultimately falls into decay. Its free government becomes a tyranny. The principles that should preserve the government are disregarded, and finally it degenerates into despotism. The distinctive feature of small republics is permanence: that of large republics varies, but always with a tendency toward empire. Almost all small republics have had long lives. Among the larger republics, only Rome lasted for several centuries, for its capital was a republic. The rest of her dominions were governed by divers laws and institutions.

The policy of a king is very different. His constant desire is to increase his possessions, wealth, and authority; and with justification, for his power grows with every acquisition, both with respect to his neighbors and his own vassals, who fear him because his power is as formidable as his empire, which he maintains by war and conquest. For these reasons I think that the Americans, being anxious for peace, science, art, commerce, and agriculture, would prefer republics to kingdoms. And, further, it seems to me that these desires conform with the aims of Europe.

We know little about the opinions prevailing in Buenos Aires, Chile, and Perú. Judging by what seeps through and by conjecture, Buenos Aires will have a central government in which the military, as a result of its internal dissensions and external wars, will have the upper hand. Such a constitutional system will necessarily degenerate into an oligarchy or a monocracy, with a variety of restrictions the exact nature of which no one can now foresee. It would be unfortunate if this situation were to follow because the people there deserve a more glorious destiny.

The Kingdom of Chile is destined, by the nature of its location, by the simple and virtuous character of its people, and by the example of its neighbors, the proud republicans of Arauco, to enjoy the blessings that flow from the just and gentle laws of a republic. If any American republic is to have a long life, I am inclined to believe it will be Chile. There the spirit of liberty has never been extinguished; the vices of Europe and Asia arrived too late or not at all to corrupt the customs of that distant corner of the world. Its area is limited; and, as it is remote from other peoples, it will always remain free from contamination. Chile will not alter her laws, ways, and practices. She will preserve her uniform political and religious views. In a word, it is possible for Chile to be free.

Perú, on the contrary, contains two factors that clash with every just and liberal principle: gold and slaves. The former corrupts everything; the latter are themselves corrupt. The soul of a serf can seldom really appreciate true freedom. Either he loses his head in uprisings or his self-respect in chains. Although these remarks would be applicable to all America, I believe that they apply with greater justice to Lima, for the reasons I have given and because of the coöperation she has rendered her masters against her own brothers, those illustrious sons of Quito, Chile, and Buenos Aires. It is plain that he who aspires to obtain liberty will at least attempt to secure it. I imagine that in Lima the rich will not tolerate democracy, nor will the freed slaves and *pardos* accept aristocracy. The former will prefer the tyranny of a single man, to avoid the tumult of rebellion and to provide, at least, a peaceful system. If Perú intends to recover her independence, she has much to do.

From the foregoing, we can draw these conclusions: The American provinces are fighting for their freedom, and they will ultimately succeed. Some provinces as a matter of course will form federal and some central republics; the larger areas will inevitably establish monarchies, some of which will fare so badly that they will disintegrate in either present or future revolutions. To consolidate a great monarchy will be no easy task, but it will be utterly impossible to consolidate a great republic.

It is a grandiose idea to think of consolidating the New World into a single nation, united by pacts into a single bond. It is reasoned that, as these parts have a common origin, language, customs, and religion, they ought to have a single government to permit the newly formed states to unite in a confederation. But this is not possible. Actually, America is separated by climatic differences, geographic diversity, conflicting interests, and dissimilar characteristics. How beautiful it would be if the Isthmus of Panamá could be for us what the Isthmus of Corinth was for the Greeks! Would to God that some day we may have the good fortune to convene there an august assembly of representatives of republics, kingdoms, and empires to deliberate upon the high interests of peace and war with the nations of the other three-quarters of the globe. This type of organization may come to pass in some happier period of our regeneration. But any other plan, such as that of Abbé St. Pierre, who in laudable delirium conceived the idea of assembling a European congress to decide the fate and interests of those nations, would be meaningless.

Among the popular and representative systems, I do not favor the federal system. It is over-perfect, and it demands political virtues and talents far superior to our own. For the same reason I reject a monarchy that is part aristocracy and part democracy, although with such a government England has achieved much fortune and splendor. Since it is not possible for us to select the most perfect and complete form of government, let us avoid falling into demagogic anarchy or monocratic tyranny. These opposite extremes would only wreck us on similar reefs of misfortune and dishonor; hence, we must seek a mean between them. I say: Do not adopt the best system of government, but the one that is most likely to succeed.

By the nature of their geographic location, wealth, population, and character, I expect that the Mexicans, at the outset, intend to establish a representative republic in which the executive will have great powers. These will be concentrated in one person, who, if he discharges his duties with wisdom and justice, should almost certainly maintain his authority for life. If through incompetence or violence he should excite a popular revolt and it should be successful, this same executive power would then, perhaps, be distributed among the members of an assembly. If the dominant party is military or aristocratic, it will probably demand a monarchy that would be limited and constitutional at the outset, and would later inevitably degenerate into an absolute monarchy; for it must be admitted that there is nothing more difficult in the political world than the maintenance of a limited monarchy. Moreover, it must also be agreed that only a people as patriotic as the English are capable of controlling the authority of a king and of sustaining the spirit of liberty under the rule of sceptre and crown.

The states of the Isthmus of Panamá, as far as Guatemala, will perhaps form a confederation. Because of their magnificent position between two mighty oceans, they may in time become the emporium of the world. Their canals will shorten distances throughout the world, strengthen commercial ties between Europe, America, and Asia, and bring to that happy area tribute from the four quarters of the globe. There some day, perhaps, the capital of the world may be located—reminiscent of the Emperor Constantine's claim that Byzantium was the capital of the ancient world.

New Granada will unite with Venezuela, if they can agree to the establishment of a central republic. Their capital may be Maracaibo or a new city to be named Las Casas (in honor of that humane hero) to be built on the borders of the two countries, in the excellent port area Bahía-Honda. This location, though little known, is the most advantageous in all respects. It is readily accessible, and its situation is so strategic that it can be made impregnable. It has a fine, healthful climate, a soil as suitable for agriculture as for cattle raising, and a superabundance of good timber. The Indians living there can be civilized, and our territorial possessions could be increased with the acquisition of the Goajira Peninsula. This nation should be called Colombia as a just and grateful tribute to the discoverer of our hemisphere. Its government might follow the English pattern, except that in place of a king there will be an executive who will be elected, at most, for life, but his office will never be hereditary, if a republic is desired. There will be a hereditary legislative chamber or senate. This body can interpose itself between the violent demands of the people and the great powers of the government during periods of political unrest. The second representative body will be a legislature with restrictions no greater than those of the lower house in England. The Constitution will draw on all systems of government, but I do not want it to partake of all their vices. As Colombia is my country, I have an indisputable right to desire for her that form of government which, in my opinion, is best. It is very possible that New Granada may not care to recognize a central government, because she is greatly addicted to federalism; in such event, she will form a separate state which, if it endures, may prosper, because of its great and varied resources.

"Great and beneficial changes," you say, "can frequently be brought about through the efforts of individuals." The South Americans have a tradition to this effect: When Quetzalcoatl, the Hermes or Buddha of South America, gave up his ministry and left his people, he promised them he would return at an ordained time to reëstablish his government and revive their prosperity. Does not this tradition foster a conviction that he may shortly reappear? Can you imagine the result if an individual were to appear among these people, bearing the features of Quetzalcoatl, their Buddha of the forest, or those of Mercury, of whom other nations have spoken? Do you suppose that this would affect all regions of America? Is it not unity alone that is needed to enable them to expel the Spaniards, their troops, and the supporters of corrupt Spain and to establish in these regions a powerful empire with a free government and benevolent laws?

Like you, I believe that the specific actions of individuals can produce general results, especially in revolutions. But is that hero, that great prophet or God of Anáhuac, Quetzalcoatl, capable of effecting the prodigious changes that you propose? This esteemed figure is not well known, if at all, by the Mexican people: such is the fate of the defeated, even if they be gods. Historians and writers, it is true, have undertaken a careful investigation of his origin, the truth or falsity of his doctrine, his prophesies, and the account of his departure from Mexico. Whether he was an apostle of Christ or a pagan is openly debated. Some would associate his name with St. Thomas; others, with the Feathered Serpent; while still others say he is the famous prophet of Yucatán, Chilan-Cambal. In a word, most Mexican authors, polemicists, and secular historians have discussed, at greater or lesser length, the question of the true character of Quetzalcoatl. The fact is, according to the historian, Father Acosta, that he established a religion which, in its rites, dogmas, and mysteries, bore a remarkable similarity to the religion of Jesus, the faith that it probably most resembles. Nevertheless, many Catholic writers have tried to dismiss the idea that he was a true prophet, and they refuse to associate him with St. Thomas, as other celebrated writers have done. The general opinion is that Quetzalcoatl was a divine law-giver among the pagan peoples of Anáhuac; that their great Montezuma was his lieutenant, deriving his power from that divinity. Hence it may be inferred that our Mexicans would not follow the pagan Quetzalcoatl, however ingratiating the guise in which he might appear, for they profess the most intolerant and exclusive of all religions.

Happily, the leaders of the Mexican independence movement have made use of this fanaticism to excellent purpose by proclaiming the famous Virgin of Guadalupe the Queen of the Patriots, invoking her name in all difficult situations and placing her image on their banners. As a result, political enthusiasms have been commingled with religion, thus producing an intense devotion to the sacred cause of liberty. The veneration of this image in Mexico is greater than the exaltation that the most sagacious prophet could inspire.

Surely unity is what we need to complete our work of regeneration. The division among us, nevertheless, is nothing extraordinary, for it is characteristic of civil wars to form two parties, *conservatives* and *reformers*. The former are commonly the more numerous, because the weight of habit induces obedience to established powers; the latter are always fewer in number although more vocal and learned. Thus, the physical mass of the one is counterbalanced by the moral force of the other; the contest is prolonged, and the results are uncertain. Fortunately, in our case, the mass has followed the learned.

I shall tell you with what we must provide ourselves in order to expel the Spaniards and to found a free government. It is *union,* obviously; but such union will come about through sensible planning and well-directed actions rather than by divine magic. America stands together because it is abandoned by all other nations. It is isolated in the center of the world. It has no diplomatic relations, nor does it receive any military assistance; instead, America is attacked by Spain, which has more military supplies than any we can possibly acquire through furtive means.

When success is not assured, when the state is weak, and when results are distantly seen, all men hesitate; opinion is divided, passions rage, and the enemy fans these passions in order to win an easy victory because of them. As soon as we are strong and under the guidance of a liberal nation which will lend us her protection, we will achieve accord in cultivating the virtues and talents that lead to glory. Then will we march majestically toward that great prosperity for which South America is destined. Then will those sciences and arts which, born in the East, have enlightened Europe, wing their way to a free Colombia, which will cordially bid them welcome.

Such, Sir, are the thoughts and observations that I have the honor to submit to you, so that you may accept or reject them according to their merit. I beg you to understand that I have expounded them because I do not wish to appear discourteous and not because I consider myself competent to enlighten you concerning these matters.

I am, Sir, etc., etc.

SIMÓN BOLÍVAR

The Angostura Address*

Though independence was only half won in 1819, Bolívar called a Congress to meet at Angostura, in the heart of the llanos, to begin the administration of the phoenix Venezuelan Republic and to unite it to the provinces of New Granada. This keynote address, which opened that Congress, is the first developed statement of Bolívar's political thought. It reveals a strong classical and French influence, an admiration for British institutions, and a deeply-rooted suspicion of the United States example. Popular election of the legislature was Bolívar's tribute to democracy. The strong executive, hereditary Senate, and Chamber of Censors to modulate the general will were his adaptations to assure permanence and stability. The delegates elected Bolívar President, with a four-year term; approved his anti-federalist principles; and rejected his hereditary Senate in favor of a life-term one. Bolívar had cast a mold for a conservative republic.

Angostura, February 15, 1819.

Gentlemen:

Fortunate is the citizen, who, under the emblem of his command, has convoked this assembly of the national sovereignty so that it may exercise its absolute will! I, therefore, place myself among those most favored by Divine Providence, for I have had the honor of uniting the representatives of the people of Venezuela in this august Congress, the source of legitimate authority, the custodian of the sovereign will, and the arbiter of the Nation's destiny.

In returning to the representatives of the people the Supreme Power which was entrusted to me, I gratify not only my own innermost desires but also those of my fellow-citizens and of future generations, who trust to your wisdom, rectitude, and prudence in all things. Upon the fulfillment of this grateful ob-

---

* Simón Bolívar, *Selected Writings of Bolívar,* 2 vols., compiled by Vicente Lecuna, ed. Harold A. Bierck, Jr., translated by Lewis Bertrand, published by Banco de Venezuela (New York, 1951), I, 173-197. Reprinted with the permission of Banco de Venezuela. Footnotes in original not included.

ligation, I shall be released from the immense authority with which I have been burdened and from the unlimited responsibility which has weighed so heavily upon my slender resources. Only the force of necessity, coupled with the imperious will of the people, compelled me to assume the fearful and dangerous post of *Dictator and Supreme Chief of the Republic.* But now I can breathe more freely, for I am returning to you this authority which I have succeeded in maintaining at the price of so much danger, hardship, and suffering, amidst the worst tribulations suffered by any society.

The period in the history of the Republic over which I presided was not one of mere political storm; nor was it simply a bloody war or merely popular anarchy. It was, indeed, the culmination of every disruptive force. It was the flood-tide of a devastating torrent which overran the good earth of Venezuela. What barriers could one man—a man such as myself—erect to stay the onrush of such devastation? In the midst of that sea of troubles, I was but a mere plaything in the hurricane of revolution that tossed me about like so much straw. I could do neither good nor evil. Irresistible forces directed the course of our events. To attribute these forces to me would not be just, for it would place upon me an importance that I do not merit. Do you wish to know who is responsible for the events of the past and the present? Consult the annals of Spain, of America, and of Venezuela; examine the Laws of the Indies, the one-time system of *mandatarios,* the influence of religion and of foreign rule; observe the first acts of the republican government, the ferocity of our enemies, and our national character. Do not question me about the effects of these ever-to-be-lamented catastrophes; for I am but a simple instrument of the great driving forces that have left their mark on Venezuela. Nevertheless, my life, my conduct, my every public and private action—all are subject to public censure. Representatives! You must judge my actions. I submit the record of my rule for your impartial verdict: I shall add nothing in its favor, for I have already said all that can be said in my behalf. If I obtain your approbation, I shall have achieved the sublime title of Good Citizen, which I prefer to that of *Liberator* given me by Venezuela, or that of *Pacificator* accorded me by Cundinamarca, or to any title the world at large might confer upon me.

Legislators! I deliver into your hands the supreme rule of Venezuela. Yours is now the august duty of consecrating yourselves
to the achievement of felicity of the Republic; your hands hold
the scales of our destiny, the measure of our glory. They shall
seal the decrees that will insure our liberty. At this moment the
Supreme Chief of the Republic is no more than just a plain
citizen, and such he wishes to remain until his death. I shall,
however, serve as a soldier so long as any foe remains in Venezuela. Our country has a multitude of worthy sons who are
capable of directing her progress. Talent, virtue, experience, and
all else needed to command free men are the heritage of many
who represent the people here; and outside this Sovereign Body
there are citizens who at all times have shown courage in facing
danger, prudence in avoiding it, and the ability, moreover, to
govern themselves and others. These illustrious men will undoubtedly deserve the support of the Congress, and they will be
entrusted with the government which I now so sincerely and
gladly relinquish forever.

The continuance of authority in the same individual has frequently meant the end of democratic governments. Repeated
elections are essential in popular systems of government, for
nothing is more perilous than to permit one citizen to retain
power for an extended period. The people become accustomed
to obeying him, and he forms the habit of commanding them;
herein lie the origins of usurpation and tyranny. A just zeal is
the guarantee of republican liberty. Our citizens must with good
reason learn to fear lest the magistrate who has governed them
long will govern them forever.

Since, therefore, by this profession of mine in support of Venezuela's freedom I may aspire to the glory of being reckoned
among her most faithful sons, allow me, Gentlemen, to expound,
with the frankness of a true republican, my respectful opinion
on a *Plan of a Constitution,* which I take the liberty of submitting to you as testimony of the candor and sincerity of my
sentiments. As this plan concerns the welfare of all, I venture to
assume that I have the right to be heard by the representatives
of the people. I well know that your wisdom needs no counsel,
and I know also that my plan may perhaps appear to be mis-
taken and impracticable. But I implore you, Gentlemen, receive
this work with benevolence, for it is more a tribute of my sincere

deference to the Congress than an act of presumption. Moreover, as your function is to create a body politic, or, it might be said, to create an entire society while surrounded by every obstacle that a most peculiar and difficult situation can present, perhaps the voice of one citizen may reveal the presence of a hidden or unknown danger.

Let us review the past to discover the base upon which the Republic of Venezuela is founded.

America, in separating from the Spanish monarchy, found herself in a situation similar to that of the Roman Empire when its enormous framework fell to pieces in the midst of the ancient world. Each Roman division then formed an independent nation in keeping with its location or interests; but this situation differed from America's in that those members proceeded to reëstablish their former associations. We, on the contrary, do not even retain the vestiges of our original being. We are not Europeans; we are not Indians; we are but a mixed species of aborigines and Spaniards. Americans by birth and Europeans by law, we find ourselves engaged in a dual conflict: we are disputing with the natives for titles of ownership, and at the same time we are struggling to maintain ourselves in the country that gave us birth against the opposition of the invaders. Thus our position is most extraordinary and complicated. But there is more. As our rôle has always been strictly passive and our political existence nil, we find that our quest for liberty is now even more difficult of accomplishment; for we, having been placed in a state lower than slavery, had been robbed not only of our freedom but also of the right to exercise an active domestic tyranny. Permit me to explain this paradox.

In absolute systems, the central power is unlimited. The will of the despot is the supreme law, arbitrarily enforced by subordinates who take part in the organized oppression in proportion to the authority that they wield. They are charged with civil, political, military, and religious functions; but, in the final analysis, the satraps of Persia are Persian, the pashas of the Grand Turk are Turks, and the sultans of Tartary are Tartars. China does not seek her mandarins in the homeland of Genghis Khan, her conqueror. America, on the contrary, received everything from Spain, who, in effect, deprived her of the experience that she would have gained from the exercise of an active tyr-

anny by not allowing her to take part in her own domestic
affairs and administration. This exclusion made it impossible
for us to acquaint ourselves with the management of public
affairs; nor did we enjoy that personal consideration, of such
great value in major revolutions, that the brilliance of power
inspires in the eyes of the multitude. In brief, Gentlemen, we
were deliberately kept in ignorance and cut off from the world
in all matters relating to the science of government.

Subject to the threefold yoke of ignorance, tyranny, and vice,
the American people have been unable to acquire knowledge,
power, or [civic] virtue. The lessons we received and the models
we studied, as pupils of such pernicious teachers, were most
destructive. We have been ruled more by deceit than by force,
and we have been degraded more by vice than by superstition.
Slavery is the daughter of Darkness: an ignorant people is a
blind instrument of its own destruction. Ambition and intrigue
abuse the credulity and experience of men lacking all political,
economic, and civic knowledge; they adopt pure illusion as reality; they take license for liberty, treachery for patriotism, and
vengeance for justice. This situation is similar to that of the robust
blind man who, beguiled by his strength, strides forward with
all the assurance of one who can see, but, upon hitting every
variety of obstacle, finds himself unable to retrace his steps.

If a people, perverted by their training, succeed in achieving
their liberty, they will soon lose it, for it would be of no avail
to endeavor to explain to them that happiness consists in the
practice of virtue; that the rule of law is more powerful than
the rule of tyrants, because, as the laws are more inflexible,
everyone should submit to their beneficent austerity; that proper
morals, and not force, are the bases of law; and that to practice
justice is to practice liberty. Therefore, Legislators, your work is
so much the more arduous, inasmuch as you have to reëducate
men who have been corrupted by erroneous illusions and false
incentives. Liberty, says Rousseau, is a succulent morsel, but one
difficult to digest. Our weak fellow-citizens will have to strengthen
their spirit greatly before they can digest the wholesome nutriment
of freedom. Their limbs benumbed by chains, their sight dimmed
by the darkness of dungeons, and their strength sapped by the
pestilence of servitude, are they capable of marching toward the
august temple of Liberty without faltering? Can they come near

enough to bask in its brilliant rays and to breathe freely the pure air which reigns therein?

Legislators, meditate well before you choose. Forget not that you are to lay the political foundation for a newly born nation which can rise to the heights of greatness that Nature has marked out for it if you but proportion this foundation in keeping with the high plane that it aspires to attain. Unless your choice is based upon the peculiar tutelary experience of the Venezuelan people—a factor that should guide you in determining the nature and form of government you are about to adopt for the well-being of the people—and, I repeat, unless you happen upon the right type of government, the result of our reforms will again be slavery.

The history of bygone ages affords you examples of thousands of governments. Visualize the nations that have shone in brightest splendor and you will be grieved to see that virtually all the world has been, and still is, the victim of its governments. You will note numerous systems of governing men, but always their purpose has been to oppress them. If our habit of looking upon the human species as being led by its own shepherds did not diminish the horror of so distressing a spectacle, we should be stunned to see our docile species grazing upon the surface of the earth, like meek flocks destined to feed their cruel keepers. Nature, in truth, endows us at birth with the instinctive desire for freedom; but, be it laziness or some tendency inherent in humanity, it is obvious that mankind rests unconcerned and accepts things as they are, even though it is bound forcibly in fetters. As we contemplate humanity in this state of prostitution, it would appear that we have every right to persuade ourselves that most men hold this humiliating maxim to be the truth: It is harder to maintain the balance of liberty than to endure the weight of tyranny. Would that this maxim, which goes counter to the morality of Nature, were false. Would that this axiom were not sanctioned by man's lack of concern respecting his most sacred rights!

Many ancient and modern nations have shaken off oppression; yet those who have enjoyed even a few precious moments of liberty are rare, as they have speedily returned to their old political vices; because peoples rather than governments repeatedly drag tyranny in their train. The habit of being ruled makes them insensible to the attractions of honor and national prosperity, and they regard with indifference the glory of living in the free sway of liberty, under the protection of laws dictated by their own free will. The records of the universe proclaim this awful truth.

Only democracy, in my opinion, is amenable to absolute liberty. But what democratic government has simultaneously enjoyed power, prosperity, and permanence? On the other hand, have not aristocracy and monarchy held great and powerful empires together century after century? Is there any government older than that of China? What republic has lasted longer than Sparta or Venice? Did not the Roman Empire conquer the earth? Has not France had fourteen centuries of monarchy? Is there any nation greater than England? Yet these nations have been or still are aristocracies and monarchies.

Despite these bitter reflections, I experience a surge of joy when I witness the great advances that our Republic has made since it began its noble career. Loving what is most useful, animated by what is most just, and aspiring to what is most perfect, Venezuela, on breaking away from Spain, has recovered her independence, her freedom, her equality, and her national sovereignty. By establishing a democratic republic, she has proscribed monarchy, distinctions, nobility, prerogatives, and privileges. She has declared for the rights of man and freedom of action, thought, speech, and press. These eminently liberal acts, because of the sincerity that has inspired them, will never cease to be admired. The first Congress of Venezuela has indelibly stamped upon the annals of our laws the majesty of the people, and, in placing its seal upon the social document best calculated to develop the well-being of the nation, that Congress has fittingly given expression to this thought.

I am forced to gather all my strength and to exert every effort of which I am capable in order to perceive the supreme good embodied in this immortal Code of our rights and laws. But how can I venture to say it! Shall I dare, by my criticism, to profane the sacred tablets of our laws . . . [*sic*]? There are some feelings that a true patriot cannot retain in his heart. They overflow, forced out by their own violence, and in spite of one's efforts to restrain them an inner force will make them known. I am thoroughly imbued with the idea that the government of Venezuela should be reformed; and, although many prominent citizens think as I do, not all of them possess the courage necessary to recommend publicly the adoption of new principles. This consideration obliges me to take the initiative in a matter of the greatest importance—a matter in which the utmost audacity is required—the offering of advice to the councilors of the people.

The more I admire the excellence of the federal Constitution of Venezuela, the more I am convinced of the impossibility of its application to our state. And, to my way of thinking, it is a marvel that its prototype in North America endures so successfully and has not been overthrown at the first sign of adversity or danger. Although the people of North America are a singular model of political virtue and moral rectitude; although that nation was cradled in liberty, reared on freedom, and maintained by liberty alone; and—I must reveal everything—although those people, so lacking in many respects, are unique in the history of mankind, it is a marvel, I repeat, that so weak and complicated a government as the federal system has managed to govern them in the difficult and trying circumstances of their past. But, regardless of the effectiveness of this form of government with respect to North America, I must say that it has never for a moment entered my mind to compare the position and character of two states as dissimilar as the English-American and the Spanish-American. Would it not be most difficult to apply to Spain the English system of political, civil, and religious liberty? Hence, it would be even more difficult to adapt to Venezuela the laws of North America. Does not *L'Esprit des lois* state that laws should be suited to the people for whom they are made; that it would be a major coincidence if those of one nation could be adapted to another; that laws must take into account the physical conditions of the country, climate, character of the land, location, size, and mode of living of the people; that they should be in keeping with the degree of liberty that the Constitution can sanction respecting the religion of the inhabitants, their inclinations, resources, number, commerce, habits, and customs? This is the code we must consult, not the code of Washington!

The Venezuelan Constitution, although based upon the most perfect of constitutions from the standpoint of the correctness of its principles and the beneficent effects of its administration, differed fundamentally from the North American Constitution on one cardinal point, and, without doubt, the most important point. The Congress of Venezuela, like the North American legislative body, participates in some of the duties vested in the executive power. We, however, have subdivided the executive power by vesting it in a collective body. Consequently, this executive body has been subject to the disadvantages resulting from the periodic existence of a government which is suspended and dissolved whenever its members adjourn. Our executive triumvirate lacks, so to speak, unity, continuity, and individual responsibility. It is deprived of prompt action, continuous existence, true uniformity, and direct responsibility. The government that does not possess these things which give it a morality of its own must be deemed a nonentity.

Although the powers of the President of the United States are limited by numerous restrictions, he alone exercises all the governmental functions which the Constitution has delegated to him; thus there is no doubt but that his administration must be more uniform, constant, and more truly his own than an administration wherein the power is divided among a number of persons, a grouping that is nothing less than a monstrosity. The judicial power in Venezuela is similar to that of North America: its duration is not defined; it is temporary and not for life; and it enjoys all the independence proper to the judiciary.

The first Congress, in its federal Constitution, responded more to the spirit of the provinces than to the sound idea of creating an indivisible and centralized republic. In this instance, our legislators yielded to the ill-considered pleadings of those men from the provinces who were captivated by the apparent brilliance of the happiness of the North American people, believing that the blessings they enjoy result exclusively from their form of government rather than from the character and customs of the citizens. In effect, the United States' example, because of their remarkable prosperity, was one too tempting not to be followed. Who could resist the powerful attraction of full and absolute enjoyment of sovereignty, independence, and freedom? Who could resist the devotion inspired by an intelligent government that has not only blended public and private rights but has also based its supreme law respecting the desires of the individual upon common consent? Who could resist the rule of a beneficent government which, with a skilled, dextrous, and powerful hand always and in all regions, directs its resources toward social perfection, the sole aim of human institutions?

But no matter how tempting this magnificent federative system might have appeared, and regardless of its possible effect, the Venezuelans were not prepared to enjoy it immediately upon casting off their chains. We were not prepared for such good, for good, like evil, results in death when it is sudden and excessive. Our moral fibre did not then possess the stability necessary to derive benefits from a wholly representative government; a government so sublime, in fact, that it might more nearly befit a republic of saints.

Representatives of the People! You are called upon to confirm or to suppress whatever may appear to you worthy of preservation, modification, or rejection in our social compact. The task of correcting the work of our first legislators is yours. I should like to say that it is your duty to cloak some of the charms that are displayed in our political code; for not every heart is capable of admiring all beauty, nor are all eyes able to gaze upon the heavenly light of perfection. The Book of the Apostles, the teachings of Jesus contained in that divine work, so sublime and so sacred, that Providence has sent us for the betterment of mankind, is now a rain of fire in Constantinople; indeed, Asia would burst into fiery flames if this Book of Peace were suddenly imposed upon her as a code of religion, law, and customs.

Permit me to call the attention of the Congress to a matter that may be of vital importance. We must keep in mind that our people are neither European nor North American; rather, they are a mixture of African and the Americans who originated in Europe. Even Spain herself has ceased to be European because of her African blood, her institutions, and her character. It is impossible to determine with any degree of accuracy where we belong in the human family. The greater portion of the native Indians has been annihilated; Spaniards have mixed with Americans and Africans, and Africans with Indians and Spaniards. While we have all been born of the same mother, our fathers, different in origin and in blood, are foreigners, and all differ visibly as to the color of their skin: a dissimilarity which places upon us an obligation of the greatest importance.

Under the Constitution, which interprets the laws of Nature, all citizens of Venezuela enjoy complete political equality. Al-

though equality may not have been the political dogma of
Athens, France, or North America, we must consecrate it here
in order to correct the disparity that apparently exists. My
opinion, Legislators, is that the fundamental basis of our political system hinges directly and exclusively upon the establishment
and practice of equality in Venezuela. Most wise men concede
that men are born with equal rights to share the benefits of
society, but it does not follow that all men are born equally gifted
to attain every rank. All men should practice virtue, but not all
do; all ought to be courageous, but not all are; all should possess talents, but not everyone does. Herein are the real distinctions which can be observed among individuals even in the most
liberally constituted society. If the principle of political equality
is generally recognized, so also must be the principle of physical
and moral inequality. Nature makes men unequal in intelligence,
temperament, strength, and character. Laws correct this disparity
by so placing the individual within society that education, industry, arts, services, and virtues give him a fictitious equality
that is properly termed political and social. The idea of a
classless state, wherein diversity increases in proportion to the
rise in population, was an eminently beneficial inspiration. By
this step alone, cruel discord has been completely eliminated.
How much jealousy, rivalry, and hate have thus been averted!

Having dealt with justice and humanity, let us now give attention to politics and society, and let us resolve the difficulties
inherent in a system so simple and natural, yet so weak that the
slightest obstacle can upset and destroy it. The diversity of
racial origin will require an infinitely firm hand and great tact-
fulness in order to manage this heterogeneous society, whose
complicated mechanism is easily damaged, separated, and disintegrated by the slightest controversy.

The most perfect system of government is that which results
in the greatest possible measure of happiness and the maximum
of social security [seguridad social] and political stability. The
laws enacted by the first Congress gave us reason to hope that
happiness would be the lot of Venezuela; and, through your laws,
we must hope that security and stability will perpetuate this happiness. You must solve the problem. But how, having broken all
the shackles of our former oppression, can we accomplish the
enormous task of preventing the remnants of our past fetters

from becoming liberty-destroying weapons? The vestiges of Spanish domination will long be with us before we can completely eradicate them: the contagion of despotism infests the atmosphere about us, and neither the fires of war nor the healing properties of our salutary laws have purified the air we breathe. Our hands are now free, but our hearts still suffer the ills of slavery. When man loses freedom, said Homer, he loses half his spirit.

Venezuela had, has, and should have a republican government. Its principles should be the sovereignty of the people, division of powers, civil liberty, proscription of slavery, and the abolition of monarchy and privileges. We need equality to recast, so to speak, into a unified nation, the classes of men, political opinions, and public customs. Let us now consider the vast field of problems yet to be traversed. Let us focus our attention upon the dangers we must avoid. Let history serve us as a guide in this survey. First, Athens affords us the most brilliant example of an absolute democracy, but at the same time Athens herself is the most melancholy example of the extreme weakness of this type of government. The wisest legislator in Greece did not see his republic survive ten years; and he suffered the humiliation of admitting that absolute democracy is inadequate in governing any form of society, even the most cultured, temperate, and limited, because its brilliance comes only in lightning flashes of liberty. We must recognize, therefore, that, although Solon disillusioned the world, he demonstrated to society how difficult it is to govern men by laws alone.

The Republic of Sparta, which might appear to be but a chimerical invention, produced more tangible results than all the ingenious labors of Solon. Glory, virtue, morality, and consequently, national felicity, were the results of Lycurgus' legislation. Although two kings in one state meant two monsters to devour it, Sparta had little to regret because of its dual throne; whereas Athens promised itself a most brilliant future replete with absolute sovereignty, free and frequent election of magistrates, and moderate, wise, and politic laws. Pisistratus, the usurper and tyrant, accomplished more for Athens than did her laws; and Pericles, although also an usurper, was her most useful citizen. The Republic of Thebes existed only during the lifetimes of Pelopidas and Epaminondas; because there are times when men, not principles, constitute governments. Codes, systems, statutes, wise as they may be, are useless works having but small influence on societies: virtuous men, patriotic men, learned men make republics.

The Roman Constitution brought power and fortune such as no other people in the world have ever known. It did not provide for an exact distribution of powers. The consuls, senate, and people were alternately legislators, magistrates, and judges; everyone participated in all powers. The executive, comprising two consuls, was subject to the same weakness as was that of Sparta. Despite this weakness, the Republic did not experience the disastrous discord that would appear to have been unavoidable in a magistrature composed of two individuals with equal authority, each possessing the powers of a monarch. A government whose sole purpose was conquest would hardly seem destined to insure the happiness of a nation; but an enormous and strictly warlike government lifted Rome to the highest splendor of virtue and glory, and made of this earth a Roman dominion, thereby demonstrating to man what political virtues can accomplish and the relative unimportance of institutions.

Passing from ancient to modern times, we find England and France attracting the attention of all nations and affording them a variety of lessons in matters of government. The evolution [*revolución*] of these two great peoples, like a flaming meteor, has flooded the world with such a profusion of political enlightenment that today every thinking person is aware of the rights and duties of man and the nature of the virtues and vices of governments. All can now appreciate the intrinsic merit of the speculative theories of modern philosophers and legislators. In fact, this political star, in its illuminating career, has even fired the hearts of the apathetic Spaniards, who, having also been thrown into the political whirlpool, made ephemeral efforts to establish liberty; but, recognizing their incapacity for living under the sweet rule of law, they have returned to their immemorial practices of imprisonment and burnings at the stake.

Here, Legislators, is the place to repeat what the eloquent Volney says in the preface of his *Ruins of Palmyra*: "To the newborn peoples of the Spanish Indies, to the generous leaders who guide them toward freedom: may the mistakes and misfortures of the Old World teach wisdom and happiness to the New." May the teachings of experience be not lost; and may the schools of Greece, Rome, France, England, and North America instruct us in the difficult science of creating and preserving nations through laws that are proper, just, legitimate, and, above all, useful. We must never forget that the excellence of a government lies not in its theories, not in its form or mechanism, but in its being suited to the nature and character of the nation for which it is instituted.

Among the ancient and modern nations, Rome and Great Britain are the most outstanding. Both were born to govern and to be free and both were built not on ostentatious forms of freedom, but upon solid institutions. Thus I recommend to you, Representatives, the study of the British Constitution, for that body of laws appears destined to bring about the greatest possible good for the peoples that adopt it; but, however perfect it may be, I am by no means proposing that you imitate it slavishly. When I speak of the British government, I only refer to its republican features; and, indeed, can a political system be labelled a monarchy when it recognizes popular sovereignty, division and balance of powers, civil liberty, freedom of conscience and of press, and all that is politically sublime? Can there be more liberty in any other type of republic? Can more be asked of any society? I commend this Constitution to you as that most worthy of serving as model for those who aspire to the enjoyment of the rights of man and who seek all the political happiness which is compatible with the frailty of human nature.

Nothing in our fundamental laws would have to be altered were we to adopt a legislative power similar to that held by the British Parliament. Like the North Americans, we have divided national representation into two chambers: that of Representatives and the Senate. The first is very wisely constituted. It enjoys all its proper functions, and it requires no essential revision, because the Constitution, in creating it, gave it the form and powers which the people deemed necessary in order that they might be legally and properly represented. If the Senate were hereditary rather than elective, it would, in my opinion, be the basis, the tie, the very soul of our republic. In political storms this body would arrest the thunderbolts of the government and would repel any violent popular reaction. Devoted to the government because of a natural interest in its own preservation, a hereditary senate would always oppose any attempt on the part of the people to infringe upon the jurisdiction and authority of their magistrates. It must be confessed that most men are unaware of their best interests and that they constantly endeavor to assail them in the hands of their custodians—the individual clashes with the mass, and the mass with authority. It is necessary, therefore, that in all governments there be a neutral body to protect the injured and disarm the offender. To be neutral, this body must not owe its origin to appointment by the government or to election by the people, if it is to enjoy a full measure of independence which neither fears nor expects anything from these two sources of authority. The hereditary senate, as a part of the people, shares its interests, its sentiments, and its spirit. For this reason it should not be presumed that a hereditary senate would ignore the interests of the people or forget its legislative duties. The senators in Rome and in the House of Lords in London have been the strongest pillars upon which the edifice of political and civil liberty has rested.

At the outset, these senators should be elected by Congress. The successors to this Senate must command the initial attention of the government, which should educate them in a *colegio* designed especially to train these guardians and future legislators of the nation. They ought to learn the arts, sciences, and letters that enrich the mind of a public figure. From childhood they should understand the career for which they have been destined by Providence, and from earliest youth they should prepare their minds for the dignity that awaits them.

The creation of a hereditary senate would in no way be a violation of political equality. I do not solicit the establishment of a nobility, for, as a celebrated republican has said, that would simultaneously destroy equality and liberty. What I propose is an office for which the candidates must prepare themselves, an office that demands great knowledge and the ability to acquire such knowledge. All should not be left to chance and the outcome of elections. The people are more easily deceived than is Nature perfected by art; and, although these senators, it is true, would not be bred in an environment that is all virtue, it is equally true that they would be raised in an atmosphere of enlightened education. Furthermore, the liberators of Venezuela are entitled to occupy forever a high rank in the Republic that they have brought into existence. I believe that posterity would view with regret the effacement of the illustrious names of its first benefactors. I say, moreover, that it is a matter of public interest and national honor, of gratitude on Venezuela's part, to honor gloriously, until the end of time, a race of virtuous, prudent, and persevering men who, overcoming every obstacle, have founded the Republic at the price of the most heroic sacrifices. And if the people of Venezuela do not applaud the elevation of their benefactors, then they are unworthy to be free, and they will never be free.

A hereditary senate, I repeat, will be the fundamental basis of the legislative power, and therefore the foundation of the entire government. It will also serve as a counterweight to both government and people; and as a neutral power it will weaken the mutual attacks of these two eternally rival powers. In all conflicts the calm reasoning of a third party will serve as the means of reconciliation. Thus the Venezuelan senate will give strength of this delicate political structure, so sensitive to violent repercussions; it will be the mediator that will lull the storms and it will maintain harmony between the head and the other parts of this political body.

No inducement could corrupt a legislative body invested with the highest honors, dependent only upon itself, having no fear of the people, independent of the government, and dedicated solely to the repression of all evil principles and to the advancement of very good principle—a legislative body that would be deeply concerned with the maintenance of a society, for it would share the consequences, be they honorable or disastrous. It has rightly been said that the upper house in England is invaluable to that nation because it provides a bulwark of liberty; and I would add that the Senate of Venezuela would be not only a bulwark of liberty but a bastion of defense, rendering the Republic eternal.

The British executive power possesses all the authority properly appertaining to a sovereign, but he is surrounded by a triple line of dams, barriers, and stockades. He is the head of the government, but his ministers and subordinates rely more upon law than upon his authority, as they are personally responsible; and not even decrees of royal authority can exempt them from this

responsibility. The executive is commander in chief of the army
and navy; he makes peace and declares war; but Parliament annually determines what sums are to be paid to these military
forces. While the courts and judges are dependent on the executive power, the laws originate in and are made by Parliament.
To neutralize the power of the King, his person is declared inviolable and sacred; but, while his head is left untouched, his
hands are tied. The sovereign of England has three formidable
rivals: his Cabinet, which is responsible to the people and to
Parliament; the Senate [*sic*], which, representing the nobility
of which it is composed, defends the interests of the people; and
the House of Commons, which serves as the representative body
of the British people and provides them with a place in which
to express their opinions. Moreover, as the judges are responsible
for the enforcement of the laws, they do not depart from them;
and the administrators of the exchequer, being subject to prose-
cution not only for personal infractions but also for those of
the government, take care to prevent any misuse of public funds.
No matter how closely we study the composition of the English
executive power, we can find nothing to prevent its being judged
as the most perfect model for a kingdom, for an aristocracy, or
for a democracy. Give Venezuela such an executive power in
the person of a president chosen by the people or their representatives, and you will have taken a great step toward national
happiness.

No matter what citizen occupies this office, he will be aided
by the Constitution, and therein being authorized to do good, he
can do no harm, because his ministers will coöperate with him
only insofar as he abides by the law. If he attempts to infringe
upon the law, his own ministers will desert him, thereby isolating
him from the Republic, and they will even bring charges against
him in the Senate. The ministers, being responsible for any
transgressions committed, will actually govern, since they must
account for their actions. The obligation which this system places
upon the officials closest to the executive power, that is, to take
a most interested and active part in governmental deliberations
and to regard this department as their own, is not the smallest
advantage of the system. Should the president be a man of no
great talent or virtue, yet, notwithstanding his lack of these
essential qualities, he will be able to discharge his duties satis-

factorily, for in such a case the ministry, managing everything by itself, will carry the burdens of the state.

Although the authority of the executive power in England may appear to be extreme, it would, perhaps, not be excessive in the Republic of Venezuela. Here the Congress has tied the hands and even the heads of its men of state. This deliberative assembly has assumed a part of the executive function, contrary to the maxim of Montesquieu, to wit: A representative assembly should exercise no active function. It should only make laws and determine whether or not those laws are enforced. Nothing is as disturbing to harmony among the powers of government as their intermixture. Nothing is more dangerous with respect to the people than a weak executive; and if a kingdom has deemed it necessary to grant the executive so many powers, then in a republic these powers are infinitely more indispensable.

If we examine this difference, we will find that the balance of power between the branches of government must be distributed in two ways. In republics the executive should be the stronger, for everything conspires against it; while in monarchies the legislative power should be superior, as everything works in the monarch's favor. The people's veneration of royal power results in a self-fascination that tends greatly to increase the superstitious respect paid to such authority. The splendor inherent in the throne, the crown, and the purple; the formidable support that it receives from the nobility; the immense wealth that a dynasty accumulates from generation to generation; and the fraternal protection that kings grant to one another are the significant advantages that work in favor of royal authority, thereby rendering it almost unlimited. Consequently, the significance of these same advantages should serve to justify the necessity of investing the chief magistrate of a republic with a greater measure of authority than that possessed by a constitutional prince.

A republican magistrate is an individual set apart from society, charged with checking the impulse of the people toward license and the propensity of judges and administrators toward abuse of the laws. He is directly subject to the legislative body, the senate, and the people: he is the one man who resists the combined pressure of the opinions, interests, and passions of the social state and who, as Carnot states, does little more than struggle constantly with the urge to dominate and the desire to escape domination. He is, in brief, an athlete pitted against a multitude of athletes.

This weakness can only be corrected by a strongly rooted force. It should be strongly proportioned to meet the resistance which the executive must expect from the legislature, from the judiciary, and from the people of a republic. Unless the executive has easy access to all the [adminstrative] resources, fixed by a just distribution of powers, he inevitably becomes a nonentity or abuses his authority. By this I mean that the result will be the death of the government, whose heirs are anarchy, usurpation, and tyranny. Some seek to check the executive authority by curbs and restrictions, and nothing is more just; but it must be remembered that the bonds we seek to preserve should, of course, be strengthened, but not tightened.

Therefore, let the entire system of government be strengthened, and let the balance of power be drawn up in such a manner that it will be permanent and incapable of decay because of its own tenuity. Precisely because no form of government is so weak as the democratic, its framework must be firmer, and its institutions must be studied to determine their degree of stability. Unless this is done, we must plan on the establishment of an experimental rather than a permanent system of government; and we will have to reckon with an ungovernable, tumultuous, and anarchic society, not with a social order where happiness, peace, and justice prevail.

Legislators, we should not be presumptuous. We should be moderate in our pretensions. It is not likely that we will secure what mankind has never attained or that which the greatest and wisest nations have not acquired. Complete liberty and absolute democracy are but reefs upon which all republican hopes have foundered. Observe the ancient republics, the modern republics, and those of most recent origin: Virtually all have attempted to establish themselves as absolute democracies, and almost all have seen their just aspirations thwarted. The men who covet legitimate institutions and social perfection are indeed worthy of commendation. But who has told these men that they now possess the wisdom or practice the virtue that is so forcefully demanded by the union of power with justice? Only angels, not men, can exist free, peaceful, and happy while exercising every sovereign power.

The people of Venezuela already enjoy the rights that they may legitimately and easily exercise. Let us now, therefore, restrain the growth of immoderate pretensions which, perhaps, a form of government unsuited to our people might excite. Let us abandon the federal forms of government unsuited to us; let us put aside the triumvirate which holds the executive power and center it in a president. We must grant him sufficient authority to enable him to continue the struggle against the obstacles inherent in our recent situation, our present state of war, and every variety of foe, foreign and domestic, whom we must battle for some time to come. Let the legislature relinquish the powers that rightly belong to the executive; let it acquire, however, a new consistency, a new influence in the balance of authority. Let the courts be strengthened by increasing the stability and independence of the judges and by the establishment of juries and civil and criminal codes dictated, not by antiquity nor by conquering kings, but by the voice of Nature, the cry of Justice, and the genius of Wisdom.

My desire is for every branch of government and administration to attain that degree of vigor which alone can insure equilibrium, not only among the members of the government, but also among the different factions of which our society is composed. It would matter little if the springs of a political system were to relax because of its weakness, so long as this relaxation itself did not contribute to the dissolution of the body social and the ruination of its membership. The shouts of humanity, on the battlefields or in tumultuous crowds, denounce to the world the blind, unthinking legislators who imagined that experiments with chimerical institutions could be made with impunity. All the peoples of the world have sought freedom, some by force of arms, others by force of law, passing alternately from anarchy to despotism, or from despotism to anarchy. Few peoples have been content with moderate aims, establishing their institutions according to their means, their character, and their circumstances. We must not aspire to the impossible, lest, in trying to rise above the realm of liberty, we again descend into the realm of tyranny. Absolute liberty invariably lapses into absolute power, and the mean between these two extremes is supreme social liberty. Abstract theories create the pernicious idea of unlimited freedom. Let us see to it that the strength of the public is kept within the limits prescribed by reason and interest; that the national will is confined within the bonds set by a just power; that the judiciary is rigorously controlled by civil and criminal laws, analogous to those in our present Constitution—then an equilibrium between the powers of government will exist, the conflicts that hamper the progress of the state will disappear, and those complications which tend to hinder rather than unite society will be eliminated.

The formation of a stable government requires as a foundation a national spirit, having as its objective a uniform concentration on two cardinal factors, namely, moderation of the popular will and limitation of public authority. The extremes, which these two factors theoretically establish, are difficult to define in practice; but it can well be conceived that the maxim that must guide them is mutual limitation and concentration of power, in order that there may be the least possible friction between the popular will and the constituted public authority. The science of achieving this balance is acquired almost imperceptibly, through practice and study. Progress in the practice of this science is hastened by progress in the enlightenment of the people, and integrity of mind and spirit speeds the progress of enlightenment.

Love of country, love of law, and respect for magistrates are the exalted emotions that must permeate the soul of a republic. The Venezuelans love their country, but they cannot love her laws, because these, being sources of evil, have been harmful; neither can they respect their magistrates, as they have been unjust, while the new administrators are scarcely known in the calling which they have just entered. Unless there is a sacred reverence for country, laws, and authority, society becomes confused, an abyss—an endless conflict of man versus man, group versus group.

All our moral powers will not suffice to save our infant republic from this chaos unless we fuse the mass of the people, the government, the legislation, and the national spirit into a single united body. Unity, unity, unity must be our motto in all things. The blood of our citizens is varied: let it be mixed for the sake of unity. Our Constitution has divided the powers of government: let them be bound together to secure unity. Our laws are but a sad relic of ancient and modern despotism. Let this monstrous edifice crumble and fall; and, having removed even its ruins, let us erect a temple to Justice; and, guided by its sacred inspiration, let us write a code of Venezuelan laws. Should we wish to consult monuments of legislation, those of Great Britain, France, and the United States of North America afford us admirable models.

Popular education should be the primary concern of the paternal love of Congress. Morality and enlightenment are the foundations of a republic; morality and enlightenment constitute our primary needs. From Athens let us take her Areopagus and her guardians of custom and law; from Rome, her censors and domestic tribunals; and, having effected a holy alliance of these moral institutions, let us revive in the world the idea of a people who, not content to be free and strong, desire also to be virtuous. From Sparta let us take her austere institutions; and, when from these three springs we have made a fountain of virtue, let us endow our republic with a fourth power having jurisdiction over the youth, the hearts of men, public spirit, good customs, and republican ethics. Let us establish an Areopagus to watch over the education of our youth and to promote national enlightenment, in order that it may purify every instance of corruption in the Republic and denounce ingratitude, selfishness, indifferent love of country, and idleness and negligence on the part of the citizens, that it may judge the first signs of corruption and of evil example, using moral penalties to correct violations of customs, even as criminals are punished by corporal penalties. Such action should be taken not only against that which conflicts with customs, but also against that which mocks them; not only against that which attacks them, but against that which weakens them; not only against that which violates the Constitution, but also against that which outrages public decency. The jurisdiction of this truly sacred tribunal should be effective with respect to education and enlightenment, but advisory only with regard to penalties and punishments. But its annals or registers containing its acts and deliberations, which will, in effect, record the ethical precepts and the actions of citizens, should be the public books of virtue and vice. These books would be consulted [for guidance] by the people in elections, by the magistrates in their decisions, and by the judges in rendering verdicts. Such an institution, chimerical as it may appear, is infinitely more feasible than others which certain ancient and modern legislators have established with less benefit to mankind.

Legislators! In the plan of a constitution that I most respectfully submit to your better wisdom, you will observe the spirit in which it was conceived. In proposing to you a division of citizens into active and passive groups, I have endeavored to promote the national prosperity by means of the two greatest levers of industry: work and knowledge. By activating these two powerful mainsprings of society, we can achieve the most difficult of accomplishments among men—that of making them honest and happy. By setting just and prudent restrictions upon the primary and electoral assemblies, we can put the first check on popular license, thereby avoiding the blind, clamorous conventions that have in all times placed the stamp of error on elections, an error that consequently carries over to the magistrates and in turn to the conduct of the government; for the initial act of election is the one by which a people creates either liberty or slavery.

By augmenting Congress' weight in the balance of powers through an increase in the number of legislators and a change in the character of the Senate, I have endeavored to provide this first legislative body in the nation with a firm basis and to endow it with an eminence that will better insure the fulfillment of its sovereign functions.

In separating the executive jurisdiction from that of the legislature by means of well-defined boundaries, it is my intention not to divide but rather to unite these supreme powers through those bonds that are born of independence, for any prolonged conflict between these powers has never failed to destroy one of the contenders. In seeking to vest in the executive authority a sum total of powers greater than that which it previously enjoyed, I have no desire to grant a despot the authority to tyrannize the Republic, but I do wish to prevent deliberative despotism from being the immediate source of a vicious circle of despotic situations, in which anarchy alternates with oligarchy and monocracy. In requesting tenure for judges and the establishment of juries and a new code of law, I have asked the Congress to guarantee civil liberty, the most precious, the most just, the most necessary, in a word, the only liberty, since without it the others are nothing. I have solicited the correction of the most lamentable abuses in our judiciary. These abuses had their vicious origin in that welter of Spanish legislation which, like time itself, was collected from all ages and from all men, whether the works of the sane or of the demented, whether the creations of brilliant or of extravagant minds, and whether gathered from monuments of human thought or of human caprice. This judicial compendium, a monster of ten thousand heads, which, to this day, has been the curse of the Spanish peoples, is the most subtle punishment that the wrath of Heaven could have inflicted upon this unfortunate empire.

After meditating upon the most effective means of regenerating the characteristics and customs bred in us by tyranny and war, I have dared to devise a moral power, drawn from the depths of remote antiquity and specifically from those forgotten laws that long maintained qualities of virtue among the Greeks and Romans. It may well be looked upon as sheer delirium, but it is not an impossibility, and I flatter myself that you may not wholly reject an idea which, if perfected by experience and learning, may prove to be very effective.

Horrified by the disagreement that has reigned and will continue to reign among us owing to the subtle nature which characterizes the federal government, I am impelled to request that you adopt a central form of government, uniting all the states of Venezuela into a republic, one and indivisible. This measure, which I regard as urgent, vital, and redeeming is of such a nature that, unless it is adopted, death will be the fruit of our rebirth.

It is my duty, Legislators, to present you with a detailed and faithful picture of my political, civil, and military administration; but to do so would weary you and distract your valuable attention at this critical time when every moment is precious. Consequently, the secretaries of state will report to Congress on their respective departments, submitting at the same time the documents and records that will serve as supporting data in order that you may gain an exact picture of the true and positive state of the Republic.

I would not dwell upon the most notable acts of my command did they not concern the majority of Venezuelans. I refer, Gentlemen, to the more important resolutions of this most recent period. The dark mantle of barbarous and profane slavery covered the Venezuelan earth, and our sky was heavy with stormy clouds, which threatened to rain a deluge of fire. I implored the protection of the God of Humanity, and redemption soon dispersed the tempests. Slavery broke its fetters, and Venezuela was filled with new sons, grateful sons who have forged the instruments of their captivity into weapons of freedom. Yes, those who once were slaves are now free: those who once were the embittered enemies of a stepmother are now the proud defenders of their own country. To describe the justice, the necessity, and the beneficent results of this measure would be superfluous, for you know the history of the Helots, of Spartaco, and of Haiti; and because you know that one cannot be both free and enslaved at the same time, without simultaneously violating every natural, political, and civil law, I leave to your sovereign decision the reform or the repeal of all my statutes and decrees; but I plead for the confirmation of the absolute freedom of the slaves, as I would plead for my very life and for the life of the Republic.

To recount for you the military history of Venezuela would be to recall the history of republican heroism among the ancients; it would but point out to you that Venezuela has her place in the great record of sacrifices made on the altar of liberty. Nothing could fill the noble breasts of our generous warriors except the sublime honors that are granted to the benefactors of mankind. As they have fought neither for power, nor for fortune, nor even for glory, but for liberty alone, the title of Liberators of the Republic is their just reward. I, therefore, have founded a sacred society of these illustrious men and created the Order of the Liberators of Venezuela. Legislators! Yours is the power to grant honors and decorations; it is your duty to carry out this august act of national gratitude.

Men who have given up all the pleasures and possessions that they have acquired by their diligence and talents; men who have experienced every cruelty of a horrible war and who have suffered the bitterest privations and the severest torments; men so well-deserving of the nation demand the attention of the government; therefore, I have ordered them to be compensated out of the public domain. If I have earned any merit whatsoever in the eyes of the people, I ask their representatives simply to heed my petition as reward for my humble services. Let the Congress order the distribution of the national property pursuant to the law which I, in the name of the Republic, have decreed in behalf of the soldiers of Venezuela.

Now, after endless victories, we have succeeded in annihilating the Spanish hosts. The court of Madrid has desperately and vainly endeavored to play upon the conscience of the magnanimous sovereigns who have just rid Europe of usurpation and tyranny, and who are certain to support the legality and justice of the American cause. Incapable of obtaining our submission by force of arms, Spain has reverted to her insidious policy; unable to conquer us, she desires to employ her techniques in creating suspicion. Ferdinand has so humbled himself as to confess that he needs foreign aid in order to return us to his ignominious yoke—a yoke that all the force in the world cannot impose! Venezuela, convinced that she possesses sufficient strength to repel her oppressors, has announced, through her government, her absolute determination to fight unto the death in defense of her political existence, not only against Spain but against all men, were all men to degrade themselves by coming to the aid of a rapacious government whose only mobile weapons are the sword of extermination and the flames of the Inquisition —a government that today does not seek dominions, but deserts; not cities, but ruins, not vassals, but tombs. The Declaration of [Independence of] the Republic of Venezuela is a most glorious act, a most heroic act, one most worthy of a free people. It is the one act which, with the greatest satisfaction, I have the honor to submit to the Congress, as it has been sanctioned by the unanimous expression of the free people of Venezuela.

During the second period of the Republic our army lacked military supplies; always unarmed and without munitions, it was poorly equipped. But now the soldiers who defend our independence are armed not only with justice but also with might. Our troops are comparable to the best in Europe, as there is no inequality in weapons of destruction. These great advantages we owe to the unbounded liberality of certain generous-hearted foreigners who, having heard the pitiful cries of humanity, were moved by the cause of righteousness. These foreigners did not view these events as idle spectators; they hastened to supply their aid and assistance. To guarantee the triumph of their philanthropic principles, they provided the Republic with whatever it needed. These friends of humanity have been the guardian angels of America, and we owe them an eternal debt of gratitude as well as the religious fulfillment of the sacred obligations that we have contracted with them. Our national debt, Legislators, is the repository of Venezuelan faith, honor, and gratitude. Respect it as the Holy Covenant that contains not only the claims of our benefactors but also the glory of our honor. Let us perish rather than break a pledge that has saved our country and the life of her sons.

The reuniting[1] of New Granada and Venezuela into one great state has been the constant wish of the peoples and governments of these republics. The fortunes of war have effected this merger so earnestly desired by all Colombians: in fact, we are now a single state. These brother peoples have already entrusted to you their interests, their rights, and their destinies.

As I contemplate the reunion of this territory, my soul ascends to the heights necessary to view the mighty panorama afforded by this astounding picture. My imagination, taking flight to the ages to come, is captured by the vision of future centuries, and when, from that vantage point, I observe with admiration and amazement the prosperity, the splendor, the fullness of life which will then flourish in this vast region, I am overwhelmed. I seem to behold my country as the very heart of the universe, its far-flung shores spreading between those oceans which Nature kept apart but which our country will have joined by an imposing system of extensive canals. I can see her serving as the bond, the center, and the emporium of the human race. I behold her shipping to all corners of the earth the treasures of silver and gold which lie hidden in her mountains. I can see her dispensing, by means of her divine plants, health and life to the ailing of the Old World. I can see her confiding her precious secrets to the learned men who do not know that her store of knowledge is superior to the wealth with which Nature has prodigally endowed her. I can see her crowned by glory, seated upon the throne of liberty with the sceptre of Justice in her hand, disclosing to the Old World the majesty of the New.

I pray you, Legislators, receive with indulgence this profession

---

[1] *Reunión*. The republican areas of Venezuela and Colombia were once united politically in the colonial era. Bolívar's persistent reference to past history demands the above translation, although union is implied (ed.).

of my political faith, these innermost yearnings of my heart, these fervent pleas, which, on behalf of the people, I venture to place before you. I pray you, grant to Venezuela a government preëminently popular, preëminently just, preëminently moral; one that will suppress anarchy, oppression, and guilt—a government that will usher in the reign of innocence, humanity, and peace; a government wherein the rule of inexorable law will signify the triumph of equality and freedom.

Gentlemen: you may begin your labors, I have finished mine.

BOLÍVAR

READING NO. 14

A Prediction of Unfavorable Things to Come*

By the close of the struggles for independence many leaders had developed serious doubts about the future of the new states. Here, the independence hero and statesman Santander in a letter of May 9, 1826 to a friend prophesies that intellectuals, priests, and armed forces officers will produce an explosive combination in Gran Colombia.

This republic [Gran Colombia] is immoderately overwrought. The discontent of the military is spreading because soldiers are distrusted, even scorned, everywhere, partly because of the bad conduct and worse manners of some of our officers and partly because ambitious lawyers (*letrados*) want to destroy everyone who might become a counterpoise. The lack of anything for the military to do, their dissatisfaction with salaries and benefits, the contempt with which they are treated, and the insults which the press is wont to vent upon them has the army extremely

---

* Francisco de Paula Santander, *Cartas de Santander,* 3 vols., obra formada por Vicente Lecuna, translated by Doris M. Ladd (Caracas, 1942), II, 166-167. Reprinted with the permission of Fundación Vicente Lecuna.

discontented, including men as moderate as Urdaneta, Soublette, Fortoul, etc. The anxious clergy is bursting with rage at the liberality of the Congress and at the insults published daily against them. The influence of the clergy, which some believe insignificant, seems to me powerful and capable of doing harm; from this it is easy to conclude that if the military and ecclesiastical powers unite and incorporate the *godos* [Spaniards] who tend to join the party that is promoting upheaval, the republic is likely to suffer terribly. The liberated, more numerous than the liberators, are taking exclusive possession of the countryside, and since there is a large number of ambitious and fickle lawyers, they are trying hard to exclude the military, the clergy, and everyone who will not submit to their opinions and desires for offices and advancement. The issue is joined, the Congress and the press have served as arena, and it is impossible that an explosion, which may begin by tumbling the theatre that the lawyers have built for the fray, can long be averted. Thus we must tremble for the fate of Colombia and whoever comes to govern must shudder with horror. The fuel is gathered, the elements of disunity are on collision course; at the slightest clash, the spark will leap, and this poor land will burn.

READING NO. **15**

The Bolivian Constitution of 1826*

The Bolivian Constitution of 1826 was essentially the creation of Bolívar, who grew more conservative in his political thinking

* *Documentos referentes a la creación de Bolivia,* 2 vols., ed. by Vicente Lecuna, translated by Doris M. Ladd (Caracas, 1924), II, 323-327, 329-339, 343-353. Reprinted with the permission of the Fundación Vicente Lecuna. The complete text of the Constitution may be found in translation in Great Britain, Foreign Office, British and Foreign State Papers, XII (London, 1841), 875-893. It is instructive to compare Bolívar's address to the Congress on the occasion of his presentation of his proposed constitution with the Constitution itself. The address may be found in Great Britain, Foreign Office, *op. cit.,* 865-874, and in Bolívar, *Selected Writings,* II, 596-606.

as he grew older and the independence of Spanish America was assured. As the following document shows, he and the members of the Bolivian Congress discovered numerous ways to guarantee elite control of the Republic and to protect private property. The moralistic character of Bolívar and his political allies in the Congress is evident in those sections of the Constitution dealing with the Catholic Church, citizenship, the qualifications for office-holding and the responsibilities of the fourth branch of Bolívar's government, the Censors. The Liberator insisted that he had written a constitution that tied the hands and severed the head of the chief executive. However, his contention is belied by the fact that his chief executive was given nearly complete control over the armed forces. This meant that as long as he could keep the armed forces satisfied, the chief executive was free to exercise almost unlimited power. It should be noted that few documents of the era treat the question of local government in as much detail as does the Bolivian Constitution of 1826.

Bolívar's recommendations appear in roman type. All amendments, additions, and suppressions made by the Bolivian Congress are set in italics.

IN THE NAME OF GOD

The General Constituent Congress of the Bolivian Republic, named by the people to form the constitution of the state, decrees the following:

TITLE I: OF THE NATION

Chapter I: Of the Bolivian Nation

Article 1. The nation of Bolivia is the union of all Bolivians.

2. Bolivia is and ever shall be independent of all foreign domination; and cannot be the patrimony of any person or family.

Chapter II: Of the Territory

*   *   *

Added as Article 6. The Roman Catholic and Apostolic religion is the religion of the republic, to the exclusion of all other public worship. The government will protect it and make it respected, recognizing the principle that there is no human power over the conscience.

TITLE II: OF THE GOVERNMENT

Chapter I: Form of the Government

6. The Government of Bolivia is popular and representative.
7. Sovereignty emanates from the people, and its exercise resides in powers that this Constitution establishes.
8. Supreme power is divided . . . into four sections: electoral, legislative, executive, and judicial.

*   *   *

Chapter II: Of Bolivians

10. Bolivians are:

1st—All who are born in the territory of the republic.

2nd—Children born of Bolivian father or mother outside the territory so soon as they may legally indicate their willingness to domicile themselves in Bolivia.

3rd—The Liberators of the republic, so declared by the law of 11 August 1825.

[Defined as *Those who fought for liberty at Junín or Ayacucho.*]

4th—Foreigners who obtain a naturalization certificate or who have resided in the territory of the republic for three years.

5th—All those who up to now have been slaves and who are de facto free by the publication of this constitution; a special law shall determine the indemnification to be made to their former owners.

[Amended: *All those who up to now have been slaves and who are by law free by the publication of this constitution; but they cannot abandon the house of their former owners until a special law determines the procedure.*]

*   *   *

13. To be a citizen it is necessary:

1st—To be a Bolivian

2nd—To be married or over 21 years of age.

3rd—To know how to read and write.

[Amended: *To know how to read and write well; this condition will be required only after 1836.*]

4th—To have some vocation or trade; or to profess some art or science, without being subject to another in the capacity of a domestic servant.

14. Citizens are:

1st—The liberators of the republic (Art. 10, 3rd).

2nd—Foreigners who have obtained naturalization certificates.

3rd—Foreigners married to Bolivian women [and] who fulfill the 3rd and 4th conditions of Article 13.

4th—Unmarried foreigners who have resided four years in the republic, and [fulfill] the same conditions.

15. Citizens of the nations of America, previously Spanish, shall enjoy the rights of citizenship in Bolivia according to treaties which may be made with those nations.

16. Only those who are actually citizens can hold public offices and employments.

17. Citizenship shall be suspended:

1st—for insanity

2nd—for the stigma of fraudulent debtor

3rd—for being criminally prosecuted

4th—for being a notorious drunkard, gambler or beggar

5th—for buying or selling votes in the elections, or by disturbing their order. . . .

* * *

TITLE III: OF THE ELECTORAL POWER

Chapter I: Of Elections

19. The electoral power shall be directly exercised by actual citizens, one elector being chosen for every ten.

Amended: *One elector for every 100.*

* * *

Chapter II: Of the Electoral Body

22. The electoral body is composed of electors named by popular suffrage.

Added: *To be an elector it is indispensable to be a ctitzen and to know how to read and write.*

23. The electors, assembled in the capital of the province, shall name by a plurality of votes a president, two censors, and a

secretary from their midst; these [officers] shall function for the duration of the organization.

This article was suppressed.

24. Each electoral body shall last for four years. . . .

25. [Electors' functions:]

1st—To qualify citizens who begin exercising their rights and to suspend those who are disqualified under Articles 17 and 18.

Modified: *To qualify citizens who begin exercising their rights and to declare disqualified those who may fall under the provisions of Articles 17 and 18.*

Added: *To appoint for the first time the individuals who will constitute the chambers.*

2nd—To elect and propose *en terna* [by nominating three]: 1st to each respective chamber the members which will constitute it or fill its vacancies; 2nd, to the executive power, candidates for the prefecture of their department, for the government of their province, and for the corregidores of their cantons and towns; 3rd, to the prefect of the department, the alcaldes and justices of the peace . . . ; 4th, to the senate, the members of district courts . . . and judges ôf the first instance; 5th, to the executive power priests and vicars for the vacancies in their province.

Amended: *To elect and propose en terna:*

1st, to the respective chambers the members which are to renew them or fill their vacancies; 2nd, to the senate the members of the district courts . . . and judges of the first instance; 3rd, to the prefect of the department the justices of the peace . . . 4th, to propose: first, to the executive power from six to ten candidates for the prefecture of their department; a similar quantity for the governorship of the province and for corregidores of their cantons and towns; second, to the ecclesiastical government a list of priests and vicars for the vacancies of their provinces.

3rd—To receive election returns; to examine the identity of the newly elected, and to declare them constitutionally appointed.

4th—To petition the chambers for whatever they may deem favorable for the welfare of citizens; and to complain of grievances and injustices which they may experience from constituted authorities.

TITLE IV: OF THE LEGISLATIVE POWER

Chapter I: Of the Division, Prerogatives, and Restrictions of this Power.

26. Legislative power emanates directly from the electoral bodies named by the people. Its exercise resides in three chambers: tribunes; senators; censors.

27. Each chamber shall consist of thirty members for the first twenty years.
Amended: *To 20 members each.*

*   *   *

Chapter II: Of the Chamber of Tribunes

41. In order to be a tribune, it is necessary:
    1st—to be an actual citizen.
    Further restricted: (1) *same qualifications as for electors* and (2) *to have been born in Bolivia or resided there for six years.*
    2nd—To be twenty-five years old.
    3rd—Never to have been convicted in a criminal offense.
42. The chamber of tribunes has the initiative:
    1st—In regulation of the territorial division of the republic.
    2nd—In the annual contributions and public expenditures.
    3rd—In authorizing the executive power to negotiate loans; and in adopting ways and means of extinguishing the public debt.
    4th—In the value, type, standard, weight, and denomination of money, and in the regulation of weights and measures.
    5th—In equipping all kinds of port facilities.
    6th—In the construction of roads, causeways, bridges, public buildings, and in the improvement of the police and branches of industry.
    7th—In the salaries of public functionaries.
    8th—In the reforms which they may deem necessary in the field of finance and war.

9th—On the proposal tendered by the government, in making war or peace.

10th—In alliances.

11th—In permitting passage to foreign troops.

12th—Concerning naval and land forces for the year, on the proposal tendered by the government.

13th—In giving ordinances to the navy, army, and national militia on the proposal of the government.

14th—In foreign affairs.

15th—In granting certificates of naturalization and citizenship.

16th—In granting general pardons.

43. The Chamber of Tribunes shall be renewed by halves every two years and shall have four years' duration. In the first legislature, the half which is to retire at the expiration of two years shall be determined by lot.

44. Tribunes may be re-elected.

Chapter III: Of . . . Senators

45. To be a Senator, it is necessary:

1st—[To have] the qualifications required for electors.

Amended: *The same qualifications as tribunes.*

2nd—To be thirty-five years of age.

Amended: *to age 30.*

46. The prerogatives of the senate are:

1st—To form the civil and criminal codes, [codes] of procedure and commerce, and ecclesiastical regulations.

2nd—To initiate all laws concerning reform of judicial matters.

3rd—To watch over the prompt administration of civil and criminal justice.

4th—To originate laws which prevent infringement of the constitution and of the law on the part of magistrates, judges, and ecclesiastics.

5th—To exact responsibility of the superior tribunals of justice, of prefects, of magistrates, and subaltern judges.

6th—To propose *en terna* to the chamber of censors the individuals who will constitute the supreme tribunal of justice, the archbishops, bishops, dignitaries, canons, and prebends of cathedrals.

7th—To approve or reject the prefects, governors, and corregidores which the government has selected from the list of
three candidates submitted by the electoral bodies.

8th—To elect from the list of three candidates submitted by the
electoral bodies the district judges and the subalterns for
every department.

9th—To regulate the exercise of the patronato and to draft
laws relating to all ecclesiastical business which has relation to the government.

10th—To examine Council decisions, bulls, rescripts, and
pontifical briefs in order to approve them or not.

47. The term of senators shall be eight years, and the Chamber
shall be renewed by one-half every four years, the half of the
first legislature which is to retire being determined by lot.

48. Senators may be re-elected.

Chapter IV: Of the . . . Censors

49. To be a censor, it is necessary:

1st—To possess the qualifications required for senators.

2nd—To be forty years of age.
Amended: *to age 35.*

3rd—Never to have been condemned, not even for trifling
offenses.

50. [Function of the Censors]

1st—To see that the government complies with and enforces
compliance with the Constitution, laws, and public treaties.

2nd—[When necessary] to bring before the Senate charges
against the Executive for having infringed the constitution,
laws, and public treaties.

3rd—To petition the senate to suspend the vice-president and
secretaries of state should the well-being of the republic
urgently demand it.

51. To the censors belong exclusively the obligation to impeach
the vice-president and secretaries of state before the senate in
cases of treason, extortion, or manifest violation of the fundamental laws of the republic.

*   *   *

59. Furthermore, the chamber of censors:

1st—Chooses from a list of three candidates presented by the senate the individuals who are to form the supreme tribunal and those who are to be presented for vacant archbishoprics, bishoprics, canonries, and prebends.

2nd—Executes laws relating to the press, economy, regulation of studies, and method of public instruction.

3rd—Protects the liberty of the press and appoints the judges who will decide appeals regarding it.

4th—Proposes regulations for development of arts and sciences.

5th—Grants rewards and compensations to those who, by their services to the republic, may deserve them.

6th—Decrees public honors to the memory of great men and for the virtues and services of citizens.

7th—Condemns to eternal disgrace usurpers of public authority, great traitors, and flagrant criminals.

Added as 8th: *Concedes to Bolivians admission to employment, titles, and distinctions accorded to them by another government. . . .*

60. Censors shall be appointed for life.

Chapter V: Of the Formation and Promulgation of Laws

62. The vice-president and secretaries of state may attend the sessions and discuss laws and other topics; but they may not vote or be present when the votes are taken.

*   *   *

69. If the president of the republic believes a law inexpedient, he must, within ten days, return it to the chamber which originated it, together with his observations. . . .

*   *   *

71. When the executive returns the law . . . to the Chambers, they shall meet in a joint session; and whatever they determine by a majority vote shall be carried out without further discussion or observation.

*   *   *

74. Projects of law which originate in the senate shall pass to the censors and, if there approved, shall have the force of law. If the censors do not approve, the project will pass to the tribunes, whose decision shall be definitive. . . .

75. Projects of law which originate in the censors shall pass to the senate; its sanction shall have the force of law. But in case its assent is not given, the project will pass to the tribunes. . . .

TITLE V: OF THE EXECUTIVE POWER

76. The exercise of the executive power resides in a life president, a vice-president, and three secretaries of state.

Chapter I: Of the President

*   *   *

78. In order to be nominated for president of the republic it is necessary:

1st—To be an actual citizen and a native of Bolivia.

Added: *To profess the religion of the republic.*

2nd—To be more than thirty years old.

3rd—To have rendered important services to the republic.

4th—To possess known talents for the administration of the state.

5th—Never to have been convicted by the tribunals, even of slight offenses.

79. The president of the republic is the chief of state, without responsibility for the acts of the administration.

80. In case of the resignation, death, infirmity, or absence of the president of the republic, the vice-president will succeed him at once.

*   *   *

82. The prerogatives of the president of the republic are:

1st—To open the sessions of the chambers and to present to them a message on the state of the republic.

2nd—To propose the vice-president to the Chambers; and by himself to appoint the secretaries of state.

3rd—To dismiss the vice-president and secretaries of state whenever he shall deem it expedient.

Modified: *to dismiss the vice-president with the consent of the legislature, and the secretaries of state whenever he deems it expedient.*

4th—To publish, circulate, and enforce the laws.

5th—To authorize regulations and orders for the better fulfillment of the constitution, laws, and public treaties.

6th—To order and enforce the sentences of the tribunals. . . .

7th—To demand of the legislative body its adjournment for up to thirty days.

8th—To convoke the legislative body for extraordinary sessions, when absolutely necessary.

9th—To dispose of the permanent forces of the army and navy for the external defense of the republic.

10th—To command in person the armies of the republic in peace and in war. When the president is absent from the capital, the vice-president shall take charge of the government of the republic.

Amended: *To command the armies of the republic in peace and in war, and in person, when he believes it expedient.* . . .

11th—To reside in any part of the territory occupied by the national armed forces when he is directing the war in person.

12th—To dispose of the national militia for internal security within the limits of its departments; and outside their boundaries with the consent of the legislative body.

13th—To appoint all army and naval officers.

14th—To establish military and naval academies.

15th—To order established military hospitals and rest homes.

16th—To grant furloughs and retirement. To concede pensions to the military and their families, according to the laws, and to regulate, according to the laws, everything else pertaining to this department.

17th—To declare war, previously decreed by the legislative body, in the name of the republic.

18th—To grant letters of marque.

19th—To superintend the collection and investment of public revenues. . . .

20th—To appoint officials of [the Ministry of] Finance.

21st—To direct diplomatic negotiations and to conclude treaties of peace, friendship, confederation, alliance, armistice, armed neutrality, commerce, and any others; always with the prior approval of the legislature.

22nd—To appoint the ministers, consuls, and subalterns of the ministry of foreign affairs.

23rd—To receive foreign ministers.

24th—To authorize or suspend council decisions, pontifical bulls, briefs, and rescripts, with the approval of the corresponding authority.

25th—To present to the senate for its approval one of the list of three candidates proposed by the electoral body for prefects, governors, and corregidores.

26th—To present to the ecclesiastical government one of the list of three candidates proposed by the electoral body as curates and vicars.

27th—To suspend functionaries for up to three months, always for cause.

28th—To commute capital punishment decreed by the tribunals. . . .

Defined: *To commute capital punishment to exile for ten years or perpetual banishment.*

29th—To expedite, in the name of the republic, the commissions and appointments of all functionaries.

83. The restrictions on the president . . . are:

1st—The president may not deprive any Bolivian of his liberty or impose any punishment whatsoever by his own authority.

2nd—When the safety of the republic demands the arrest of one or more citizens, the accused must be placed at the disposition of the proper judge or tribunal within forty-eight hours.

3rd—He cannot deprive any individual of his property, unless the public interest urgently demand it; and a just indemnification . . . be made to the proprietor in advance.

4th—He cannot impede elections nor any other function delegated by law to the powers of the republic.

5th—He cannot absent himself from the territory of the republic without the permission of the legislature.

Modified: *He may leave the capital without legislative consent.*

Chapter II: Of the Vice-President

84. The vice-president is named by the president of the republic and approved by the legislature. . . .

*   *   *

86. The qualifications for vice-president are the same as for president.

87. The vice-president . . . is the prime minister.
88. He shall be responsible, together with the secretary of each respective department, for the administration of the state.
89. He shall dispatch and sign, in the name of the republic and of the president, all the affairs of administration. . . .

*   *   *

Chapter III: Of the Secretaries of State

91. There shall be three secretaries of state. One shall be charged with the department of government and foreign affairs; another with that of finance; and the other with that of war and navy.
92. These three secretaries shall function immediately under the orders of the vice-president.

*   *   *

96. To be a secretary of state, it is necessary:
   1st—To be an actual citizen.
   2nd—To be thirty years old.
   3rd—Never to have been convicted of a criminal offense.

*   *   *

TITLE VII: OF LOCAL GOVERNMENT

124. The supreme political authority in each department resides in a prefect.
125. That of each province in a governor.
   Added: *To be prefect or governor it is necessary*
   1st—*To be an actual citizen.*
   2nd—*Thirty years of age.*
   3rd—*Never to have been convicted in a criminal offense.*
126. That of the cantons in a corregidor.
127. In each town over a hundred . . . there shall be a justice of the peace.
   Defined: *The population no less than 100, no more than 2,000.*
128. When the population of a town or its surroundings exceeds one thousand, there shall be an alcalde . . . , and for every five hundred in excess of one thousand a justice of the peace, and for every two thousand an alcalde.
   Amended: *When the population of a town and its environs*

exceeds two thousand, there shall be a justice of the peace for each two thousand; if the excess is more than five hundred there shall be another.

129. The function of alcaldes and justices of the peace are to give advice; and no citizen, without just cause, may be exempt from obeying them.

    Amended: *alcaldes were suppressed.*

130. Prefects, governors, and corregidores shall serve for four years, but they may be re-elected.

131. Alcaldes and justices of the peace shall be renewed every two years, but they may be re-elected.

    Amended: *Justices of the peace shall be renewed every year and they may be re-elected only twice.*

132. The prerogatives of prefects, governors, corregidores, and alcaldes shall be determined by law to maintain order and public safety, duly subordinate to the supreme government.

*   *   *

TITLE VIII: OF THE ARMED FORCES

134. There shall be a permanent armed force in the republic.

135. The armed force shall consist of the army . . . and a squadron.

136. In each province there shall be corps of national militia, composed of its respective inhabitants.

137. There shall also be a military guard, whose principal duty shall be to prevent all clandestine commerce. A special regulation shall detail its organization and constitution. . . .

*   *   *

TITLE X: OF GUARANTEES

144. Civil liberty, individual security, property, and equality under law are guaranteed to citizens by the constitution.

145. All may communicate their thoughts verbally or in writing and may publish them through the medium of the press without previous censorship; but the law shall determine responsibility.

146. Every Bolivian may remain in or leave the territory of the republic at will, taking his property with him, but observing the regulations of the police and the rights of others.

147. The house of every Bolivian is an inviolable asylum. It cannot be entered at night except by his consent, and in the

daytime only . . . in the manner which the law shall determine.

148. Contributions shall be levied proportionately without any exceptions or privileges.

149. All hereditary offices and privileges and entails are abolished; all property is alienable even though it belong to pious or religious institutions or other groups.

150. No type of work, industry, or commerce can be prohibited unless it opposes public custom, or the security and health of Bolivians.

151. Every inventor shall have the proprietorship of his discoveries and of his inventions. The law shall secure for him an exclusive privilege for a [specific] time or compensation for loss in the event that it be made public.

152. Constitutional powers cannot suspend the Constitution nor the rights of Bolivians except in the cases and under the circumstances defined in the Constitution itself; on those occasions the period of suspension must without exception be specified.

READING NO. 16

Collapse*

Bolívar had dominated his surroundings for so long that he was, until the end, unable fully to comprehend how far he had fallen. In this short selection one of his biographers, Gerhard Masur, makes abundantly clear that Bolívar had no real choice but to accept his rejection by the leaders of Colombia.

. . . the attacks of his mortal illness increased and although he knew that he lacked the strength to guide the affairs of the nation, he was again and again to feel the magical attraction of politics. About the middle of March [1830] news indicating the complete decline of the Republic reached Bogotá. A regiment,

* Gerhard Masur, *Simón Bolívar* (Albuquerque: The University of New Mexico Press, 1949), pp. 672-73. Reprinted with the permission of the University of New Mexico Press. Footnotes in original not included.

quartered in the coastal region, had deserted, and its commanding officer had placed himself under Páez' command. Bolívar's first thought was to take up his office again, believing that his dictatorship would avert greater calamity. He did not realize that he lacked support for this venture, that his colleagues of 1828 were now estranged from him and his views. He was still confident that Urdaneta, Herrán, París, and Castillo y Rada would follow his lead; accordingly, he invited them to a conference at his place of retirement. This memorable meeting took place on the twentieth of March. Bolívar proposed that he should assume authority and declare war on the Venezuelan secessionists. The gentlemen ventured to say that such a war would be unpopular; the separation of Venezuela was a fact and should be accepted as such. It was quite clear that the majority was opposed to the plan. Up to this moment Urdaneta had remained silent, and Bolívar now turned to him for an expression of his opinion. But this was Urdaneta's opportunity to take his revenge. He had never forgotten that Bolívar had called Sucre the most worthy of all the generals, and he also resented Bolívar's accusation that he, Urdaneta, was responsible for the chaotic state of the Republic. He gave Bolívar a vehement and cruel answer. The separation from Venezuela, he said, had been consummated as early as 1827, when Bolívar himself had sounded the death knell of the Republic by pardoning Páez. Bolívar could not refute the accusation; moreover, he was without support from his former friends. Castillo y Rada, after excusing himself from the meeting, had sent a letter which the Liberator now read, his voice trembling with fury as he apprehended its contents. Renounce the power forever, his former prime minister advised; the separation from Venezuela is a fact; the war you contemplate would be unpopular; the issue must be faced, and an independent government for New Granada must be constituted—a government without Bolívar! In his rage Bolívar heaped accusations and reproaches on his erstwhile co-workers. They would have him desert the wheel of state—but he would not go; he would stay in spite of them, in spite of everything! The meeting broke up without having reached any decision. Returning to Bogotá through the fog and rain, the politicians felt that they had been in attendance at the agony of a great man.

There were many who feared that Bolívar might attempt to seize dictatorship even without political reassurances, relying entirely upon the army. Those who entertained this fear wanted Bolívar to leave the country; they would have considered his death a dispensation of Providence. Insulting references to the Liberator appeared in the press; in Bogotá slanderous remarks again spread from house to house, from street corner to street corner. . . .

READING NO. 17

The Burden of the Past*

One of Mexico's most distinguished contemporary scholars, Leopoldo Zea, historian and philosopher, presents a decidedly unsanguine view of what the wars of independence accomplished. Note the attention the author gives to the area's colonial heritage as a factor in accounting for its backwardness.

Spain, the past, was in the mind, in the habits and customs of Hispanic-American man. It was so deeply rooted in him that he felt he was unable to develop as other peoples were doing. He felt that all his efforts to transform his past had failed. He could do nothing to change it. He felt that everything attempted toward this end was futile. . . . The past, Spain, was always present in the flesh and blood of the liberators themselves. They, who had aspired to give to Hispanic America a form of life that was alien to Spain, had failed because in their own blood they carried the very roots of his failure. It was all to no avail; the colonial past imposed by Spain always appeared. . . .

The leaders of the new Hispanic-American emancipation were fully aware of this situation and hoped to end it. The revolution of independence, they said, had been animated more by the Hispanic imperial spirit than by the spirit of liberty. It had been a

* From *The Latin-American Mind,* by Leopoldo Zea, translated from the Spanish by James H. Abbott and Lowell Dunham. Copyright 1963 by the University of Oklahoma Press.

political revolution, argued the leadership, and not a social revolution. They had only sought to replace one master by another. The scepter had been wrested from Spain, but they kept its spirit. The legislative bodies of the period of liberation, the liberators, and the soldiers of the political emancipation of Hispanic America had acted only in accordance with the spirit which Spain had imposed upon them. The struggle had not been between America and Spain, but between Spain and Spain. A younger Spain, but Spain, after all, had conquered the old Spain. Nothing had changed, the same old privileges continued to exist, the liberators themselves had seen to it that it would be so. Hispanic America continued to be a colony.

Bibliography

Alamán, Lucas. *Historia de Méjico desde los primeros movimientos que prepararon su independencia en el año 1808, hasta la época presente.* 5 vols. Méjico, 1849-52.

Arnade, Charles W. *The Emergence of the Republic of Bolivia.* Gainesville, Florida, 1957.

Arnade, Charles W., Arthur P. Whitaker, Bailey W. Diffie. "Causes of Spanish American Wars of Independence," *Journal of Inter-American Studies,* II (April 1960), 125-144.

Basadre, Jorge. "Chile, Perú, y Bolivia independientes," A. Ballesteros (ed.), *Historia de América.* Vol. XXV, Barcelona, 1948.

————. *La promesa de la vida peruana y otros ensayos.* Lima, 1958.

Batllori, Miguel, S. I. *El Abate Viscardo: historia y mito de la intervención de los jesuítas en la independencia.* Caracas, 1953.

Belaúnde, Víctor Andrés. *Bolívar and the Political Thought of the Spanish American Revolution.* Baltimore, 1938.

————. "Factors of the Colonial Period in South America Working Toward a New Regime," *Hispanic American Historical Review,* IX (May 1929), 144-153.

Benítez, Fernando. *The Century After Cortés.* Translated by Joan MacLean. Chicago, 1965.

Benson, Nettie Lee (ed.). *Mexico and the Spanish Cortes: 1810-1822.* Austin, Texas, 1966.

Bierck, Harold A., Jr. "The Struggle for Abolition in Gran Colombia," *Hispanic American Historical Review,* XXXIII (August 1953), 365-386.

Blanco-Fombona, Rufino. *La evolución política y social de Hispano-América.* Madrid, 1911.

Bolívar, Simón. *Cartas del Libertador, corregidas conforme a los* [sic] *originales.* (ed.) Vicente Lecuna. 12 vols. Published by Banco de Venezuela, Caracas, 1929-1959.

————. *Escritos del Libertador,* published by Sociedad Bolivariana de Venezuela, Caracas, 1964.

————. *Selected Writings of Bolívar.* Compiled by Vicente Lecuna, (ed.) Harold A. Bierck, Jr. Translated by Lewis Bertrand. 2 vols. Published by Banco de Venezuela, New Ycrk, 1951.

Bushnell, David. *The Santander Regime in Gran Colombia.* Newark, Delaware, 1954.

Castro, Américo. *The Structure of Spanish History.* Translated by Edmund L. King. Princeton, 1954.

Congreso Hispanoamericano de Historia, 1st. *Causas y caracteres de la independencia hispanoamericana.* Madrid, 1953.

218

Cosío Villegas, Daniel. *American Extremes.* Translated by Américo Paredes. Austin, Texas, 1964.

Donoso, Ricardo. *Las ideas políticas en Chile.* Mexico, 1946.

Fisher, Lillian Estelle. *The Background of the Revolution.* Boston, 1934.

Friede, Juan. "La legislación indígena en la Gran Colombia," *Boletín de historia y antigüedades.* Bogotá, XXXVI (abril-junio 1949), 286-298.

Gandía, Enrique de. *La independencia americana.* Buenos Aires, 1961.

Gilmore, Robert L. *Caudillism and Militarism in Venezuela, 1810-1910.* Athens, Ohio, 1964.

Griffin, Charles C. *Los temas sociales y económicos en la época de la independencia.* Caracas, 1962.

——. *The United States and the Disruption of the Spanish Empire, 1810-1822.* London, 1937.

Hale, Charles A. "José María Luis Mora and the Structure of Mexican Liberalism," *Hispanic American Historical Review,* XLV (May, 1965), 196-227.

Hanke, Lewis. "Simón Bolívar and Neutral Rights," *Hispanic American Historical Review,* XXI (May 1941), 258-291.

Haring, Clarence H. *The Spanish Empire in America.* New York, 1947.

Herr, Richard. *The Eighteenth-Century Revolution in Spain.* Princeton, 1958.

Humboldt, Alexander von. *Personal Narrative of Travels to the Equinoctial Regions of the New Continent During the Years 1799-1804. . . .* Translated by Helen Maria Williams. 4 vols. (3rd ed.). London, 1822.

——. *Political Essay on the Kingdom of New Spain.* Translated by John Black. 4 vols. New York, 1811.

Humphreys, Robert A. *The Evolution of Modern Latin America.* London, 1946.

Humphreys, Robert A. and John Lynch. *The Origins of the Latin American Revolutions, 1808-1826.* New York, 1965.

Jane, Cecil. *Liberty and Despotism in Spanish America.* Oxford, 1929.

Jones, Tom B. *South America Rediscovered.* Minneapolis, 1949.

King, James F. "The Colored Castes and the American Representation in the Cortes of Cádiz," *Hispanic American Historical Review,* XXXIII (February 1953), 33-64.

——. "A Royalist View of the Colored Castes in the Venezuelan War of Independence," *Hispanic American Historical Review,* XXXIII (November 1953), 526-537.

Lanning, John Tate. *The Eighteenth-Century Enlightenment in the University of San Carlos de Guatemala.* Ithaca, New York, 1956.

Lecuna, Vicente. *Crónica razonada de las guerras de Bolívar.* 3 vols. New York, 1950.

————. compiler, *Documentos referentes a la creación de Bolivia*. 2 vols. Caracas, 1924.

Lewin, Boleslao. *Los movimientos de emancipación en Hispanoamérica y la independencia de Estados Unidos*. Buenos Aires, 1952.

Lockey, Joseph Byrne. *Pan Americanism: Its Beginnings*. New York, 1920.

Lynch, John. *Spanish Colonial Administration, 1782-1810, the Intendant System in the Viceroyalty of the Río de la Plata*. London, 1958.

McAlister, Lyle N. *The "Fuero Militar" in New Spain, 1764-1800*. Gainesville, Florida, 1957.

Madariaga, Salvador de. *Bolívar*. London, 1952.

————. *The Fall of the Spanish American Empire*, New York, 1948.

Malagón Barceló, Javier (ed.). *Las actas de independencia de América*, Pan-American Union. Washington, D.C., 1955.

Manning, William Ray. (ed.). *Diplomatic Correspondence of the United States Concerning the Independence of the Latin American Nations*. 3 vols. New York, 1925.

Martin, Percy Alvin. *Simón Bolívar, the Liberator*. Stanford, 1931.

Masur, Gerhard. *Simón Bolívar*. Albuquerque, New Mexico, 1948.

Mijares, Augusto, Mariano Picón Salas, *et al*. *Venezuela independiente, 1810-1960*. Caracas: Fundación Mendoza, 1962.

Mitre, Bartolomé. *The Emancipation of South America*. Translated and condensed by William Pilling. London, 1893.

Mora, José María Luis. *Méjico y sus revoluciones*. 3 vols. Paris, 1836.

Mörner, Magnus. "The History of Race Relations in Latin America: Some Comments on the State of Research," *Latin American Research Review*, I (Summer 1966), 17-44.

Mörner, Magnus. (ed.). *The Expulsion of the Jesuits from Latin America*. New York, 1965.

Motten, Clement G. *Mexican Silver and the Enlightenment*. Philadelphia, 1950.

O'Leary, Daniel F. *Bolívar y la emancipación de Sur-América*. Translated from the English by Simón B. O'Leary. 2 vols. Madrid, 1915.

Páez, José Antonio. *Autobiografía del general José Antonio Páez*. 2 vols. (3rd ed.). New York, 1878.

Pan American Institute of Geography and History, Comisión de Historia. *El movimiento emancipador de Hispanoamérica*. Caracas, 1961.

Pan American Union. *Simón Bolívar*, special issue of the "Bulletin" (December 1930) with articles by José Rodó, Víctor Andrés Belaúnde, Raimundo Rivas, *et al*.

————. Columbus Memorial Library, Bibliographic Series No. 1. *Bibliography of the Liberator, Simón Bolívar* (rev.). Washington, D.C., 1933.

Peru de Lacroix, Louis. *Diario de Bucaramanga*, ed. Nicolás E. Navarro. Caracas, 1949.

Picón Salas, Mariano. *A Cultural History of Spanish America, From*

Conquest to Independence. Translated by Irving A. Leonard. Berkeley, 1962.

Pons, François Raymond Joseph de. *A Voyage to the Eastern Part of Terra Firma or the Spanish Main in South America, During the Years 1801, 1802, 1803, and 1804.* Translated by an American Gentleman. 3 vols. New York, 1806.

Priestley, Herbert Ingram, *José de Gálvez. Visitor-General of New Spain, 1765-1771.* Berkeley, 1916.

Restrepo, José Manuel. *Historia de la revolución de la república de Colombia en la América Meridional.* 8 vols. Bogotá, 1942-1950.

Robertson, William S. *France and Latin American Independence.* Baltimore, 1939.

———. *The Life of Miranda.* 2 vols. Chapel Hill, North Carolina, 1929.

———. *Rise of the Spanish American Republics as Told in the Lives of Their Liberators.* New York, 1918.

Rodríguez, Simón. *Escritos de Simón Rodríguez.* Compiled by Pedro Grases. 3 vols. Caracas, 1954.

Romero, José Luis. *A History of Argentine Political Thought.* Translated by Thomas F. McGann. Stanford, 1963.

Ruíz Rivas, Guillermo. *Simón Bolívar más allá del mito.* 2 vols. Bogotá, 1964.

Rydjord, John. *Foreign Interest in the Independence of New Spain: An Introduction to the War for Independence.* Durham, North Carolina, 1935.

Samper, José María. *Ensayo sobre las revoluciones políticas y la condición social de las repúblicas colombianas (hispano-americanas).* Paris, 1861.

Santander, Francisco de Paula, *Cartas de Santander,* ed. Vicente Lecuna. 3 vols. Caracas, 1942.

Schmitt, Karl M. "The Clergy and the Independence of New Spain," *Hispanic American Historical Review,* XXXIV (August 1954), 289-312.

Shafer, Robert Jones. *The Economic Societies in the Spanish World, 1763-1821.* Syracuse, New York, 1958.

Spell, Jefferson Rea. *Rousseau in the Spanish World Before 1833; A Study in Franco-Spanish Literary Relations.* Austin, Texas, 1938.

Stevenson, William B. *On the Disturbances in South America.* London, 1830.

Torres, Carlos Arturo. *Idola fori, ensayo sobre las supersticiones políticas.* Bogotá, 1944.

Trend, John B. *Bolívar and the Independence of Spanish America.* Published by Bolivarian Society of Venezuela. Clinton, Massachusetts, 1951.

Ulloa, Antonio de and Jorge Juan. *A Voyage to South America.* Translated by John Adams (abridged). New York, 1964.

Unamuno, Miguel de. (ed.). *Simón Bolívar, libertador de la América del Sur, por los más grandes escritores americanos.* Madrid, 1914. Contains articles by Juan Montalvo, José Martí, José Rodó, Rufino

Blanco-Fombona, Francisco García Calderón, and Juan Bautista Alberdi.

Villalobos, Sergio. *Tradición y reforma en 1810.* Santiago, 1961.

Villanueva, Carlos A. *La monarquía en América.* 4 vols. Paris [1912].

Webster, Charles K. (ed.). *Britain and the Independence of Latin America, 1812-1830; Select Documents from the Foreign Office Archives.* 2 vols. London, 1938.

Whitaker, Arthur P. *The United States and the Independence of Latin America, 1800-1830.* Baltimore, 1941.

Whitaker, Arthur P. (ed.). *Latin America and the Enlightenment* (2nd ed.). Ithaca, New York, 1961.

Zea, Leopoldo. *The Latin American Mind.* Translated by James H. Abbott and Lowell Dunham. Norman, Oklahoma, 1963.

Zimmermann, Arthur F. "Spain and its Colonies, 1808-1820," *Hispanic American Historical Review,* XI (November 1931), 439-463.

Zum Felde, Alberto. *Proceso histórico del Uruguay y esquema de su sociología.* Montevideo, 1963.

Index

[Entries in italic indicate topic headings.]